Trauma and the Memory

In this original study, Jenny Edkins explores how we remember traumatic events such as wars, famines, genocides and terrorism, and questions the assumed role of commemorations as simply reinforcing state and nationhood. Taking examples from the World Wars, Vietnam, the Holocaust, Kosovo and September 11 Edkins offers a thorough discussion of practices of memory such as memorials, museums, remembrance ceremonies, the diagnosis of post-traumatic stress and the act of bearing witness. She examines the implications of these commemorations in terms of language, political power, sovereignty and nationalism. She argues that some forms of remembering do not ignore the horror of what happened but rather use memory to promote change and to challenge the political systems that produced the violence of wars and genocides in the first place. This wide-ranging study embraces literature, history, politics and international relations, and makes a significant contribution to the study of memory.

Jenny Edkins is Senior Lecturer in International Politics at the University of Wales Aberystwyth. Her publications include *Whose Hunger? Concepts of Famine, Practices of Aid* (2000), *Poststructuralism and International Relations: Bringing the Political Back In* (1999) and, with Nalini Persram and Véronique Pin-Fat, *Sovereignty and Subjectivity* (1999).

Trauma and the Memory of Politics

Jenny Edkins
University of Wales Aberystwyth

CAMBRIDGE UNIVERSITY PRESS
Cambridge, New York, Melbourne, Madrid, Cape Town, Singapore, São Paulo

Cambridge University Press
The Edinburgh Building, Cambridge CB2 8RU, UK

Published in the United States of America by Cambridge University Press, New York

www.cambridge.org
Information on this title: www.cambridge.org/9780521826969

First published 2003

A catalogue record for this publication is available from the British Library

ISBN 978-0-521-82696-9 hardback
ISBN 978-0-521-53420-8 paperback

Transferred to digital printing 2007

For John

Know what has happened, do not forget, and at the same time never will you know.

– Maurice Blanchot

Contents

Illustrations

All photographs are from the author's collection unless otherwise indicated

Preface

This book was prompted by a curiosity about how what we call 'politics' draws on a particular linear notion of time. Thinking about time and politics led me to explore what have become two growth areas of recent scholarship in a range of academic fields – history, anthropology, cultural studies and psychoanalysis – questions of trauma and memory. At the beginning of the new century it appears that a large number of people are interested in how, to what purposes and with what effects, we memorialise the traumatic events of the twentieth century. Places such as Flanders, Auschwitz, Hiroshima and Vietnam all hold our attention now not only as events, but in relation to the question of memory. And following the events of September 11, 2001 in New York and Washington this interest in trauma and memory has intensified and become more personal for many. Two things are recognised. First, from work on trauma it is acknowledged that memories such as these are distinct – traumatic memory is not the same as everyday memory. Second, from work on collective or cultural memory it is argued that many contemporary forms of memorialisation function to reinforce the idea of the nation. What I do in this study is put these two understandings together and explore what they imply in political terms. It has already been argued that memorialisation often constitutes a form of forgetting. I explore how this works, but I am more particularly interested in asking how it can be and is challenged, by whom and in what contexts. I argue that such challenges constitute a questioning of the power of the sovereign state itself, as a form of political community, and its legitimation through 'politics'.

Increasingly a distinction is being drawn between what we call 'politics' – the routine, regular processes that take place in parliaments, elections, political parties and the institutions of government – and something more lively, less dogmatic, less predictable, which some writers have begun to call 'the political'. This latter is the arena of innovation and revolution, a field of sudden, unexpected and abrupt change, a point at which the status quo is challenged. It is where what we might call 'real politics' resurfaces, challenging the claims of the impostor that has taken its place. Quite often, such challenges and the changes they produce are so startling that we don't quite know how to describe them until some time after they have taken place. Occasionally, they appear traumatic. They upset, or escape, the straightforward linear temporality associated with the regularity of so-called 'politics' and appear to occupy another form of time: a time that I call in this book 'trauma time'.

In the linear time of the standard political processes, which is the time associated with the continuance of the nation-state, events that happen are part of a well-known and widely accepted story. What happens fits into a pattern. We know almost in advance that such events have a place in the narrative. We know what they are. In trauma time, in contrast, we have a disruption of this linearity. Something happens that doesn't fit, that is unexpected – or that happens in an unexpected way. It doesn't fit the story we already have, but demands that we invent a new account, one that will produce a place for what has happened and make it meaningful. Until this new story is produced we quite literally do not know what has happened: we cannot say what it was, it doesn't fit the script – we only know that 'something happened'.

The events of September 11 are an example of this traumatic disruption to the linearity of time and expectations. Television viewers around the world heard reporters in New York and Washington struggling to find words to describe what had happened. People on the streets of New York stood frozen, horror-struck, staring up at the twin towers, unable to believe that what they saw in front of their eyes was actually taking place. Although the newsrooms responded in the main by replaying over and over again the point of impact and, later, the images of the collapse of the towers, eventually they needed to make a 'story'. They needed to put titles across the screen. And later, New Yorkers needed to talk: hundreds gathered in Union Square that night to debate and discuss – and to mourn. However, even one year on the term 'events' survived as perhaps the best that could be managed by way of description and the date 'September 11', or '9/11', stood in as the most evocative designation for what had happened.

Of course, the distinction I have made between trauma time and the linear time of the state is not quite as straightforward as I have described it. For the nation-state and its so-called 'politics' to work, the linear time associated with it has to be produced and reproduced all the time. This time is not a natural phenomenon, but one that is socially constituted – it is a notion that exists because we all work, in and through our everyday practices, to bring it into being. In the main, the production and reproduction of linear time take place by people assuming that such a form of time does exist, and specifically that it exists as an empty, homogeneous medium in which events take place. This is a very Newtonian conception of time, one long since called into question by Einstein's re-thinking of natural science. Our everyday thinking about social events has yet to catch up with what are now our accepted scientific notions of time. Even though we are happy to explore the new Einsteinian cosmology in science fiction, we have not yet begun to think about how it would affect our ideas about politics if we were to take it seriously.

However, it is no accident that we haven't done this. Nor can it be put down to intellectual laziness or a reluctance to change our ways of thinking. I will argue in this book that the old Newtonian way of thinking about time persists not because we just haven't got round to re-thinking these ideas in the light of new scientific analysis, but because linear, homogeneous time suits a particular form of power – sovereign power, the power of the modern nation-state. Sovereign power produces and is itself produced by trauma: it provokes wars, genocides and famines. But it works by concealing its involvement and claiming to be a provider not a destroyer of security. It does this, of course, directly, through discourses of international security that centre around the state as well as through claiming to provide security internally for its citizens. In addition, however, the state does this in no small part through the way in which it commemorates wars, genocides and famines. By rewriting these traumas into a linear narrative of national heroism, this book will argue, the state conceals the trauma that it has, necessarily, produced. Resistance to this re-scripting – resistance to state narratives of commemoration – constitutes resistance to sovereign power. As Milan Kundera reminds us in his *Book of Laughter and Forgetting*: 'the struggle of man against power is the struggle of memory against forgetting'.[1]

-o0o-

My interest in time and the political was initially provoked by an invitation to contribute to a panel on 'time' at a conference of the International Studies Association in Vienna in 1998. My thanks go to Mike Shapiro and David Campbell for the invitation, and to participants at the session for their comments. Since then, work in progress has been presented in a number of seminars and conference panels. I would like to thank participants in the International Studies Association conferences at Washington in 1999, and at Chicago and Hong Kong in 2001. Thanks to Cindy Weber and François Debrix, the convenors of the series 'Mediating Internationals' and participants in the seminar at the University of Leeds in February 2000. Tarak Barkawi's colloquium

[1] Milan Kundera, *The Book of Laughter and Forgetting*, trans. Aaron Asher (London: Faber and Faber, 1996).

in Aberystwyth was a valuable occasion to air some of the debates engaged in here, and many thanks go to participants Susie Carruthers, Huw Evans, Sue Ferguson, Steve Hobden, Jasmina Husanovic, Adam Morton and Priscilla Netto. A number of people have read and commented on drafts of parts of the book at various stages, including Mick Dillon, Nicky Gregory, Len Scott, Steve Smith, Annick Wibben and Maja Zehfuss, and many more have contributed to the book's development in different ways: Diana Bankston, Aida Hozic, Véronique Pin-Fat, Patricia Owens, Daniel Warner and Marysia Zalewski, among others. Thanks to Edith and Horst Zehfuss for hospitality, and to staff of the Dachau concentration camp memorial archive in Munich, and the Imperial War Museum archive and the Public Record Office in London for their assistance. Thanks to Katherine Tomlinson and to Olivia Bennett of the Oral Testimony Programme at the Panos Institute in London. And, finally, thanks to the two anonymous reviewers at Cambridge University Press for their encouraging comments.

Parts of this book draw on material published elsewhere, and I am grateful for permission to include this here. Part of Chapter 4 is revised from 'Sovereign Power, Zones of Indistinction and the Camp', *Alternatives: Global, Local, Political*, 25, no. 1 (January–March 2000), copyright © Lynne Rienner Publishers, used with permission of the publisher. Part of Chapter 3 appeared as 'Authenticity and Memory at Dachau', *Cultural Values*, 5, no. 4 (2001): 405–20.

I would like to thank the Leverhulme Trust and the Economic and Social Research Council for funding the early parts of the research, including visits to Washington DC in the spring of 1999 and to London to work in the Public Records Office at Kew, the University of Wales for two periods of six months' sabbatical leave in 1999 and 2000 and the University Research Fund for funding trips to Dachau, London and Beijing in 2001.

As always I am grateful to my family for contributing to the development of my ideas and thoughts in all sorts of different ways. Two family members warrant special mention in the context of this particular book. The first is my grandmother, the late Elizabeth Smith. Her husband died on 3 July 1925 from tuberculosis brought on by injuries sustained in the 1914–18 war. Their daughter (my mother) was two-and-a-half at the time. Richard Smith had served as a private in the Lancashire Fusiliers and was with the BEF from 13 March to 20 October 1917. The second, John Roy Pierpoint Edkins, who died in 1960, was a psychiatrist at Woodside Hospital during the Second World War. He worked with trauma victims and published papers on treatment by abreaction. My immediate family are the ones who I must thank the most, however:

John, David and Tim. I apologise to Tim and David if my preoccupation with my computer for long hours at a stretch has put them off writing and the academic life for good, and wish them much joy in their chosen alternatives. John has always supported me, and my work, way beyond the call of duty and I dedicate this book to him.

The epigraph at the start of the book is taken from Maurice Blanchot, *The Writing of the Disaster: L'écriture du désastre*, trans. Ann Smock, new edn (Lincoln and London: University of Nebraska Press, 1995), 82.

1 Introduction: trauma, violence and political community

> The essence of the trauma is precisely that it is too horrible to be remembered, to be integrated into our symbolic universe. All we have to do is to mark repeatedly the trauma as such.
>
> – Slavoj Žižek[1]

In the aftermath of a war or catastrophe comes the reckoning. The dead and the missing are listed, families grieve and comfort each other, and memorials are erected. If it is a war that has been won, commemoration endorses those in power, or so it seems at first glance. Victory parades, remembrance ceremonies and war museums tell of glory, courage and sacrifice. The nation is renewed, the state strengthened. Private grief is overlaid by national mourning and blunted – or eased – by stories of service and duty. The authorities that had the power to conscript citizens and send them to their deaths now write their obituaries.

But returning combatants tell a different tale. Survivors are subdued, even silent. Many witnessed the deaths of those around them. They cannot forget, and some are haunted by nightmares and flashbacks to scenes of unimaginable horror. In their dreams they re-live their battlefield experiences and awake again in a sweat. First World War veterans were said to be suffering from shell shock. By the end of that war, 80,000 cases of shell shock had been treated in units of the Royal Army Medical Corps and 30,000 evacuated for treatment in Britain. Some 200,000 veterans received pensions for nervous disorders after the war.[2] This epidemic led to a reconsideration of psychoanalytic theory, then based on the notion of dreams as the fulfilment of unconscious wishes. Much contemporary work that seeks to understand what is now called trauma stems from

[1] Slavoj Žižek, *For They Know Not What They Do: Enjoyment as a Political Factor* (London: Verso, 1991), 272–3.

[2] Martin Stone, 'Shellshock and the psychologists' in *The Anatomy of Madness: Essays in the History of Psychiatry*, ed. W. F. Bynum, R. Porter and M. Shepherd (London: Tavistock, 1988), II: 242–71, quoted in Allan Young, *The Harmony of Illusions: Inventing Post-Traumatic Stress Disorder* (Princeton University Press, 1997), 41–2.

this period and from an attempt to understand why traumatic events are re-lived time and time again by survivors.

By the Second World War it was no longer only service personnel (not themselves necessarily volunteers) who were intimately affected by state-organised violence. Aerial bombing campaigns drew civilian populations into the conflict. The bombing of Hiroshima and Nagasaki in August 1945 was horrific and overwhelming in its brutality. And the genocidal policies of the Nazi régime in Germany led to the deaths of millions in concentration camps, open-air shootings and ghettos.

In the aftermath of genocide, when a state has turned on people who considered themselves its citizens, the dead have no names and no burial place because their families are killed too. Memorialisation is difficult if not impossible. It can be many years before memory surfaces in the public arena or indeed before there is a willingness to listen to survivors' testimony. States are implicated more thoroughly than in the case of war, both the state in which the genocide occurred and those that stood by while it happened. Nevertheless, eventually, after a lapse of time or a change in the political landscape, a narrative takes shape. Events are named, memorials and museums set up, and the identity of at least some of the victims established.

Following the Nazi genocide of the 1940s, many of the survivors emerged with a compelling need to bear witness and an overwhelming conviction of the importance of doing so. They were largely ignored. It was not until much later that what became known as 'the Holocaust' grew into a topic of fascination. But whereas traumatic stress as a result of combat is thought far-fetched by some, the status of Holocaust survivor has generally had a special aura.[3] What survivors have witnessed has long been recognised as 'unimaginable' and 'unspeakable', although these epithets have often served as an excuse for neither imagining it nor speaking about it. The Holocaust has been a largely proprietary event: it was 'narrated by Jews and non-Jews alike as a collective (and sole) property of the Jews, as something to be left to, or jealously guarded by, those who escaped the shooting and the gassing, and by the descendants of the shot and gassed'.[4] It belongs to the Jews (or to the Jewish state) and others feel debarred from talking about it.

Work by feminists in the 1970s argued that the symptoms of victims of rape and incest were similar to those of combat survivors. After a lengthy

[3] In Israel in the 1950s the aura was one of failure: survivors were regarded as 'the epitome of the Jew as helpless schlemiel, a counterexample to the new Israeli Jew' (Yaron Ezrahi, *Rubber Bullets: Power and Conscience in Modern Israel* (Berkeley: University of California, 1997), 147.

[4] Zygmunt Bauman, *Modernity and the Holocaust* (Cambridge: Polity, 1989), viii–ix.

campaign that included Vietnam veterans, the term 'post-traumatic stress' was finally written into the American Psychiatric Association's manual in 1980.[5] Childhood abuse and trauma, although still controversial, became something that could be discussed, first in women's groups and later more widely. Sigmund Freud's work in Vienna in the 1890s had led him to conclude that symptoms of what was then called hysteria in his women patients could be traced back to childhood abuse. He published his findings and conclusions in 1896 in a paper entitled 'The Aetiology of Hysteria', where he put forward the view that 'at the bottom of every case of hysteria there are *one or more occurrences of premature sexual experience*. . . . I believe this is an important finding'.[6] But he did not pursue this line; it was unacceptable to him and to his contemporaries.[7] He argued instead that women were in some sense responsible for their own abuse. He replaced his original analysis of hysteria (the seduction theory) with theories of infantile sexuality and the Oedipus complex. Ironically, it was only during his work with shell shock after the First World War that Freud returned to the study of what we now call psychic trauma. Of course, in the case of childhood abuse and rape as with shell shock and earlier with hysteria, the people concerned were regularly regarded as having either caused their traumatic experiences – by their own behaviour, or as a fulfilment of their unconscious wishes – or imagined something that had not actually occurred. Women were accused of having wanted to be raped, soldiers of faking their illness in a cowardly attempt to avoid fighting, and children's reports were seen as exaggerated and unbelievable.

Events that give rise to what we categorise today as symptoms of trauma generally involve force and violence. Often this is a threat to those people involved, their lives and integrity, as in rape, torture or child abuse; sometimes it also involves witnessing the horrific deaths of others, for example in wartime combat or in concentration camps. The victim of trauma feels they were helpless in their enforced encounter with death, violence and brutality. This is not always the case. For example, on the whole, Vietnam veterans were not in situations where they were trapped in the same way as First World War soldiers in the trenches or concentration camp victims. In most cases, they were perpetrators of violence

[5] Judith Lewis Herman, *Trauma and Recovery: from Domestic Abuse to Political Terror* (London: Pandora, 1992), 32.

[6] Sigmund Freud, 'The Aetiology of Hysteria', quoted in Alice Miller, *Thou Shalt Not Be Aware: Society's Betrayal of the Child*, trans. Hildegarde and Hunter Hannum, new edn (London: Pluto Press, 1998), 117.

[7] Herman, *Trauma and Recovery*, 19. Alice Miller discusses this issue and quotes extensively from Freud's 1896 lecture (Miller, *Thou Shalt Not Be Aware*, 109–20). I am grateful to Annick Wibben for this reference.

rather than victims.[8] But it seems that to be called traumatic – to produce what are seen as symptoms of trauma – an event has to be more than just a situation of utter powerlessness. In an important sense, it has to entail something else. It has to involve a betrayal of trust as well. There is an extreme menace, but what is special is where the threat of violence comes from. What we call trauma takes place when the very powers that we are convinced will protect us and give us security become our tormentors: when the community of which we considered ourselves members turns against us or when our family is no longer a source of refuge but a site of danger.

This can be devastating because who we are, or who we think we may be, depends very closely on the social context in which we place and find ourselves. Our existence relies not only on our personal survival as individual beings but also, in a very profound sense, on the continuance of the social order that gives our existence meaning and dignity: family, friends, political community, beliefs. If that order betrays us in some way, we may survive in the sense of continuing to live as physical beings, but the meaning of our existence is changed. Commonplace solutions to do with who and what we are and what life might be provided by culture, religious beliefs, patriotic sentiment or close family relationships are overwhelmed. Any illusion of safety or security is broken. Events seen as traumatic seem to reflect a particular form of intimate bond between personhood and community and, most importantly, they expose the part played by relations of power. For the child, abuse involves betrayal by the person the child should most be able to trust. For the conscript, it is the state that breaks faith and deceives. Both cases involve relations of power.

Witnessing violence done to others and surviving can seem to be as traumatic as suffering brutality oneself. Here a sense of shame is paramount. The survivor feels complicit in the betrayal perpetrated by others. In this sense the survivor of a rape or of incest is ashamed for the protagonist of violence against them as well as for themselves. Taking part in violence oneself can evoke a similar shame – as was the case with Vietnam veterans – though this of course is *not at all to be equated with* witnessing violence done by others.[9] The camp survivor is filled with shame for the deeds done by the guards, and because the inmates were powerless to prevent them. As Primo Levi remembers, 'the shame . . . drowned us after the selections, and every time we had to watch or submit to some outrage: the shame . . . that such a crime should exist, that it should be

[8] Young, *Harmony of Illusions*, 283.

[9] See, for example, Primo Levi, *The Drowned and the Saved*, trans. Raymond Rosenthal (London: Abacus, 1989), 2.

introduced irrevocably into the world of things that exist'.[10] The combat veteran has not only seen his comrades killed or mutilated but has himself brutally slaughtered enemy soldiers – and in some cases betrayed his own supposed code as a warrior (or as a person) when he has terrorised and victimised civilians.

Events of the sort we call traumatic are overwhelming but they are also a revelation. They strip away the diverse commonly accepted meanings by which we lead our lives in our various communities. They reveal the contingency of the social order and in some cases how it conceals its own impossibility. They question our settled assumptions about who we might be as humans and what we might be capable of. Those who survive often feel compelled to bear witness to these discoveries.

On the whole, the rest of us would rather not listen. A frequent excuse is that the horrors survivors testify to are too terrible. They are 'unimaginable': we need not listen because we cannot hear. Robert Antelme, describing the encounter of the American liberators with camp survivors at Dachau in Germany at the end of the Second World War, says that the word 'unimaginable' is 'the most convenient word. When you walk around with this word as your shield, this word for emptiness, your step becomes better assured, more resolute, your conscience pulls itself together.'[11] But in particular those who would try to prevent survivors from speaking out are the powerful, those who have perhaps more of a stake than most in concealing the contingency of forms of social and political organisation. This may include, for example, governments who have sent soldiers into battle, men who benefit from a structure in which women and children are subservient and vulnerable, states who have turned on a section of their own citizens in genocides or deportations. The testimony of survivors can challenge structures of power and authority. Moreover, this challenge can in some regards transcend boundaries of culture and social group.[12] It is what Michel Foucault referred to as 'the solidarity of the shaken'.

On the other hand, do contemporary forms of political community have an ironic connection with the events that we have been discussing? Do political communities such as the modern state survive in part through the scripting of these events as emergencies, or even, indeed, as traumatic? Or even by the production of events that can appear as exceptional, beyond

[10] Primo Levi, *If This is a Man and The Truce*, trans. Stuart Woolf (London: Abacus, 1987), 188.

[11] Robert Antelme, *The Human Race*, 289–90, quoted in Sarah Kofman, *Smothered Words*, trans. Madeleine Dobie (Evanston, Illinois: Northwestern University Press, 1998), 38.

[12] Cathy Caruth, *Unclaimed Experience: Trauma, Narrative, and History* (Baltimore: Johns Hopkins University Press, 1996), 56.

the norm? In modern political communities in the west, our faith in the social order and our search for security are invested in systems that themselves are productive of and produced by force and violence. This point is no surprise to women of course, who have long had to separate their notions of safety from the patriarchal structures in which they live. Battered women would not recognise the picture of the family as a source of protection and stability, for example. The contemporary form of political community, the state, relies for its existence on the assumption that it can compel its citizens to fight (and die) for its sovereignty. It proffers security in return for obedience. As a political unit it is produced and defined by organised violence. States are founded on violence, whether it takes the form of war, revolution or civil conflict. And although once formed a state may appear peaceable enough, internally and externally, physical violence remains a tool that only the state is allowed to use. Attempts by others – vigilante groups, opposition movements, criminals – to use violence are seen as unacceptable. In Max Weber's definition, 'the state is that human community which (successfully) lays claim to the monopoly of legitimate physical violence within a certain territory'.[13] The right to use violence, in other words, is the prerogative of the state. And it makes use of this prerogative. For example, the modern nation-state works by processes of enforced exclusion, and it can change the definition of who precisely will be excluded at any time. Exclusion does not always entail expulsion: there is also the excluded 'enemy within', a label famously used by Prime Minister Margaret Thatcher in Britain at the time of the miners' strike in 1984. The modern state, then, is a contradictory institution: a promise of safety, security and meaning alongside a reality of abuse, control and coercion.

As we saw, some feminists came to the conclusion that relations between the sexes are like a war, with the casualties being rape victims, battered wives and sexually abused children. The parallel between women and war veterans was used in the 1970s and 1980s to draw attention to the plight of women and the widespread exploitation of patriarchal power by men, which had, apart from the early work by Freud and Joseph Breuer on hysteria, been neglected.[14] If we push the similarities further, taking the insights gained from the study of sexual abuse in families and applying them to other events categorised as traumatic, what do we find? What if,

[13] Max Weber, *Weber: Political Writings*, trans. Ronald Spiers, ed. Peter Lassman and Ronald Spiers (Cambridge University Press, 1994), 310–11.

[14] Sigmund Freud and Joseph Breuer, *Studies on Hysteria*, trans. James Strachey and Alix Strachey, The Penguin Freud Library, vol. III, ed. James Strachey and Alix Strachey (London: Penguin, 1974); Herman, *Trauma and Recovery*.

instead of likening family relations to a war, we compare the treatment of populations in wartime with the treatment of women in families? It turns out that we have a parallel exploitation of power in political communities, which we might call political abuse. Political authorities are using their power over their citizens to abuse and torture them or to compel them to take part in abhorrent acts, acts which violate their sense of self-worth and which provoke intense shame, humiliation and anger. According to US Marine veteran Michael Norman, survivors of Vietnam were angry. They were not unlike survivors of previous wars, however. Their anger was not new. It was 'old, atavistic. We were angry as all civilised men who have ever been sent to make murder in the name of virtue were angry.'[15] States abuse citizens on the battlefield, in captivity, in concentration camps. The modern state cannot be assumed to be a place of safety, any more than the patriarchal family can. Political abuse in one parallels sexual abuse in the other.[16] Both give rise to what we call symptoms of trauma.

In both cases what has happened is beyond the possibility of communication. There is no language for it. Abuse by the state, the fatherland, like abuse by the father within the family, cannot be spoken in language, since language comes from and belongs to the family and the community. Survivors of political abuse in the contemporary west have something compelling to say, but it is something that is unsayable in the vocabulary of the powerful, and it is dangerous to the political institutions in place. The use of the term 'unspeakable' in relation to trauma is not only an excuse to avoid the need to listen to what is being said. It also reflects the view of survivors that what they have been through cannot be communicated. Communication takes place in language and language itself is social and political, not individual. Relations of power are produced through and reflected in language. Words get their meaning from their place in chains of meaning, through their associations with other words based on sound, metaphor and layers of usage. Meaning can shift and words can be re-articulated with new associations and new contexts. For language to work at a particular time and in a particular context, it is necessary for there to be a linguistic community that shares or is subject to something that will temporarily fix meanings. There has to be some provisional agreement, accepted ideology or central authority structure that will halt the fluidity of terms and make language meaningful. In psychoanalytic theory it is

[15] Quoted by Herman, *Trauma and Recovery*, 27.

[16] Of course, the notion of 'abuse' relies on the possibility of a legitimate, contractual power. Michel Foucault, 'Two lectures', in *Power/Knowledge: Selected Interviews and Other Writings 1972–1977 by Michel Foucault*, ed. Colin Gordon (Brighton: Harvester, 1980), 78–108; 92.

not just language that works like this. The unconscious mind is structured like a language; in other words, who we think we are is shifting and fluid, until fixed by the social context or the dominant group. But this group does not exist independently of the people of whom it is made up. We produce this group at the same time as becoming members of it. By assuming a community exists we produce one. By situating ourselves as citizens of a state or political authority or as members of a family, we reproduce that social institution at the same time as assuming our own identity as part of it. As we have seen, in what we call a traumatic event this group betrays us. We can no longer be who we were, and the social context is not what we assumed it to be. It is not all-powerful, it does not have all the answers: in fact, its answers are flawed. As Jean Amery puts it: 'Every morning when I get up I can read the Auschwitz number on my forearm.... Every day anew I lose my trust in the world.'[17] The cause of his oppression and restlessness is society: 'it and only it robbed me of my trust in the world'.[18] As a survivor of catastrophe, he lives in constant fear of its return: 'nothing can again lull me into the slumber of security from which I awoke in 1935'.[19] It has become plain to a survivor that the appearance of fixity and security produced by the social order is just that: an appearance. Of course, the language we speak is part of the social order, and when the order falls apart around our ears, so does the language. What we *can* say no longer makes sense; what we *want* to say, we can't. There are no words for it. This is the dilemma survivors face. The only words they have are the words of the very political community that is the source of their suffering. This is the language of the powerful, the words of the status quo, the words that delimit and define acceptable ways of being human within that community.

What survivors seek is perhaps impossible. They seek a way of resistance. For some, Sarah Kofman for example, this means a way of 'writing without power'. Such a writing or speech was forbidden in the concentration camps, 'yet also withheld, preserved, protected against all straying, all corruption, against all violent abuse that might have exposed it to the suspicion of playing along with boundless violence, and therefore have discredited it forever'.[20] Such a way of speaking implies a form of community that does not entail a circuit of power between oppressors and victims, a community that does not produce forms of subjection where human beings are indistinguishable from what Giorgio Agamben calls

[17] Jean Amery, *At the Mind's Limits: Contemplations by a Survivor on Auschwitz and its Realities*, trans. Sidney Rosenfeld and Stella P. Rosenfeld (London: Granta, 1999), 94.

[18] Amery, *At the Mind's Limits*, 100.

[19] *Ibid.*, 95

[20] Kofman, *Smothered Words*, 41.

'bare life'.[21] It is a form of community that is hardly found in the modern western state.

What the state attempts in contrast is a normalisation or medicalisation of survivors; we shall see an example of this in Chapter 2. The aim is recovery, or the reinsertion of survivors into structures of power. Survivors are helped to verbalise and narrate what has happened to them; they receive counselling to help them accommodate once more to the social order and re-form relationships of trust. In the case of the military these days, those suffering from symptoms of traumatic stress are treated swiftly with the aim of being returned to active service within a matter of hours or days.[22] If this fails, then the status of victim of post-traumatic stress disorder serves to render the survivor more or less harmless to existing power structures. In contemporary culture victimhood offers sympathy and pity in return for the surrender of any political voice.

The concept of trauma oscillates between victimhood and protest and can be linked with or articulated to either. Its invocation registers a movement in the boundaries of acceptability of the use and abuse of violence in relations of power and forms of authority or political community. When there is a mismatch between expectation and event we have what is experienced as a betrayal – or in other words, as traumatic. This is not a sufficient condition for us to call something 'trauma' of course, though we soon get into difficulties if we try to probe further into the matter of scale. We end up asking impossible questions such as 'Can one *measure* trauma? Is there a hierarchy of trauma?'[23] Nevertheless, when our expectations of what community is, and what we are, are shown to be misplaced, then our view of ourselves has to be altered – or we have to fight for political change, in other words a reformulation of community.

The traumatic dimension of the political

This book explores the connections between violence, the effects of trauma that it produces, and forms of political community. It aims to contribute to understandings of the particular way in which power, the social order and the person are constituted in the contemporary west, through a study of practices of trauma, memory and witness. Its focus is

[21] Giorgio Agamben, *Homo Sacer: Sovereign Power and Bare Life*, trans. Daniel Heller-Roazen (Stanford University Press, 1998).

[22] During the Second World War the American Army Medical Corps treated psychiatric casualties with food, rest and reassurance before they were returned to their units, usually in a couple of days. Young, *Harmony of Illusions*, 92.

[23] Tim Woods, 'Mending the Skin of Memory: Ethics and History in Contemporary Narratives', *Rethinking History*, 2, no. 3 (1998): 339–48; 345.

firmly on western conceptions of personhood and political community in the modern period. It does not examine, except in passing, how practices of trauma or memory may have been exported beyond what might be considered the geographical bounds of a western paradigm, nor does it discuss, except to point up the specificity of a western approach, how people seemingly located outside that paradigm differ in their practices. Of course, these distinctions (west and the rest) are arbitrary and contestable, and they reflect a western tendency to dichotomise at the same time as promoting western power relations. There are many people located within the contemporary west in geographical or ideological terms who would not adopt what I am regarding as 'western' conceptions of self and society.

By taking as its route an examination of extreme situations and events seen as traumatic, the book reflects Giorgio Agamben's analysis of contemporary sovereign power as based on a state of emergency or exception.[24] His work is discussed in Chapter 5. My examination of practices of memorialisation and testimony arises out of and is framed against a more general interest in the formation of sovereign power and western subjectivity or personhood. The form of power that underlies the modern state and the violence it entails often goes unanalysed in political science or international relations studies. Both political science, in its focus on the internal (supposedly peaceable) workings of the state, and international politics, with its concern for external conflict and war, seem to ignore the production of the self and the state, which takes place at the traumatic intersection between peace and war, inside and outside.[25] The way we see the democratic state rests on not questioning that particular form of political community or the forms of individuality or personhood on which it is based.

The account of statehood in the liberal view is a story of individual citizens banding together to form democratic institutions which (more or less) represent the views of those citizens and which (more or less) have their interests at heart. The state possesses power (and can use violence), in this narrative, because the people legitimise its authority. However, according to a Foucauldian view, power is not centralised but dispersed; it is not something that can be possessed, but a relationship.[26] We should speak of relations of power, not of power plain and simple. Because it is

[24] Agamben, *Homo Sacer*.

[25] R. B. J. Walker, *Inside/Outside: International Relations as Political Theory* (Cambridge University Press, 1993).

[26] Foucault, 'Truth and power', in *Power/Knowledge*, ed. Gordon, 109–33. For an overview see Barry Hindess, *Discourses of Power: from Hobbes to Foucault* (Oxford: Blackwell, 1996).

a relation, power always exists alongside resistance. How does this play out in the trauma situation? In this case it means that what happens is not straightforward; there is not a perpetrator and a victim with no ambiguity. That in many ways is what is most difficult. Primo Levi talks of the concentration camp as a 'grey zone' where all feel implicated in some way in what happens.[27] As far as memory is concerned, how we remember a war, for example, and the way in which we acknowledge and describe what we call trauma can be very much influenced by dominant views, that is, by the state. However, it is not determined by them: their influence, and the state structure itself, can be contested and challenged. Forms of statehood in contemporary society, as forms of political community, are themselves produced and reproduced through social practices, including practices of trauma and memory.

Like the liberal account of the state, the form of personhood that fits alongside it often goes unchallenged too. The sovereign state in the modern world relies on a notion of a separate, autonomous, sovereign individual. But this is a historically specific concept of personhood, one that arose alongside state structures and particular family organisation in the early modern era.[28] Other accounts question this liberal view, and argue that the person or 'subject' does not exist independently of or prior to the social order, but is formed through its interaction with that order. A further position regards both social order and person as inherently incomplete and insecure. According to this account, which derives from psychoanalytic work, in the west both state and subject pretend to a security, a wholeness and a closure that is not possible. From this point of view, an event can be described as traumatic if it reveals this pretence. It is experienced as a betrayal.

In the psychoanalytic account the subject is formed around a lack, and in the face of trauma. We become who we are by finding our place within the social order and family structures into which we are born. That social order is produced in symbolic terms, through language. Language does not just name things that are already there in the world. Language divides up the world in particular ways to produce for every social grouping what it calls 'reality'. Each language – each symbolic or social order – has its own way of doing this. Crucially, none of these are complete; none of them can find a place for everything. This is a logical limitation, not a question of a symbolic or social order being insufficiently developed. Completeness or closure is impossible. There is always, inevitably, something that is missed out, something that cannot be symbolised, and this is one part of

[27] Levi, *The Drowned and the Saved.* [28] Walker, *Inside/Outside.*

what psychoanalytic theory calls 'the real'. In its birth into the symbolic or social order, into language, the subject is formed around, and through a veiling of, that which cannot be symbolised – the traumatic real. The real is traumatic, and has to be hidden or forgotten, because it is a threat to the imaginary completeness of the subject. The 'subject' only exists in as far as the person finds their place within the social or symbolic order. But no place that the person occupies – as a mother, friend, consumer, activist – can fully express what that person is. There is always something more. Again, this is not a question of people not fitting into the roles available for them and a call for more person-friendly societies. Nor does it concern multiple or fragmented identities in a postmodern world. It is a matter of a structural impossibility. If someone is, say, a political activist, there is always the immediate question of whether they are sufficiently involved to count as an activist: don't activists have to be more committed, to take part in more than just demonstrations, shouldn't they stand for office? On the other hand, are they perhaps more than an activist – does that description do justice to what they are, to their role in the party? There is always an excess, a surplus, in one direction or the other. However, we choose on the whole to ignore this – to forget this impossibility, and to act as if completeness and closure were possible. We hide the traumatic real, and stick with the fantasy of what we call social reality.

As I have argued elsewhere, the political is that which enjoins us not to forget the traumatic real but rather to acknowledge the constituted and provisional nature of what we call social reality.[29] Politics refers to the sphere of activity and institutions that is called 'politics' as opposed to 'economics' or 'society'. Politics is part of what we call social reality. It exists within the agendas and frameworks that are already accepted within the social order. The political, in its 'properly traumatic dimension',[30] on the other hand, concerns the real. It refers to events in which politics of the first sort and its institutions are brought into being. This can be the day-to-day production and reproduction of the social and symbolic order. This continual process has to take place; the social order is not natural, it doesn't exist unless it is produced continually. The political also takes place at moments when major upheavals occur that replace a preceding social and legal system and set up a new order in its place. At such points, the symbolism and ideology that concealed the fragile and contingent

[29] Jenny Edkins, *Poststructuralism and International Relations: Bringing the Political Back In* (Boulder, Colorado: Lynne Rienner, 1999); Jenny Edkins and Véronique Pin-Fat, 'The subject of the political', in *Sovereignty and Subjectivity*, ed. Jenny Edkins, Nalini Persram and Véronique Pin-Fat (Boulder, Colorado: Lynne Rienner, 1999), 1–19.

[30] Slavoj Žižek, *The Ticklish Subject: The Absent Centre of Political Ontology* (London: Verso, 1999), 190.

nature of authority collapse altogether and there is a brief interregnum before the new order imposes a different form of concealment.

The way that time figures in the psychoanalytic account is interesting. A certain non-linearity is evident: time no longer moves unproblematically from past through present to future. In a sense, subjects only retrospectively become what they already are – they *only ever will have been*.[31] And the social order too shares this retroactive constitution. The subject and the social order in which the subject finds a place are both in a continual process of becoming. Neither exists as a fixed entity in the present moment, as the common-sense view in western culture might lead us to expect. Both are always in the process of formation. This is because the two are so intimately related. The person is formed, not through a process of interaction with the social order (since that would mean thinking of the social as already there), but by imagining or supposing that the social order exists. This supposing by the individual is what brings the social into being. We have to imagine that others will respond to us before we speak, but it is only our speaking, of course, that enables them to respond. But supposing that the social exists does not only produce the social order, it also, simultaneously, brings the individual into existence too. When our speaking elicits a response, we recognise ourselves as subjects in that response. This recognition is belated when viewed through the lens of a linear temporality: it is not at the moment we decide to speak that we see who we are, but only a moment later, when we get a response. The response tells us not who we are now, since we are no longer that – we have already changed. It tells us who we were, at the moment when we spoke. This is the sense in which we never *are*, we *only ever will have been*. Like the distant stars, whose past we know from the light that has taken millions of years to reach us but whose present we can only guess at, we can only know what we were, not what we are. And even that is also a guess, of course. In a similar way, when we listen to a sentence being spoken, we can predict what is being said, but we cannot be sure we were right until the sentence is completed and over. Some forms of speech – rhetoric and jokes for example – play on that unpredictability.

The uncertainty and unpredictability that this involves can be unsettling. In the rational west, we tend to seek certainty and security above all. We don't like not knowing. So we pretend that we do. Or that if we don't we could, given sufficient scientific research effort and enough money. We forget the uncertainties involved and adopt a view that what we call social reality – which Slavoj Žižek calls social fantasy – is basically knowable.

[31] Jacques Lacan, *Écrits: A Selection*, trans. Alan Sheridan (London: Routledge, 1980), 86.

We adopt an ontology – a view of being and the nature of things – that depends on a progressive linear notion of time. Things can 'be' in our modern western sense only in the context of this temporality. They 'are' because they have a history in time, but they are at the same time separate from that history.

But central to this solution to doubt is forgetting, as we have seen. The fantasy is only convincing if, once it has been put in place, we can forget that it is a fantasy. What we are forgetting – some would say deliberately – is the real, that which cannot be symbolised, and that which is produced as an excess or surplus by any attempt at symbolisation. We do not remember the trauma that lies at the root of subjectivity, the lack or gap that remains, even within what we call social reality. This position leads to a depoliticisation. We forget that a complete, non-antagonistic society is impossible. We strive for completion and closure, often at any price. There are a number of ways in which this is done, according to Žižek.[32] The first is communitarian attempts to produce a close homogeneous society – *arche-politics*. Political struggle disappears because everyone agrees on everything. The second, most common in the liberal west, Žižek calls *para-politics*. Here the political is replaced by politics. Standardised competition takes place between accepted political parties according to pre-set rules, the prize being a turn at executive control of the state bureaucracy. Politics has become policing or managerial control. In the third – *meta-politics* – political conflict is seen as a shadow theatre, with the important events taking place in another scene, that of economic processes. Politics should be cancelled when economic processes have worked themselves out (as scientific materialism predicts) and matters can be decided by rational debate and the collective will. Finally, we have *ultra-politics*, where political struggle becomes warfare, and the military are called in. There is no common ground for debate and politics is militarised.

If we are to resist such attempts to 'gentrify' or depoliticise the political we have to recall the constituted, provisional and historically contingent nature of every social order, of every ontology. This position, which Žižek calls 'traversing the fantasy', 'tarrying with the negative' or fidelity to the ontological crack in the universe, is uncomfortable.[33] It involves an acceptance of the lack of trauma at the centre of the subject and the non-existence of any complete, closed social order.

[32] Žižek, *The Ticklish Subject*, 190.

[33] For the ontological crack, see Slavoj Žižek, *The Plague of Fantasies* (London: Verso, 1997), 214; for tarrying with the negative, Slavoj Žižek, *Tarrying with the Negative: Kant, Hegel and the Critique of Ideology* (Durham, North Carolina: Duke University Press, 1993), 237; and for traversing the fantasy, see, for example, Slavoj Žižek, *The Sublime Object of Ideology* (London: Verso, 1989), 126.

Although we have been talking about an intellectual act of traversing the fantasy, in fact facing trauma, facing the way being is ungrounded and how it relies on a particular, constituted notion of linear temporality is something that in any case takes place. It happens. It takes place in security crises, in wars, revolutions or other social upheavals – where the symbolic order itself and its institutions are under threat or in suspense – and where people as individuals face the horrors of battle, persecution, famine or bombing. It takes place also, as feminists in particular remind us, in the everyday, in the face of threats to personal security.[34]

In this book I examine the connection between trauma, violence and political community by looking at how traumas such as wars or persecutions are inscribed and re-inscribed into everyday narratives. This takes place in practices of remembrance, memorialisation and witnessing. It also takes place in political action. All these practices are the site of struggle. For example, the temporality and inexpressibility of trauma makes the role of the witness an almost unbearable one. Despite this, there is an imperative to speak, and a determination to find ways of speaking that remain true to the trauma. I argue that the process of re-inscription into linear narratives, whilst possibly necessary from some points of view – it is argued that telling the story alleviates traumatic stress, for example – is a process that generally depoliticises, and that there is an alternative, that of *encircling the trauma*. We cannot try to address the trauma directly without risking its gentrification. We cannot remember it as something that took place in time, because this would neutralise it. All we can do is 'to *encircle* again and again the site' of the trauma, 'to *mark* it in its very impossibility'.[35] Memory and forgetting are crucial, both in contesting the depoliticisation that goes under the name of politics, and in keeping open a space for a genuine political challenge by encircling the trauma rather than attempting to gentrify it. The reinstallation of time as linear and the narrating of events as history are central to the process of re-inscription. However, there are forms of memory and memorialisation (perhaps more aptly called 'not forgetting' rather than remembering) that do not produce a linear narrative, but rather retain another notion of temporality. These are ways of encircling the real.[36]

This is possible because linear time and trauma time do not exist independently; it is not a question of choosing one or the other. Rather, they define and constitute each other in a complex relationship, almost

[34] Laura S. Brown, 'Not outside the range: one feminist perspective on psychic trauma', in *Trauma: Explorations in Memory*, ed. Cathy Caruth (Baltimore: Johns Hopkins University Press, 1995), 100–12.

[35] Žižek, *For They Know Not What They Do*, 272.

[36] Žižek, *Plague of Fantasies*, 213–18.

like opposite poles of a dichotomy. Like remembering and forgetting, each implies the other: they are inextricably entwined. Trauma time is inherent in and destabilises any production of linearity. Trauma has to be excluded for linearity to be convincing, but it cannot be successfully put to one side: it always intrudes, it cannot be completely forgotten. And similarly, trauma time cannot be described in the language we have without recourse to notions of linearity, as we saw when discussing the retroactive production of the subject. Memorialisation that does not return to a linear narrative but rather retains the trace of another notion of temporality does occur. It is found when the political struggle between linear and trauma time is resolved not by a forgetting of trauma and a return to linearity, nor by attempting the impossible opposite – speaking from within trauma – but by a recognition and *surrounding* of the trauma at the heart of any social or symbolic order.

Practices of trauma

After traumatic events, there is a struggle over memory. Some forms of remembering can be seen as ways of forgetting: ways of recovering from trauma by putting its lessons to one side, refusing to acknowledge that anything has changed, restoring the pretence. In the next chapter I look at remembrance and veterans' accounts in Britain and Australia after the First World War, and at one of the responses to Vietnam veterans in the United States. In Britain, remembrance practices continue some eighty years after the 1914–18 war. They involve families as well as veterans themselves. Accounts of the war drawing on veterans' experiences have been written. An Australian study shows that memories that veterans relate depend on and interact with the public context of their remembering, and this leads to a discussion of the nature of memory. Memory is not straightforward, especially in the case of traumatic memory. The second part of Chapter 2 considers trauma and how post-traumatic stress is produced as a condition that can be diagnosed – and cured. The effect of this in the case of Vietnam veterans is to depoliticise their memories; a form of disciplinary control is instituted. This is an example of how hegemonic power can control and subjugate memory.

In the most part, memorialisation of war is a practice that reproduces stories of national glory and heroism. It produces linear time, the time of the state. But does it always do that? Is this contested? Don't these accounts have a far too unquestionably consensual view of the political community? In Chapter 3, I examine in detail two examples of memorials where at some time at least this narration of the national story did not happen: the Cenotaph in Whitehall in London, a memorial to the fallen of the British Empire in the First World War, and the US Vietnam Veterans Memorial in the Mall in Washington, the Vietnam Wall. In both cases it turns out that the role and form of the memorial were contested, and that the struggle was precisely over the processes of bearing witness to the horror of war, or forgetting it and inscribing a narrative of sacrifice and heroism. In each instance, the function of the memorial has changed through time but both have involved a certain openness to unanswered and unanswerable questions. Both can be described in part at least as encircling the event, marking its place without narrating it as part of a linear story or national myth. Both can also be seen to be later co-opted into the dominant account: they have both come to stand for the status quo. The Vietnam Wall has spawned lookalikes, in particular, ironically enough, a monument to law enforcement officers, also in Washington. The Cenotaph was daubed with graffiti during anti-capitalist protests, when it was seen as a monument to imperial wars.

Memorials to war, even to defeat, can inscribe the national myth or the imagined community. What happens when what is to be commemorated is a genocide rather than a war? How is an event like this to be embodied in stone? In Chapter 4, I examine memorials to the Irish famine, American slavery and the Nazi genocide, and the controversies and debates over how those events could be commemorated or remembered. Here memorials become abstract; some are designed to disappear, or are inverted and buried; others are never built, like the Berlin memorial where nothing has yet been constructed. Fine art and particularly installation work attempts to find other languages of remembrance. The story does get told, for example, in museums, films and at concentration camp sites. A number of powerful groups attempt to appropriate it for their own political or commercial purposes, and the voice of the survivor can be co-opted into one narrative or another. I examine three museums, in Washington, London and New York, all of which opened in the 1990s. Despite attempts by scholars to question what representations were appropriate, it came to be accepted that there was one narrative history of the Holocaust and that it had to be told. I examine debates over the so-called Holocaust industry, and the ownership of 'the Holocaust', and consider whether confronting Holocaust deniers such as David Irving serves to confine our engagement to questions of historical fact, enabling us to avoid dealing with the more difficult issues raised by survivors. At the end of the chapter, I examine a recent film account of the Dachau camp museum and its self-appointed guide, Martin Zaidenstadt. This film illustrates my argument that to require irrefutable proof of testimony is to fail to hear what is being said.

If memorials on the whole (not always, of course) support the imaginary community and reproduce the status quo, testimony is generally

expected to function as a criticism of state power and its abuse. In Chapter 5, I examine how the structure of testimony and the question of survival have been analysed. The imperative to bear witness encounters two problems. First, the survivor is not in a position to bear witness: by definition, he or she has not suffered the extremities that others, those who did not survive (those who Primo Levi calls 'the drowned') suffered. Second, there is no language in which to express what the survivor wishes to say. The testimony is a witnessing of the void or the impossibility of closure and listening to testimony has to take the form of listening to something that is not there. However, those who did not survive are the true witnesses, and this paradox forces a rethinking of what is meant by human being. It also leads to the conclusion that by virtue of its very structure testimony is a challenge to sovereign power. The testimony of survivors of the concentration camps is paradigmatic here, and is found in various forms: video testimonies, literature and second-generation accounts. How much do these forms of testimony – which include truth and reconciliation commissions and oral testimony in the aftermath of Third World development projects – how much do they allow the survivor a voice? Do they not rather result either in traumatic events being rendered a spectacle, a monstrosity, or alternatively, in trauma being legalised and medicalised?

Contemporary culture has been described as a testimonial culture, as well as a culture of victimhood, with the proliferation of programmes such as the *Jerry Springer Show*. There is a rush to collect testimony of war crimes almost while a conflict is taking place. It sometimes seems that we watch ourselves standing by while atrocities are committed – as in Kosovo, for example – safe in the knowledge that there is a war crimes tribunal in place that will avenge the deeds. I examine Giorgio Agamben's argument that sovereign power (the modern state form) operates by the production of 'bare life', as exemplified in the concentration camps but found in another form in other instances of modern life. In the second part of Chapter 5, I show how in the Kosovo intervention in the 1990s the production of trauma was part of the production of sovereign power, in this case not state power, but the sovereign power of a supra-national body, Nato.

In Chapter 6, I return in conclusion to sites of memory and landscapes of political power, this time not individual war memorials and cemeteries but entire cityscapes such as the Mall in Washington and Tiananmen Square in Beijing. Here, in a return of the repressed, we find political protest brought directly to the sites of state or imperial memory and symbolism. The protests reclaim memories of trauma and rewrite them as a form of resistance. The story is never finished: the scripting of memory by those in power can always be challenged, and such challenges are very often found at moments and in places where the very foundations of the imagined community are laid out. They often take the form of self-consciously non-violent forms of protest. Sometimes the result is violent repression, as in Beijing in 1989. Occasionally, instead, there is a moment of possibility: an opening to trauma time and a recognition of the contingency of political community.

The events at the World Trade Centre in New York and at the Pentagon in Washington on September 11, 2001 were the obscene reverse of non-violent protest. What happened was the return of trauma itself to the symbolic landscapes of impregnable imperial power when extreme, gratuitous violence was used against civilians in the centre of the cityscapes of New York and Washington. Whereas in Tiananmen Square, civilians remonstrated with soldiers face-to-face, attempting to persuade them not to behave as instruments of state power but as individuals, in New York hijackers took ordinary citizens of all nationalities and turned them into instruments for, and casualties of, indiscriminate political violence. In this sense, the hijackers behaved very much as states do when they engage in the bombing of civilian areas or in sending conscripts into battle. And in so doing, they made it easier for the state to claim that any violence it might choose to use was legitimate. The events had two contradictory effects. First, they brought trauma into the heart of the safe areas of lower Manhattan, disrupting the linear narrative of security and state control. But, second, they opened the way for the state to move quickly with its offer of revenge and retaliation as a suitable and legitimate answer to that traumatic tear in the fabric of normality. Survivors were in an impossible position. The opening to trauma time and the recognition of the contingency of political community were followed immediately, even simultaneously, by the reaffirmation of solidarity and nationhood. It was difficult to distinguish calls for a recognition of the trauma from calls for revenge.

2 Survivor memories and the diagnosis of trauma: the Great War and Vietnam

At the going down of the sun and in the morning
We will remember them

– Lawrence Binyon

The 'Great War', the war to end all wars, still has a special place in British memory over eighty years after its end. Ceremonies to commemorate the Armistice initially took place on its anniversary, the eleventh day of the eleventh month at eleven o'clock in the morning and involved 'a complete suspension of all . . . activities'.[1] Later, after the Second World War, they were moved for convenience to the second Sunday of the month. This was logical, after all. It would be less of a disruption to daily life if remembrance services could replace the standard Sunday religious ceremonies instead of bringing work to a halt in the middle of the week. But by the end of the century there was a movement to bring remembrance back to the eleventh hour of the eleventh day. At first just a few people kept silence at the appointed hour and in some places gun salutes were fired. By the last year of the twentieth century, some shops and workplaces were marking the original anniversary, while official ceremonies ran in parallel on the nearest Sunday. The campaign to return to Armistice Day proper was begun by the Royal British Legion in 1995. On the eightieth anniversary in 1998 they estimated that forty-three million people in Britain had observed the two-minute silence on 11 November.[2] This seemed a little unlikely – in most places not even the traffic stopped. It remains to be seen what will become of this campaign in subsequent

[1] Proclamation of King George V. Public Record Office: Board of Education and Predecessors: Private Office: Papers (Series 1) (ED 24): ED 24/2035, King's message on first anniversary of the Armistice.

[2] 'Britain at standstill as 43 million observe two-minute silence', *The Guardian*, London, 12 November 1998, 3. This was around 75 per cent of the population. The Legion's estimates for 1996 (57 per cent), 1997 (69 per cent) also seem a little optimistic. 'Britain pays silent tribute to war dead', *The Daily Telegraph*, London, 12 November 1998, 13. The figure of 75 per cent for 1998 is derived from research by Audience Selection and MORI ('Silence: Introduction', Royal British Legion, http://www.globalsilence.com/html/intro.html, 25 October 2000, no longer active).

years. The British Legion, who describe themselves as the 'custodian of Remembrance in the UK', called for a 'global silence' in 2000, to follow a silence throughout Commonwealth countries in 1999.[3]

Although the war and its warriors are still remembered, there is no unanimity about how that remembrance should take place. Nor is there agreement among people in Britain as to what they are remembering or why. Many people, maybe an increasing number, remember relatives who died in the war or as a result of it. In the immediate aftermath of war, family remembrances are caught up with caring for those returning disabled or scarred and rebuilding family relationships around absent members, as well as the raw mourning for loss.[4] As the generations pass and the loss becomes less immediate – or as family differences and disagreements disappear perhaps – the descendants of those who fought or of their brothers and sisters acknowledge the absence, the gap in the family. Increasingly, people are tracing the graves of family members buried in France or Belgium. The War Graves Commission, set up during the First World War as an imperial commission but now, of course, representing the Commonwealth, looks after the war cemeteries. In 1998, the eightieth anniversary of the Armistice, it received 50,000 enquiries. This wasn't just an eightieth anniversary boom, however. The number of enquiries had been rising rapidly from a figure of around 2,000 a year in 1978 and 21,000 ten years later. Of the 1998 total of 50,000, some 35,000 enquiries relate to First World War soldiers.[5] The number of visitors to the war cemeteries has seen a corresponding increase. Since First World War history has formed part of the national curriculum in the UK the number has been swollen by school parties. But there are continuing visits by groups of surviving British veterans.

The personal links that we retain colour our response to public ceremonial. When we commemorate war dead we are not just or even mainly doing so as citizens of the nation, whatever that nation may be. We may no longer have our own memories of the conflict. We may not be able to challenge state ceremonial from private experience of the war and its horrors. But we have memories of relatives and we often carry a responsibility to them to express their views even when, or perhaps especially if, they can no longer do so themselves. We have inherited the mementoes

[3] Royal British Legion, 'The history of the Two Minute Silence in the UK', http://www.globalsilence.com/html/history2.html, 25 October 2000, no longer active.

[4] Jay Winter, 'Forms of kinship and remembrance in the aftermath of the Great War', in *War and Remembrance in the Twentieth Century*, ed. Jay Winter and Emmanuel Sivan (Cambridge University Press, 1999), 40–60.

[5] Robin Stummer, 'The war we can't let go', *The Guardian Weekend*, London, 7 November 1998, 12–23; 15.

Figure 1 Field of Remembrance, Westminster Abbey

left by the soldiers who were killed – and now also in most cases of those who returned – and this brings home the immediacy in a way that a parent or grandparent's stories perhaps could not. When the old soldiers or their widows or siblings die in their turn, the surviving generations become their spokespeople rather than their rebellious children. We speak for them now that they no longer can.

We respect their attitudes to remembrance, though we do not necessarily follow them. Ian Jack describes how he planted a cross with a poppy in the Field of Remembrance at Westminster in 1998. The Field of Remembrance is an area of lawn outside Westminster Abbey in London that has been used every year since 1928 around Remembrance Day (Figure 1). Relatives and friends can pay tribute to the dead, buying a small wooden cross with a poppy in its centre, inscribing it with the dead soldier's name and then planting it in the appropriate section of lawn. The plots are marked out with the names of regiments, and the result looks like a miniature military cemetery.[6] But although Ian Jack planted a cross in memory of Company Sergeant Major J. Birmingham of the

[6] *The 2000 Field of Remembrance*, Westminster Abbey, http://www.westminster-abbey.org/press/release/991111.htm, 15 January 2003.

12th Battalion Royal Scots, one of several of his great-uncles who was killed, his father, he says, would not have approved:

> My father would not have planted a cross to his Uncle Jack, though as a boy he loved him. . . . My father would not have planted a cross with a poppy for two reasons. One, he loathed poppies. The money raised went to a fund named for General Haig, whose callous strategy, in my father's view, led to hundreds of thousands of deaths, including Uncle Jack's. Two, he hated crosses, with their Christian suggestion of sacrifice and redemption and the attempt to give meaning to meaningless slaughter.[7]

In a way though, as Ian Jack points out, 'painless memories are more easily visited'. When we are less immediately involved we can more readily participate in, and perhaps challenge, practices of remembrance. Roy Hattersley recounts the story of Private Herbert Hattersley, 7th Battalion of the Sherwood Foresters. He describes Bert's diary, 'a penny notebook fastened by elastic inside a cheap leatherette wallet that his sister Augusta had sent him in anticipation of his 17th birthday'. The diary is 'not much of a record of the war in Flanders'. It records the 'bare facts' of troop movements, battles and those killed. Bert himself died on the Somme, aged nineteen. His diary was found in his billet in Bienvilliers, with three letters from home folded inside. Roy Hattersley contrasts Bert's diary 'in all its brief inadequacy' with the efforts of war poets such as Wilfred Owen. He urges us to 'forget the poetry. Remember the men who could not spell the names of the battles in which they fought and died.'[8] Niall Ferguson's grandfather was one who survived. As Ferguson points out those who were killed and their bereaved relatives were in a minority. This was because ' "only" around 12 per cent of British servicemen died in the war, leaving a good 88 per cent who (like my grandfather) came back alive, of whom only a minority were permanently incapacitated'.[9] Private Richard Smith of the Lancashire Fusiliers – my own grandfather – came back too. But he was discharged as no longer fit for military service – he was gassed – and he died of his injuries seven years later in 1925, leaving a widow and baby daughter. His widow never received a pension, though she survived him by more than sixty years. Although they had met before the war, they had waited until he was demobbed before they married. It is an old story, shared by many others. Jay Winter estimates that the war

[7] Ian Jack, 'As I paid tribute to Uncle Jack, I thought of something else. That it was memory without pain, at least for most of us', *The Independent*, London, 7 November 1998, 1.

[8] Roy Hattersley, 'There was no poetry for Uncle Herbert', *The Wednesday Review, The Independent*, London, 11 November 1998, 4.

[9] Niall Ferguson, 'Do today's public rituals hinder our understanding of war?', *The Wednesday Review, The Independent*, London, 11 November 1998, 4.

left three million widows in Britain.[10] It is not known how many men were wounded. Of the half a million war disability pensions still being paid out in 1938, some 41,000 were for bronchitis or tuberculosis as a result of gassing.[11] These figures represent only those whose needs had been officially recognised of course. And by then many would have died. Many did not pursue claims, choosing to retain their self-respect.[12] But where one generation has a pride in self-reliance, another sees merely an injustice.

While Hattersley berates the war poets and denounces any pity to be found in their work, Ferguson does not. He supports rituals of remembrance that communicate grief to what he claims were 'the lucky majority' who had not lost relatives, while deploring the use of the language of sacrifice, such as appears on the tomb of the unknown soldier in Westminster Abbey:

> THUS ARE COMMEMORATED THE MANY
> MULTITUDES WHO DURING THE GREAT
> WAR OF 1914–1918 GAVE THE MOST THAT
> MAN CAN GIVE LIFE ITSELF
> FOR GOD
> FOR KING AND COUNTRY
> FOR LOVED ONES HOME AND EMPIRE
> FOR THE SACRED CAUSE OF JUSTICE AND
> THE FREEDOM OF THE WORLD[13]

This 'high diction' was, as Ferguson points out, 'loathed by Owen and [Siegfried] Sassoon'. Owen, in his poem *Dulce et Decorum Est*, calls it 'the old Lie'.[14] Despite Ferguson's own views, his historical account of the war published in 1998 bore on its cover a Flanders poppy.[15]

Although only a small percentage of British servicemen may have been killed in the war, Ferguson underestimates the impact on subsequent generations of those deaths – and the importance of the memories of the millions who fought and *did* return to tell the tale. In most families in Britain and other countries from which troops were enlisted there will have been someone who fought.

[10] Jay Winter, 'Forms of kinship and remembrance', 42.

[11] Lyn Macdonald, *The Roses of No Man's Land* (London: Penguin, 1983), 340–1.

[12] For a discussion of how returning Anzacs were deprived of their pensions, see Alistair Thomson, *Anzac Memories: Living with the Legend* (Melbourne: Oxford University Press, 1994).

[13] *The Unknown Warrior at Westminster Abbey*, http://www.westminster-abbey.org/library/burial/warrior.htm, 15 January 2003.

[14] Wilfred Owen, *The Collected Poems of Wilfred Owen*, ed. C. Day Lewis (London: Chatto and Windus, 1963), 55.

[15] Niall Ferguson, *The Pity of War* (London: Penguin, 1998).

Survivor memories 1914–1918

Of course, for many who returned the war was the last thing they wanted to talk about. Some kept their silence for years; George Louth, for example, 'blanked out the war and only once spoke about it from 1918 to 1990'.[16] The point is not that survivors all return with the same view of the war and how it should be remembered. Nor that their descendants are likely to agree on how it should be remembered either. They do not, as we have seen. There are bleak differences of class, experience, background. Some, according to Joanna Bourke, loved killing, and this can be part of what is unspeakable about combat.[17] Others returned traumatised by their experiences. What they are likely to share, however, is a scepticism for both official accounts and pious sentiment. Even when the Prime Minister David Lloyd George recognises that those who fought have experienced something he has not, he still uses the rhetoric of flames and sacrifice: 'I cannot think what these men have gone through. I have been at the door of the furnace and witnessed it, but that is not being in it, and I saw them march into the furnace.'[18] This is from his election speech of 24 November 1918, where he calls for a land fit for heroes. Those who fought might not have been heroes sacrificing themselves for their homeland, but neither according to Lyn Macdonald are they to be pitied as sheep led meekly to the slaughter.[19] She regards such views as demeaning to those who fought. It is perhaps disagreements like this over how the war should be remembered that meant that calls for a major interpretative museum or visitor centre were for a long time unsuccessful.[20] Or perhaps it is a continuing recognition that there will always be more than one story to tell. For many years on the British sections of the battlefields there were only small private museums – and these were often collections of artefacts left to speak largely for themselves.

By the turn of the century, there were, finally, plans in hand for a visitor centre on the Somme, close to the memorial at Thiepval. Opposed by officials at the Ministry of Defence, who feared it would turn the battlefields

[16] Quoted by Gordon Marsden, 'Unheard witnesses of war', *The Friday Review*, *The Independent*, London, 13 November 1998, 5, in a review of Richard van Emden and Steve Humphries, *Veterans: Last Survivors of the Great War* (Barnsley, South Yorkshire: Leo Cooper, 1999).

[17] Joanna Bourke, *An Intimate History of Killing: Face-to-face Killing in Twentieth Century Warfare* (London: Granta, 1999), 13–14.

[18] David Lloyd George, 'A humble recognition of heroes', *The Independent*, London, 7 November 1998.

[19] Robin Stummer, 'The war we can't let go', *The Guardian Weekend*, 7 November 1998, 12–23; 21.

[20] John Lichfield, 'The memory of war', *Friday Review*, *The Independent*, London, 6 November 1998, 1.

into a theme park, but supported by the British Legion, the Commonwealth War Graves Commission and other veterans' groups, it was to be funded in part by private contributions raised in Britain and built on French soil. The appeal for funds was launched in 2000. It was seen by its supporters as a European venture, commemorating a 'European Civil War'.[21] There is also a museum at Ypres – called Flanders Field Museum – where special exhibitions relate the history of this section of the front line. In 2002, an exhibition called 'Dead.lines: War, Media and Propaganda in the Twentieth Century' was mounted. This exhibition, like the United States Holocaust Memorial Museum displays discussed in Chapter 4, attempted to involve visitors in the exhibit in a personal way by issuing them with the name of an individual involved in the campaign. As visitors made their way around the exhibit, they could punch the name into computers that recounted the individual's history.[22]

Each year it is noted that soon there will be no surviving veterans, no one still alive who can speak of the war from personal experience. These worries are often premature. The same concern has already been expressed about the Second World War and the Nazi genocide, where the fiftieth anniversaries have only recently been marked.[23] The eightieth anniversary of the Armistice produced a resurgence of interest in the recollections of veterans who had survived to reach their century.[24] Over a period of twenty-five years Lyn Macdonald has used interviews with eyewitnesses and survivors to build accounts of the battles of Ypres and the Somme and other campaigns of the war. After the first ten years, she had amassed the contributions of some 3,000 men and women who had served in the war and her work had inspired the voluntary assistance of a veritable army of research assistants.[25] Her books do not seek to enter the controversies that still surround the war so many years on nor, she claims, to make political judgements. What she is concerned with is the experience of war, not the war as an abstraction about which views can differ and conclusions can be drawn. Her aim is give a voice to the accounts of the soldiers themselves, and to preserve these accounts when all the survivors have died. They were representatives of all walks of life and all households:

[21] John Lichfield, '£1m visitor centre will salute victims of Somme battlefields', *The Independent*, London, 11 November 1999, 3.

[22] Robert Hanks, 'All go on the Western Front', *The Independent Review*, London, 22 April 2002, 16–17. See also http://www.inflandersfields.be, under construction.

[23] John Davison, 'Almost the Last Post of all for the old men of Dunkirk', *The Independent*, London, 31 May 1999, 3.

[24] Emden and Humphries, *Last Survivors*.

[25] Lyn Macdonald, *Somme* (London: Penguin, 1983), xv. The collection of oral and written history, documents and ephemera is to go to the Imperial War Museum, London.

The whole nation experienced that war, just as, three generations on, the nation is still experiencing its repercussions. There was hardly a family in the land which, in its inner or outer circle, had not suffered bereavement and hardly a young man who was lucky enough to return who would not be affected to the end of his life by his experience... Some survive still, but the voices, like the old soldiers themselves, are rapidly fading away.... When the last of them has gone a great silence will fall. I hope these histories of their war will at least continue to transmit the echo.[26]

Macdonald sees herself as the advocate of those veterans: her aim is 'to "tell it like it was" for them'.[27] She weaves together survivors' written and oral accounts, placing them in the broader context often unknown at the time to those who fought, to form a history of the war from below. The accounts are terse but often moving. This is from Private Bill Smith of the New Zealand Machine Gun Company who was serving at Passchendaele on the morning of 13 October 1917:

I was absolutely ravenous. When I'd gone into action my haversack contained a tin of bully beef and a pair of puttees. When I'd taken it off in a shell hole that night before to try to get a bit of food, it was a sight for sore eyes. Both the beef and the puttees were riddled with bullets. They must have missed my back by a fraction of an inch, for the back of my tunic was in shreds. I was so hungry that I went over to the dead Durhams and rooted in a few haversacks looking for eats. But I wasn't the first. All I could find were four small pieces of shortbread. It was home made...[28]

Another, this time from a Canadian, Private R. Le Brun, who was on duty on 24 October carrying ammunition from Ypres to a delivery point quarter of a mile from the front line:

The very first trip back on the morning of the twenty-fifth, the day before the first attack, I heard someone nearby calling for help. I dodged round a shell-hole and over a few hummocks before I saw him. It was one of our infantrymen and he was sitting on the ground, propped up on his elbow with his tunic open. I nearly vomited. His insides were spilling out of his stomach and he was holding himself and trying to push all this awful stuff back in. When he saw me he said, 'Finish it for me, mate. Put a bullet in me. Go on. I want you to. Finish it!' He had no gun himself. When I did nothing, he started to swear. He cursed and swore at me and kept on shouting even after I turned and ran. I didn't have my revolver. All my life I've never stopped wondering what I would have done if I had.[29]

[26] Macdonald, *Somme*, xiv. Other books by Lyn Macdonald include *They Called it Passchendaele: The Story of the Battle of Ypres and of the Men Who Fought in it* (London: Penguin, 1978); and *The Roses of No Man's Land*.

[27] Macdonald, *Somme*, xiv.

[28] Macdonald, *They Called it Passchendaele*, 216.

[29] *Ibid.*, 226–7.

Alistair Thomson's aims, in his oral history work with Australian veterans of the First War, or 'diggers' as Australian soldiers called themselves, are somewhat different. His interest is in the Anzac legend, and the political and historical impact of this myth of the Australian war experience.[30] He traces the story that has grown up around the Anzacs and through interviewing the same veterans twice, the second time after a lapse of years, tries to piece together how veterans' reminiscences have altered as the context in which their memories are recounted has changed. He interviewed twenty-one working-class veterans from Melbourne. His book focuses on three veterans in particular, which enables him to tell these individual stories in some depth.

Thomson gives us not just *biographies* of his three veterans, but 'memory biographies'. He traces how memories alter with the years, in parallel with changing forms of public commemoration. For returning ex-servicemen, how they remembered the war depended not only on their experiences of the war itself, but on what happened when they returned. Percy Bird, for example, never received a war pension because he had declared himself to be well on his return – without realising the significance of the question. However, he had a relatively 'easy' time in the war. Although he spent six months on the front, in that time his unit never went 'over the top'. On his return he slotted back into civilian life without any difficulties, finding a job and returning to his fiancée. He found that 'his attitude to war and his identity as an Australian soldier were affirmed through various public practices of remembrance'; he had no grievances, bitterness or disillusionment.[31] Fred Farrall's experience was different. An awkward recruit, he suffered from seasickness on the voyage. His battalion was on the Somme; Fred was hospitalised for six months with trench foot, returning in time to take part in the attack on Polygon Wood in September 1917. Further long periods in hospital followed, including nervous problems. Of the group of friends he had made on the recruiting march in Australia, almost all were killed, leaving Fred with no companions to turn to. When he was discharged, he was unable to resume work and could not get a war pension either. He finally had a nervous breakdown in 1926. In the first years after the war, Fred maintained a silence about his experiences despite having disturbing private memories. He refused to wear his medals or attend reunions or Anzac day parades.[32] Instead, he became a political radical, active in the labour movement. It was only much later,

[30] Anzac stands for Australian and New Zealand Army Corps. While the label 'Anzac' was used by officials, 'the term "digger" was coined by the Australian and other ranks on the western front in 1916 and 1917' and did not carry the same patriotic meanings (Thomson, *Anzac Memories*, 44).

[31] Thomson, *Anzac Memories*, 159. [32] *Ibid.*, 169.

in the 1960s and 1970s, that he began to talk about the war and take part in remembrance activities. All of a sudden, accounts of the war were appearing that were different. Narratives of the horrors of the trenches became part of popular history, and Fred found that his post-war nightmares were not unique. He became active in the peace movement. By the 1980s Fred's own stories were suddenly in demand by a new generation keen to hear criticisms of the war and learn what it was 'really' like. He was happy at last to have the opportunity to speak to a receptive audience and find his experiences affirmed. As Thomson puts it, 'As public representations of Australians at war changed, Fred Farrall came to live with the legend.'[33]

Thomson concludes that 'the memories of working-class diggers had become entangled with the legend of their lives, and that veterans had adopted and used the Anzac legend because it was resonant and useful in their own remembering'.[34] How they used the legend was an individual matter; different veterans would make use of it in different ways, and these uses would change with the general social context of the period. Thomson uses the concept of composure to understand this practice, where this term refers to two inseparable processes: 'In one sense we compose or construct memories using the public languages and meaning of our culture. In another sense we compose memories that help us feel relatively comfortable with our lives and identities, that give us a feeling of composure.'[35] The first requires a cultural approach to remembering, the second a more psychological one. Thomson's work is fascinating as a study of the processes of memory and highlights its complexities. It clearly has implications for the use of oral testimony, which Thomson argues 'needs to be sensitive to the ways in which such testimony is articulated in relation to public narratives and personal identities'.[36] This cuts both ways. Historians who challenge established narratives of wars 'may threaten the personal composure that veterans have found through the legend'.[37] They may revive painful memories of some veterans; on the other hand they may provide an opportunity for others, whose experiences were excluded from previous accounts, to express their memories.

Memory and trauma time

Thomson's work raises the question of how we conceptualise memory and the processes of remembering. The view of memory as composure

[33] *Ibid.*, 214. [34] *Ibid.*, 7.
[35] *Ibid.*, 8. For his notion of composure he refers to Graham Dawson, *Soldier Heroes: Britishness, Colonial Adventure and the Imagining of Masculinities* (London: Routledge, 1994).
[36] Thomson, *Anzac Memories*, 218. [37] *Ibid.*, 218.

that Thomson articulates combines both social and individual aspects. It sees the activity of remembering as the interface between the two. When veterans remember, they recall aspects of their past and recount them in particular ways: 'What memories we choose to recall and relate (and thus remember), changes over time.'[38] Remembering, as something that we *do*, seems in this account to be distinct from memories – something that we *have*. But is that the case? To what extent are the memories we have distinct from the uses we make of them? Is memory a separate thing from the activity of remembering? Are our memories inscribed somewhere, presumably in our brains, as a pristine record of what happened, when it happened, or are they produced through the social activity of remembering? And, finally, is the question 'What is memory?' one that we can answer?

In contemporary European culture we tend to think of memories in the way epitomised in the film *Blade Runner* where Rachel is convinced that what she can remember and a bundle of photographs from her childhood prove that she is a human being rather than a replicant.[39] Her memories seem to show that she was born and grew into adulthood as a human being does – whereas replicants are produced as adults, with no past. Deckard, the character whose job is to identify and hunt down replicants, is convinced at first too. The irony, of course, is that when she was made she was implanted with childhood memories – memories that belonged to someone else – and given a stack of images as proof that her memories were real. The film's questioning of what it is to be human is particularly effective when it challenges memory. Memories are what we think of as most personal and subjective, as testimony to our individuality. We also regard them as evidence of what happened – though preferably, in this doubting age, backed up by matching photographs.

Memories are pictured as traces or recordings left by the past in individual minds, like a personal archive. This view of memory is shaped by the way that in our everyday lives we are surrounded by machines that seem to 'remember' for us. We have computer systems that show exactly when we last did our shopping and what we bought, surveillance cameras that register our movements about towns and cities, and tape machines that record and play back at will. This all reinforces the image of the past as somehow inscribed somewhere in every detail – and available for us to recall if only we had the perfect memory, or unimpeded access to our memories. Neuroscience has tended to back this up with its notion of a brain with areas devoted to certain functions. We can imagine a region where memory resides and images of the past are stored as in a computer.

[38] *Ibid.*, 9. [39] *Blade Runner*, directed by Ridley Scott, Warner Brothers, 1982.

Some psychoanalytic perceptions of the mind foster this view too. It is reinforced when hypnosis or analysis appears to give access to memories that we cannot consciously recall. Survivors experience flashbacks to the scene of their trauma, and again these seem to show that a neutral, unscripted version of 'what actually happened' exists inside our heads somewhere. There is much controversy surrounding both hypnosis and traumatic recall, but these notions fit very well the idea that everything we experience is recorded in our minds and that memory is nothing much more than the rather mechanical process by which we locate and retrieve that record.

This understanding is a specifically modern idea of memory. Pierre Nora argues that in France in the 1980s and 1990s the pace of change and the movement away from local, traditional cultures had led to a memory crisis. It was for this reason, he claims, that we found a need to have special *lieux de mémoire* or 'sites of memory': 'if we still dwelt among our memories, there would be no need to consecrate sites to them'.[40] Our practices of memory had changed. Or as Nora argues, 'memory' had been replaced by 'history'. Memory and history are two different things. Memory is sacred, history profane. Memory is alive, evolving, negotiated and belongs to the present and to particular groups; history is a reconstruction of the past that has to be analytical and detached. Moreover 'memory is always suspect in the eyes of history'.[41] The concept of 'the nation' is central to the form of memory whose loss Nora laments. Now 'we no longer celebrate the nation, but we study the nation's celebrations'.[42] Modern memory is different, less immediate, more indirect. It has three characteristics. First, it is archival: 'a gigantic and breathtaking effort to store the material vestiges of what we cannot possibly remember, thereby amassing an unfathomable collection of things that we might someday need to recall'.[43] Second, memory has been transformed into a private affair, an obsession with individual psychology and a search for personal identity. Third, modern memory is alienated memory. It disconnects past from present rather than emphasising their inseparability. In other words, rephrasing Nora's analysis, modern social practice produces 'memory' as archival and private and 'the past' as distinct from the present. The view we have of memory as archival and private and our notion of time as a linear flow from past to present on

[40] Pierre Nora, 'General introduction: between memory and history', in *Realms of Memory: Rethinking the French Past*, ed. Pierre Nora and Lawrence D. Kritzman (New York: Columbia University Press, 1996), 1–20; 2.

[41] Nora, 'Between memory and history', 3. [42] *Ibid.*, 7. [43] *Ibid.*, 8.

which this view of memory depends are both specific to our historical period. They reflect 'modern memory'.

Maurice Halbwachs regards the modern understanding of memory, which makes it an appropriate topic for psychology, as astonishing. He argues that in order to explain memory at all it needs to be seen as social. He does not mean that there is something that could be called collective or cultural memory that would be a sum or combination of individual recollections. This would be to assume the existence of individual memories that could interact or be added together to produce collective memory – a circularity since this is what he is trying to explain. Nor does he mean, as Thomson argued, that the use we make of our memories, or rather how we choose to use them, depends on our social context at the time. His point is quite different. He argues that 'it is in this sense that there exists a collective memory and social frameworks for memory; it is to the degree that our individual thought places itself in these frameworks and participates in this memory that it is capable of the act of recollection'.[44] In other words, it is *only within a social context that we can remember in the first place*. He rejects the idea that the past is preserved in some area of the brain from which it can later be recalled. We do not have a store of ready-scripted memories that are held in the unconscious and then brought to our conscious mind when we need them. On the contrary, says Halbwachs, 'the past is not preserved, but is reconstructed on the basis of the present'.[45] This fits with the Freudian idea that some experiences, such as childhood abuse, do not become traumatic until they are retrospectively imbued with a meaning, for example a sexual content, that was absent earlier. Halbwachs is not disputing that we may retain our *sensory impressions* for some time, but he contends that *memories* are not at all the same thing. The difference is that memories are expressed in terms of meanings. Each impression 'leaves a lasting memory only to the extent that one has thought it over – to the extent to which it is connected with the thoughts that come to us from the social milieu'.[46] We cannot think about events in our past without connecting those events to the systems of ideas and meaning current in a particular social group of which we are, in the present, members. The function of language is crucial here. Language works not because there is any

[44] Maurice Halbwachs, 'The social frameworks of memory', in *On Collective Memory*, ed. Lewis A. Coser (University of Chicago Press, 1992), 35–189; 38. Halbwachs' proof of this is the fact that in dreams, when the individual is apparently isolated from the social context, we do not find 'the recollection of events or of complex pictures'. (Halbwachs, 'Social frameworks of memory', 174.)

[45] Halbwachs, 'Social frameworks of memory', 40. [46] *Ibid.*, 53.

natural correspondence between words and objects in the world, but because as a system it relies on the associations and connections that each word brings with it.[47] In Halbwachs' terms, each word makes sense only because it is accompanied by recollections. This works the other way too. In other words, 'we speak of our recollections before calling them to mind' and 'it is language, and the whole system of social conventions attached to it, that allows us at every moment to reconstruct our past'.[48]

Jay Winter and Emmanuel Sivan propose a somewhat different notion of memory.[49] Their version, which they propose to call 'collective remembrance' rather than 'collective memory', emphasises agency, activity and creativity.[50] It is 'the act of gathering bits and pieces of the past, and joining them together in public', and it involves 'a domain beyond that of individual memory'.[51] Memory is a social practice, 'the palpable, messy activity which produces collective remembrance'.[52] Unlike Halbwachs' collective memory, however, it retains an individualist notion of memory that underpins the collective acts of remembrance. Individuals and groups that come together to remember collectively 'bring to the task their private memories'.[53] Winter and Sivan see their position as a midpoint between those who see memory as socially determined and those who regard it as purely individual, both of which they regard as untenable. However, those two positions, and the third way that Winter and Sivan advocate, only exist within a deeper framework, one that sees the individual as distinct and distinguishable in the first place. The scientific framework they draw on, cognitive psychology, neuropsychology and social psychology, all adopt the same basic framework. Psychology relies on the notion, challenged by Ian Hacking, that there are 'facts' about memory that can be known independently of the social and historical location of memory discourse.[54] The idea is that by studying the nature of individual memory and then examining how individual memories intersect, we can learn how collective memory works – precisely the view Halbwachs wanted to distance himself from. There is another view, where the social world and

[47] Ferdinand de Saussure, *Course in General Linguistics*, trans. Wade Baskin (New York: McGraw Hill, 1966).

[48] Halbwachs, 'Social frameworks of memory', 173.

[49] Jay Winter and Emmanuel Sivan, 'Setting the framework', in *War and Remembrance in the Twentieth Century*, ed. Jay Winter and Emmanuel Sivan (Cambridge University Press, 1999), 6–39.

[50] Winter and Sivan, 'Setting the framework', 9.

[51] *Ibid.*, 6. [52] *Ibid.*, 10. [53] *Ibid.*, 9–10.

[54] Ian Hacking, *Rewriting the Soul: Multiple Personality and the Sciences of Memory* (Princeton University Press, 1995).

the individual are mutually constituted, or in other words, where social activity produces both society and individual. Neither one exists before or separately from the other. This leads back to a position closer to that of Halbwachs, where memory – and hence, the past – cannot exist other than as a historically and geographically situated social practice. Halbwachs argues that 'we should renounce the idea that the past is in itself preserved within individual memories'.[55] On the contrary, 'only those recollections subsist that in every period society, working within its present-day frameworks, can reconstruct'.[56] The past is produced in the present, rather than preceding it.

The idea that the past is separate from the present and comes before it is more or less accepted as obvious in European cultures. It is axiomatic that time is linear, a succession of past, present and future. This is despite arguments from scientists and philosophers since the beginning of the twentieth century that this notion of time does not make sense and does not square with what we see.[57] The Newtonian picture of time as continuous and linear that pervades modern common sense and western metaphysics is closely linked with the idea that objects or things have a basic nature or essence that persists in time. Time appears as a succession of 'nows', a sequence of presents, and the existence of something is confirmed by its continuing presence through a series of such moments. At each successive moment in time we can check that the object is still there and still the same. Notions of presence and essence have been widely challenged, but this seems to have made comparatively little impact on what are accepted as reasonable notions of time in academic analysis. However, it is worth noting that in popular culture even in the west, time is not such an absolute. Travel in time and parallel worlds are represented in science fiction. Ghosts and spirit mediums are not ruled out. The past is thought to be in some sense still present in buildings and places. And memorials and practices of commemoration in particular tap into these ideas.

In other parts of the world we find different concepts of past and present. In Michael Lambek's work on spirit possession in Mayotte in northwest Madagascar he describes a practice of memory where 'past

[55] Halbwachs, 'Social frameworks of memory', 173. [56] *Ibid.*, 189.

[57] See, for example, Henri Bergson, *Matter and Memory*, trans. Nancy Margaret Paul and W. Scott Palmer (New York: Zone Books, 1988); Gilles Deleuze, *Bergsonianism*, trans. Hugh Tomlinson and Barbara Habberjam (New York: Zone Books, 1988); Albert Einstein, *Relativity: The Special and the General Theory*, trans. Robert W. Lawson (London: Methuen, 1920); Martin Heidegger, *Being and Time: a Translation of Sein und Zeit*, trans. Joan Stambaugh (Albany: State University of New York Press, 1996); Stephen Mulhall, *Heidegger and Being and Time* (London: Routledge, 1996).

and present interpenetrate'.[58] Royal ancestral spirits 'possess' the bodies of living human hosts. Lambek sees this as a moral discourse. It gives us an alternative notion of memory to that prominent in, for example, contemporary America. Contemporary US devices of memory production – particularly the camera – produce a particular form of memory. Words and images are frozen, framed and rendered mechanical and impersonal. This means that 'an inherently and pre-eminently temporally constituted process like remembering is thus detemporalised'.[59] Lambek suggests imagining memory in another way, 'one which situates memory in time and sees it as a function of social relationships, in part a mutual affirmation of past interaction, in part the traces of our introjection of one another'.[60]

In Mayotte, visitors meeting an old friend are expected to greet not only their friend, but also the various spirits that possess them. New spirits are introduced and may converse with the visitor. Each spirit remembers previous encounters, and mutual obligations can be entered into. Spirits do not just possess one individual, and when they move between hosts their memories should go with them, as part of their identity. They also represent particular events and memories for their hosts. Every time they intervene they provide a new opportunity of constructing and revising the narratives of the past of which they are a part: 'Spirits [have] narrative and performative functions [and] are vehicles *for* memory rather than frozen remnants of memory.'[61]

While the possession is taking place, the host speaks with the voice of the spirit, or, rather, the spirit speaks through the host. Spirits are the ancestors of living royalty. Lambek spells out the temporal implications:

> The royal dead are not framed and frozen in objectified, textualised memory, but rendered active in the present. Reciprocally, contemporary Malagasy live not only in the present but in the past. *They do not possess memories, rather they are possessed by them.* Put another way, time is not fully consecutive; the past is not finished and done with, receding ever further into the distance, but (in grammatical terms) imperfect.[62]

Interestingly, Lambek compares spirit possession in Madagascar with cases of multiple personality disorder found in those diagnosed as suffering from trauma in the west. It is interesting to compare this with Gilles Deleuze's description of Henri Bergson's view: 'The past is "contemporaneous" with the present it *has been*. . . . The past and the

[58] Michael Lambek, 'The past imperfect: remembering as moral practice', in *Tense Past: Cultural Essays in Trauma and Memory*, ed. Paul Antze and Michael Lambek (New York: Routledge, 1996), 235–54; 246.
[59] Lambek, 'The past imperfect', 238. [60] *Ibid.* [61] *Ibid.*, 241. [62] *Ibid.*, 246.

present do not denote two successive moments, but two elements which coexist.'[63]

In his analysis of the western equivalent of spirit possession, multiple personality disorder, Ian Hacking addresses a similar issue of temporality in a rather different way. He coins the phrase 'an indeterminacy in the past', by which he means 'an indeterminacy about what people actually did, and not about what we remember them doing.... It is something about our actions, not our memories of them, that is indeterminate.'[64] For many people the issue about memory is one of truth or falsehood. Something happened in the past: how accurately do we remember what happened? In the debates over child abuse and the question of whether recovered memories are false memories, the issue is whether something happened and was experienced or whether it didn't. Both sides of the debate share the assumption that the past is determinate. It is over, and what happened happened, independently of our memory of it. The past exists prior to memory in this understanding. Even in some psychoanalytic accounts, it is the emotional meaning attached to past events that changes: the event itself still happened. We hold onto this despite the fact that we accept that 'memory is not itself like a camcorder, creating, when it works, a faithful record.... We touch up, supplement, delete, combine, interpret, shade.'[65] But Hacking argues that it is not just a question of re-interpretation, or at least not when it comes to our memories of what he calls 'human action'.

When we are concerned with human action, as we are in the case of child abuse or memories of combat, for example, what happens carries meaning and that is what we observe or remember. We don't just remember what we saw but what we consider happened. The meaning, or the intention, is central to human action according to Hacking.[66] In other words: 'the imaginary camcorder in the sky, which records everything that happens in a particular scene, does not of itself suffice to record what people were doing'.[67] As far as Hacking is concerned there are two types of thing in the past: human action, and impersonal conditions.[68] The latter is not subject to an indeterminacy; we can have definite facts about the past provided they do not concern human action. In the case of human

[63] Deleuze, *Bergsonianism*, 58–9.

[64] Hacking, *Rewriting the Soul*, 234.

[65] *Ibid.*, 247.

[66] Here his argument is similar to Max Weber's. Weber defines social action as action that carries meaning (Max Weber, *Economy and Society: an Outline of Interpretative Sociology*, ed. Guenther Roth and Claus Wittich (New York: Bedminster Press, 1968), vol. 1, 4). Of course, in Weber's definition, not all *human* action would qualify as *social* action.

[67] Hacking, *Rewriting the Soul*, 247–8.

[68] *Ibid.*, 248.

action, we can retrospectively alter what happened in the past. This change is more than just a question of re-interpretation:

> When I say that the past is revised retroactively, I do not mean only that we change our opinions about what was done, but that in a certain logical sense what was done itself is modified. As we change our understanding and sensibility, the past becomes filled with intentional actions that, in a certain sense, were not there when they were performed.[69]

Hacking treats the distinction between human actions and impersonal conditions such as natural disasters as philosophical or universal rather than historically specific and a question of practice. In addition, he extends this distinction to traumas, arguing that those produced by impersonal rather than intentional human action need to be thought of separately 'not because some different kind of memory is involved, but because of a logical difference between the events remembered'.[70] In the case of a trauma such as an earthquake 'the traumatic events were what they were, and intention or acting under a description do not arise'.[71] He goes on to argue that the distinction sometimes made between traumatic 'flashbacks', which are assumed to have a privileged truth, and 'narrative memory', which isn't, cannot be sustained. At this point he discards the view that what is important is action under a description, arguing instead that 'our common conception of remembering, as encoded in grammar, is remembering of scenes, a remembering that is presented, often, by narrating but is nevertheless a memory of scenes and episodes'. This leads him to his desired conclusion, which is that 'the flashback... is not peculiarly different from memory in general – and hence, not especially privileged'.[72]

However, there is another way of understanding traumatic memory, one that sees it as distinct in kind from other forms of memory precisely because it is the memory of events or human actions about which no interpretation has yet been formed. They are events that resist meaning. Traumatic events are so shocking, so outside our expectations, that we do not know what happened. Traumatic events are indeterminate, but in more than the way Hacking argues that all human actions are. With most human actions there are several ways of making sense of them, or several meanings that can be attributed to a single action. 'What happened' changes as different meanings are attributed to an event. A traumatic event, whether it involves human action or what Hacking calls an 'impersonal condition', is meaningless. What happens just does not make sense. When traumatic events are remembered it is not a question of remembering what we thought happened. We can only remember what we

[69] *Ibid.*, 249–50. [70] *Ibid.*, 248. [71] *Ibid.* [72] *Ibid.*, 253.

saw: there is nothing else to remember. We did not interpret what we saw at the time. We could not. This does not mean that somehow traumatic memories are more 'true' or more 'factually accurate' than other memories, however. The question at stake is not whether in some absolute, factual sense a traumatic memory is 'true' or not.

What is meant by trauma? What are we trying to grasp when we call an experience 'traumatic' in a non-trivial sense? According to Cathy Caruth

> ...trauma describes an overwhelming experience of sudden, or catastrophic events, in which the response to the event occurs in the often delayed, and uncontrolled repetitive occurrence of hallucinations and other intrusive phenomena.[73]

In Maurice Blanchot's words, trauma is 'the disaster, unexperienced. It is what escapes the very possibility of experience – it is the limit of writing. This must be repeated: the disaster de-scribes. Which does not mean that the disaster, as the force of writing, is excluded from it, is beyond the pale of writing or extratextual.'[74]

As we saw in the introduction, Freud noted with surprise the recurrence of the traumatic incident or event in dreams, which can then no longer be understood in the usual way. Freudian psychoanalysis regards dreams as produced through an elaborate, unconscious mode of thought called 'dreamwork', where repressed unconscious wishes find expression and fulfilment in a disguised or hidden form in our dreams. The nightmares that disturb survivors of war and other traumas cannot be seen as the expression of an unconscious wish. These dreams are not in any sense pleasurable. Nor are they replete with the symbolism, displacement, condensations and other 'tricks' of more general dreams that serve to conceal the motivating wish of the dream. In contrast, they are *literal*:

> The surprising *literality* and non-symbolic nature of traumatic dreams and flashbacks [means they] resist cure to the extent that they remain, precisely, literal. It is this literality and its insistent return which thus constitutes trauma and points towards its enigmatic core: the delay or incompletion in knowing, or even in seeing, an overwhelming occurrence that then remains, in its insistent return, absolutely *true* to the event.[75]

It is important to note that the term 'literal' here points to a contrast between traumatic nightmares and standard dreams. The latter are full of 'literary' devices such as metaphor and symbol; the former are not,

[73] Cathy Caruth, 'Unclaimed Experience: Trauma and the Possibility of History', *Yale French Studies*, 79, (1991): 181–92.

[74] Maurice Blanchot, *The Writing of the Disaster: l'écriture du désastre*, trans. Ann Smock, new edn (Lincoln and London: University of Nebraska Press, 1995), 7.

[75] Cathy Caruth, ed. *Trauma: Explorations in Memory* (Baltimore: The Johns Hopkins University Press, 1995), 5.

they are 'literal'. They are *true* not in the sense that they are factually accurate but in that they are to be understood in a matter-of-fact way, whereas dreams on the whole are not. The responses to trauma that we now describe as 'post-traumatic stress disorder' are not a disease or an illness: they reflect our inability to allocate meaning to the event, that's all. Caruth describes post-traumatic stress disorder as 'a symptom of history'. She notes 'the traumatised carry an impossible history within them, or they become themselves the symptom of a history they cannot entirely possess'.[76]

Originally there was a movement from body to psyche: the physical notion of injury to body tissue – long known as trauma – was adapted to signify an injury to the psyche. Present-day work is returning to the body. Ruth Leys argues that seeing the traumatic event as 'encoded in the brain' in a different way from ordinary, 'implicit or non-narrative memory' entails a belief in the traumatic memory as 'a pristine and timeless historical truth undistorted or uncontaminated by subjective meaning' that is lodged in the brain somewhere.[77] However, this is not what current work on trauma – Caruth's for example – implies. It is not the case that 'truth' is said to exist in the memory images thought to be implanted by trauma any more than it is to be found in our original perceptions. We do not have access to these images (other than as images) without interpreting or making sense of them. We cannot pass them on, unvarnished to others. Truth is not the issue here, though, of course, in some versions of the trauma discourse it can become so.

It is not just because the traumatic experience is so powerful that it is re-lived time and time again by survivors. It is because of the failure to allocate meaning to what happened. Trauma is not experienced as such – as an experience – when it occurs. Instead, in the words of war correspondent Michael Herr, it just stays 'stored there in your eyes'.[78] In a sense, we do not know what happened at all. It is rather similar to Hacking's argument about an indeterminacy in the past. With a traumatic event, we are not able, even in a preliminary way, to say 'what happened'. It is beyond the realm of what we expect as intentional action. Caruth argues that 'the historical power of the trauma is not just that the experience is repeated after its forgetting, but that it is only in and through its inherent forgetting that it is first experienced at all'.[79] To experience something we need some idea of what is happening. With trauma, by definition, we don't have this. Trauma is 'the confrontation with an event that, in

[76] Caruth, *Trauma*, 5. See also Caruth, 'Unclaimed Experience'.
[77] Ruth Leys, *Trauma: a Genealogy* (University of Chicago Press, 2000), 7.
[78] Michael Herr, *Dispatches*, quoted in Cathy Caruth, 'Unclaimed Experience', 181.
[79] Caruth, *Trauma*, 8.

its unexpectedness and horror, cannot be placed within the schemes of prior knowledge'.[80]

What does all this imply for the question of time and traumatic memory? It means that trauma and traumatic memory alter the linearity of historical, narrativised time, time which has beginnings and ends: 'since the traumatic event is not experienced as it occurs, it is fully evident only in connection with another place, and in another time'.[81] This can mean that 'traumatised persons . . . live in two different worlds: the realm of trauma and the realm of their current ordinary life'.[82] This is a sort of parallel existence; the two worlds cannot be synchronised because of the different temporalities each invokes. Events from the period of the trauma are experienced in a sense simultaneously with those of a survivor's current existence. They have not been incorporated into a narrative:

> The traumatic experience/memory is in a sense timeless. It is not transformed into a story, placed in time, with a beginning, a middle and an end (which is characteristic for narrative memory). If it can be told at all, it is still a re-experience.[83]

The symptoms of trauma precede the discovery (in therapy) of a traumatic event. The memory of the event is recovered only *after* the symptoms that the victim is experiencing have led them to try to uncover an explanation or cause. In the medical criteria for post-traumatic stress disorder (PTSD) the time line moves unproblematically from (A) traumatic event, through (B) re-experiences of the event, to (C) attempts at avoidance and (D) symptoms. In other words 'it is simply taken for granted that time and causality move from the traumatic event to the other criterial features and that the event inscribes itself on the symptoms'.[84] But, rather, like the identification and classification of PTSD itself, this sense of time 'does not emerge spontaneously from the facts'; it is not a discovery but 'an *achievement*, a product of psychiatric culture and technology'.[85]

So, to summarise, trauma is not experienced at the time; it is belated. It returns in the form of dreams or flashbacks. These re-enactments are

[80] *Ibid.*, 153.
[81] *Ibid.*, 8. I am using the word 'narrative' in this chapter in a rather loose way, in order to make a contrast between trauma time and narrative time – by which I mean time which has beginnings, middles and ends. Of course, not all narratives have this structure.
[82] Bessel A. van der Kolk and Onno van der Hart, 'The intrusive past: the flexibility of memory and the engraving of trauma', in *Trauma: Explorations in Memory*, ed. Cathy Caruth (Baltimore: Johns Hopkins University Press, 1995), 158–82; 176.
[83] Van der Kolk and van der Hart, 'The intrusive past', 177. But see my comment on narrative in note 81 above.
[84] Allan Young, *The Harmony of Illusions: Inventing Post-Traumatic Stress Disorder* (Princeton University Press, 1997), 115.
[85] Young, *Harmony of Illusions*, 116.

absolutely literal: the detail is exact. However, this does not mean in any sense that this gives us access to a 'true account' of what happened. This is not the claim, contrary to Hacking's reading. It just means that the re-enactment does not take place through a memory or narrative account. In order to produce *an account* the event still has to be interpreted; this interpretation will be no 'truer' than any other, being based on a re-living. The person re-lives the traumatic event, in its full horror. Traumatic recall possesses the survivor, rather than being possessed by them. They cannot control the way the trauma is recalled: it is often related slowly, in real time. There is no adjustment of the tale to fit the listener: no editing or condensing of the repetition.

The experiencing of the traumatic event is not only belated. It also often involves another person, a listener to whom the trauma can be recounted. As Caruth puts it: 'the history of a trauma, in its inherent belatedness, can only take place through the listening of another'. But she goes further than this, arguing that it is not solely a question of another individual to whom the event is told: 'The meaning of the trauma's address beyond itself concerns . . . not only individual isolation but a wider historical isolation that, in our time, is communicated on the level of our cultures.'[86]

Communicating trauma is very difficult, and many witnesses never either wish to recount the event, nor succeed in doing so. Bearing witness or giving testimony is problematic. In order to tell the story it has to be translated into narrative form. This loses the immediacy of the traumatic recall, but more importantly, it loses 'the force of its *affront to understanding*'.[87] This is something that cannot be conveyed in speech, but something survivors, for example survivors of the concentration camps, are reluctant to give up. This is why for so many it is both impossible to speak, and impossible not to speak. As Sarah Kofman puts it:

> About Auschwitz and after Auschwitz no story is possible, if by a story one means: to tell a story of events which makes sense. . . . There remains, nonetheless, a duty to speak, to speak endlessly for those who could not speak because to the very end they wanted to guard true speech from betrayal. To speak in order to bear witness. But how?[88]

Work with survivors, then, faces a unique problem, that of 'how to help relieve suffering, and how to understand the nature of the suffering, without eliminating the force and truth of the reality that trauma survivors

[86] Caruth, *Trauma*, 11; perhaps this is what international politics with its concern with wars and now with humanitarianism expresses.
[87] *Ibid.*, 154.
[88] Sarah Kofman, *Smothered Words*, trans. Madeleine Dobie (Evanston, Illinois: Northwestern University Press, 1998), 14, 36.

face and quite often try to transmit to us. To cure oneself... seems to many survivors to imply the giving up of an important reality or the dilution of a special truth.'[89] To integrate the memory of trauma into other memories (to make it part of one's life-story) is seen as a way of forgetting, not a way of remembering.[90]

However, working with survivors is not a process that can be abstracted from the wider social and political context. I argued in the introduction that trauma is fundamental to the production of political community. Political communities – notably the democratic state – are also the source of trauma. They send people to war; they perpetrate genocide; they condone or produce famine. Sometimes the state has an interest in *forgetting* this, and ensuring that survivors do *not* speak out. In the final part of this chapter, I want to look at memories of Vietnam veterans, and how these have been suppressed by the medicalisation and pathologisation of their trauma.

The diagnosis of trauma

Interest in trauma waxes and wanes, Judith Herman argues, depending on the political clout of interest groups such as abused women or Vietnam veterans.[91] According to the accepted history, trauma symptoms were first recognised in the 1860s in victims of what was then called 'railway spine'.[92] After a railway accident, those who suffered no visible injury at the time were later found to suffer from distress that was attributed to shock or concussion.[93] The next occurrence of the concept was in the work of Sigmund Freud with Viennese women, followed by studies of shell shock in the 1914–18 war and later in Vietnam. However, Allan Young argues that this chronology is mistaken: 'the disorder is not timeless, nor does it possess an intrinsic unity. Rather, it is glued together by the practices, technologies and narratives with which it is diagnosed, studied, treated, and represented by the various interests, institutions, and moral arguments that mobilised these efforts and resources.'[94]

In fact it is only recently that a diagnosis of PTSD has been possible and that specific treatment has been offered to sufferers. Post-traumatic stress appeared as a named disorder when it was written into the diagnostic manual of the American Psychiatric Association in 1980. It is closely linked with multiple personality disorder. These disorders and the notion

[89] Van der Kolk and van der Hart, 'The intrusive past', 177. [90] *Ibid.*
[91] Judith Lewis Herman, *Trauma and Recovery: from Domestic Abuse to Political Terror* (London: Pandora), 32.
[92] Young, *Harmony of Illusions*, 5. [93] Leys, *Trauma*, 3.
[94] Young, *Harmony of Illusions*, 5.

of trauma itself belong to a particular historic period.[95] In the nineteenth century the concept of trauma was broadened from a physical injury to a psychic or psychological one. Fundamental to the definition adopted by the American Psychiatric Association is the idea that 'owing to the emotions of terror and surprise caused by certain events, the mind is split or dissociated: it is unable to register the wound to the psyche because the ordinary mechanisms of awareness and cognition are destroyed'.[96] The specific notions of a distortion of time outlined in the last section are also fundamental to the concept. Victims of trauma are unable to remember the incident under ordinary circumstances but are haunted by dreams and nightmares during which the event replays itself. In other words 'the experience of the trauma, fixed or frozen in time, refuses to be represented *as* past, but is perpetually re-experienced in a painful, dissociated, traumatic present'.[97] In other words, traumatic stress 'is a disease of time... it permits the past (memory) to relive itself in the present, in the form of intrusive images and thoughts and in the patient's compulsion to replay old events'.[98] The notion has now become so widely adopted in discourse that trauma can refer to anything from the experience of Nazi persecution to the sexual harassment allegedly suffered by Paula Jones at the hands of President Clinton.[99]

Post-traumatic stress is not only historically but geographically specific.[100] As a diagnosis arising from notions of the self and practices of psychiatry that are located in the west, its applicability elsewhere in the world is in doubt. It draws on concepts of personhood that focus on the individual and arose in the west at a particular historical point. The export of the diagnosis and treatment of trauma as part of relief programmes and interventions needs to be examined.

It is important to emphasise that to claim a diagnosis of trauma is something that is only possible within a specific historical and geographical setting is *not* the same as to argue that those who suffer from symptoms of post-traumatic stress are malingerers. Those who make this claim do not deny the reality of the abuse or the suffering caused. This is not their argument. What they are saying is that traumatic stress as a possible diagnosis, as something people can be seen and see themselves as suffering from, has become current in a particular time period. Trauma is not something that was discovered – it is 'a man-made object [that] originates

[95] Hacking, *Rewriting the Soul*; Leys, *Trauma*; Young, *Harmony of Illusions*.
[96] Leys, *Trauma*, 2. [97] *Ibid.*
[98] Young, *Harmony of Illusions*, 7. [99] Leys, *Trauma*, 1–2.
[100] Patrick J. Bracken and Celia Petty, eds., *Rethinking the Trauma of War* (London: Free Association Press, 1998).

in the scientific and clinical discourses of the nineteenth century'.[101] In other words, it is neither 'natural' nor universal. It is a social practice. As Allan Young puts it, his job as an ethnographer 'is not to deny its reality but to explain how it and its traumatic memory have been *made* real, to describe the mechanisms through which these phenomena penetrate people's life worlds, acquire facticity, and shape the self-knowledge of patients, clinicians and researchers'.[102] I would want to extend this to how the production of trauma works in terms of relations and practices of power.

The examination of trauma as an historically situated social practice draws in various ways on the work of Michel Foucault. Foucault analysed how objects (like 'trauma') that appeared to have existed since time immemorial – though they might only have been 'discovered' recently – are actually produced in discourse. By discourse, of course, he does not just mean language. He was adamant that what he was studying was not words or texts but rather discursive formations and discursive practices, which were one among a number of social practices (disciplinary practices and technologies of the self were other social practices he examined). He described what he was doing as 'a task that consists of not – of no longer – treating discourses as groups of signs (signifying elements referring to contents or representations) but as practices that systematically form the objects of which they speak'.[103] Discourses are composed of words or signs, but they are more than just the use of those signs to refer to pre-existing objects. The objects that we talk about are produced in and through our discursive practices. As Foucault puts it: 'theory does not express, translate or serve to apply practice: it is practice'.[104] In other words, what experts or academics do when they analyse, categorise and write about memory or trauma has just as much of a practical effect as other forms of social action. Their discourse produces 'trauma' (or 'memory') as an object of study, it does not study a pre-existing object. It is not a separate, objective, independent form of knowledge, although its particular method is the one that happens to be accepted as a route to 'truth' in modern societies. The idea that theory is separate from practice is what gives this form of knowledge its particular authority and power.

It is through our social practices, and particularly through discursive practices, that 'trauma' has become something that psychiatrists study.

[101] Young, *Harmony of Illusions*, 141. [102] *Ibid.*, 6.

[103] Michel Foucault, *The Archaeology of Knowledge*, trans. A. M. Sheridan Smith (London: Tavistock, 1972), 49.

[104] Michel Foucault, 'Intellectuals and power: a conversation between Michel Foucault and Gilles Deleuze', in *Language, Counter-memory, Practice: Selected Essays and Interviews*, ed. Donald F. Bouchard (Ithaca: Cornell University Press, 1977), 205–17; 208.

Foucault has shown how the objectification of 'man' and the rise of the human sciences took place at the end of the eighteenth and beginning of the nineteenth century. Before that, it made no sense to speak of the human being as something that could be examined in the way we take for granted now. He also described how the medicalisation of the individual followed. These processes are continuing as additional subjects or objects of scientific study (it no longer makes sense to distinguish the two) are produced in discourse. In the case of 'trauma', it was only after a struggle by veterans' organisations in the USA, supported by feminists and the women's movement, that 'post-traumatic stress disorder' was listed as a category of mental disorder.[105] A Foucauldian analysis would note *not* that it was only then that PTSD was formally *recognised* as a disorder – in other words, assuming that it had always existed but gone unrecognised – but rather that it was only at that time that the disorder *came into being as a category that could be used*, and, more importantly, used with political consequences. The term 'post-traumatic stress disorder' did not just name a pre-existing complaint; it produced a syndrome that people could then be said (and feel themselves) to suffer from. This result has specific political outcomes and in turn results from a particular political configuration.

Once the concept came into being, understandings of trauma have oscillated between two irreconcilable poles, which Ruth Leys calls the mimetic and antimimetic. Roughly speaking, in the mimetic-suggestive paradigm, trauma is understood as similar to hypnotic imitation where a suggestible and abject subject later forgets what has occurred. In the antimimetic view, a sovereign if passive subject is confronted and overwhelmed by an external trauma. Leys' project is 'to reveal and investigate the tensions inherent in the mimetic–antimimetic structure, without for a moment attempting to settle those tensions'.[106] She doesn't take seriously the production of 'trauma' as a social practice and an issue of power/knowledge in the Foucauldian sense, and she finishes her book with recommendations for the 'treatment' of 'victims' without any consideration of the political implications of these terms.[107] Although she purports to offer, after Foucault, a genealogy of trauma, in fact she traces the history of the concept in a fairly standard way. Her main concern seems to be with whether certain claims made at different points in its

[105] Herman, *Trauma and Recovery*, 28.

[106] Leys, *Trauma*, 306. As she points out most authors 'use the terms "imitation", "suggestion", "mimicry" and "mimesis" interchangeably with regard to both mimetic and antimimetic processes.' (*ibid.*, 14). In Homi Bhabha's use of mimicry, failure is endemic to the process; in the colonial situation, the native is expected to be 'almost white but not quite'. In other words, mimesis involves its opposite or failure in any case.

[107] Leys, *Trauma*, 307.

history are valid or not.[108] A genealogy would focus more on the conditions of possibility that enabled various claims to be made at different times, how claims, once made, came to be regarded as tenable, and what the political result of that outcome was.

If the identification and treatment of trauma is a social practice then a series of questions arises. We need to ask how we have come to specify traumatic memory as distinct and then to medicalise and individualise it. And more important, what are the social functions of this? Who benefits? In the next section I want to explore these questions in the context of the Vietnam veterans.

Forgetting Vietnam

In the treatment and compensation of Vietnam combat veterans, the struggle to include post-traumatic stress disorder in the first standardised classification of American psychiatry was crucial. It succeeded when the third edition of the *Diagnostic and Statistical Manual of Mental Disorders* (*DSM-III*) was published in 1980. The activities of the veterans' advocates – psychiatrists and others – had been central in achieving this. This political mobilisation was essential to promote recognition of and compensation for the long-term consequences of military service. The Veterans Administration, the official US government branch involved with ex-service personnel, was aware that the inclusion of the diagnosis would have enormous fiscal and manpower implications.[109] The psychiatrists advocating inclusion were regarded by traditional veterans' organisations as anti-war activists out to milk the system.

However, once trauma exists as a mental health diagnosis, a number of consequences follow. First, the diagnosis has to be applied. People have to be slotted into the category that has been made available for them. This involves an assessment procedure that is often intrusive in the extreme as well as serving to medicalise and normalise the traumatic event. The extent of surveillance in the case of Vietnam veterans can be judged from

[108] For example, she is 'dismayed by the low quality of [Bessel] van der Kolk's scientific work. . . . There are slippages and inconsistencies in his arguments about the literal nature of traumatic memory, arguments that are inadequately supported by the empirical evidence he adduces', and she feels 'a similar impatience with the sloppiness of [Caruth's] theoretical arguments' (Leys, *Trauma*, 305). She may be right in her judgements (though I would argue that she is not). The point is that whether particular arguments are tenable or not in some abstract sense is neither relevant to a genealogy nor determinable outside any particular régime of truth. To a genealogist what is interesting is what role the arguments played in power relations and in the production of objects of study in their particular historical setting. Genealogy also has a particular interest in subjugated or forgotten knowledges.

[109] Young, *Harmony of Illusions*, 113.

descriptions of the diagnostic process as carried out at a Veterans Administration treatment centre for post-traumatic stress disorder studied by Allan Young. As would be expected, diagnostic information is collected in line with the criteria set out in *DSM-III*. But the assessment doesn't stop there. Previous psychiatric and military records are examined in depth, relatives are questioned, and a lengthy interview is conducted with the patient themselves. Prospective patients are obliged to answer questions on their life before and after the traumatic event – their family, their social life and school performance, their marital situation, employment, income – as well as describing the 'designated life event' or traumatic experience. During the interview, observations are recorded concerning the interviewee's 'appearance, behaviour (including posture, facial expression, body movements, speech, ability to interact with the interviewer), appropriateness of emotions and predominant mood, and intellectual functioning (including orientation to his surroundings, memory, insight, stream of thought, indications of delusions or hallucinations)'.[110] The person being assessed completes extensive tests, including the Minnesota Multiphasic Personality Index (MMPI) and an Impact of Event Scale. The MMPI includes a section that is supposed to identify the truthfulness or accuracy of responses to the test.

After this comprehensive procedure, the 'case' is presented to a meeting of specialists who will decide whether and in what way to treat the individual concerned. The presentation, by the staff member who interviewed the veteran, has a predetermined narrative structure, moving through the person's premilitary life, their military experiences and their return to civilian life. The 'story' is formed around 'a transformative (traumatic) experience' which connects the three segments.[111] Cases that fit easily into the expected narrative are likely to be decided swiftly and positively (i.e. the veteran will be accepted into the programme of the centre). In these cases, there tends to be a clear sense of personality behind the narrative. This is fostered by the specialist presenting the case who will inscribe motive and purpose along the way. Cases that do not fit the narrative, or where there are complications such as pre-service trauma, petty crime, doubt about the extent of in-service trauma, are puzzles. Here what happens depends as much on whether decisions can be justified as on whether the specialists consider effective treatment can be offered. A judgement not to take someone on must be defensible. The appearance of bias, for example on grounds of race, must be avoided. Young describes the case conference process as being a way the diagnosticians have developed of managing the difficulties caused by the gap between the diagnostic tests,

[110] *Ibid.*, 145–6. [111] *Ibid.*, 169.

which show PTSD, and the sufferers' own accounts, which often present a much more complicated picture. This management process is not entirely successful however, and 'when the diagnosticians are finished, a residue of indeterminacy, the suspicion that [the] nominated event is "metaphorical" rather than etiological, or that putative inscriptions have been misread, remains'.[112] It would be much simpler for the system, Young remarks, if there was some way to bypass what people say about themselves and their pasts.

From the patient's point of view, they are asked to provide a whole range of intimate information that is used by experts to impose a diagnosis that must be difficult to challenge. Those being discussed are not present at the case conference, and the intricacies on which their acceptance on the programme depends do not appear to be discussed with them. Their own views or preferences as far as treatment goes are not considered, or are overruled without consultation. They are treated as objects. The whole process of the diagnosis and admission to treatment of veterans recalls the complaint made about rape trials: that the trial is a re-raping of the victim, and the argument that questions about a victim's previous sexual history should be inadmissible. The process is one of medicalisation, and it is a process that allows a veteran's experiences to be reduced to 'stressor events'. This is, of course, not only important to the veteran as an individual. It reduces the political controversies surrounding the Vietnam war to questions of stress-related illness, treatment and maybe compensation.

Once the diagnosis is official, the veteran enters a treatment programme where therapy aims to reduce anxiety, intrusive thoughts and nightmares, and lift depression. However, what counts as a cure is debatable, both for clinicians of different persuasions, and for patients.[113] As part of the treatment, patients are required to speak about their traumatic memories. In the centre where Allan Young carried out his observations, these are generally memories of behaviour such as torturing prisoners or killing civilians or fellow US soldiers.[114] The patients on the whole were what would be labelled 'perpetrators' rather than 'victims'. Some patients resist the demand to tell their stories. One patient expressed his bitterness: 'Last time you said "Talk," I talked. You opened me up like I was a wound. But you never closed me up. You left me like that. . . .'[115] If patients become angry or complain at their treatment by psychiatrists – or by others outside the treatment situation – this is interpreted as arising from their unwillingness to confront uncomfortable memories. It is strictly controlled.[116]

[112] *Ibid.*, 175. [113] *Ibid.*, 182. [114] *Ibid.*, 189. [115] *Ibid.*, 190.
[116] *Ibid.*, 193–7.

If patients are 'cured' their entitlement to pension may be reduced or cut altogether. However, patients who resist being discharged with a positive report are not regarded as acting rationally but as employing their symptoms pathologically.[117]

Allan Young's reading of what goes on at treatment centres such as the one he studied draws attention to the contrasting attitudes of the treatment staff and the veterans to guilt, shame and anger. He points to how these emotions persist despite the best efforts of the therapeutic régime to remove them. The emotions are organised around the western concept of the self, which is 'simultaneously a *psychological* construct, identified with ideas about the "mind", and a *moral* construct, associated with ideas about obligations'.[118] The patients produce and form a moral community through their shared sense of shame, and it is within that community (which therapists are not part of) that memories – confessions – are shared. Members of the moral community, then, share a sense of shame. Shamelessness, described as a lack of self-respect, would put someone outside the community. Within the western notion of the self are a strong sense of autonomy as 'a natural right' and a component of manhood. The loss of autonomy 'is *shameful*, and the absence of anger under these conditions signifies the acceptance of this loss and is *shameless*'.[119] The therapeutic régime attempts to separate guilt from anger, putting each in a separate 'part-self'. The diagnosis of PTSD gives the veteran a new option. They can 'be' people who 'are' not, people who are split. Their discomfort has a name; they are integrated persons again, integrated this time not around the gap, the reality of human being as a being without answers, but around their identity as PTSD sufferers. Ian Hacking describes a similar process with victims of childhood abuse who are diagnosed with multiple personality disorder.[120] They are thoroughly at home in the world again, precisely as people who can never be at home in it.

However, 'when anger is separated from guilt, it loses its moral and self-signifying power; it passes into pathology'.[121] For the patients this means a loss of autonomy and leads to anger:

> Day in day out, therapists labor to transmute the patients' collective memory, a thing that is located in historical events (to which the patients have privileged access), into individual memories, a thing situated in mental events (to which the therapists have privileged access). Memory is the proof as well as the record of the self's existence, and the struggle over memory is the struggle over the self's most valued possessions.[122]

[117] *Ibid.*, 214. [118] *Ibid.*, 220. [119] *Ibid.*, 221.
[120] Hacking, *Rewriting the Soul.* [121] Young, *Harmony of Illusions*, 223.
[122] *Ibid.*, 221.

What the therapeutic process attempts to do then is to make the veterans' feelings of guilt, shame and anger into pathological symptoms. Their feelings are to be overcome, not expressed. They are to accept the route to cure suggested by therapy. Political action is ruled out. Any attempt at such action, whether in the context of complaints about the treatment process or more widely, is interpreted as an expression of their disease. It is an 'acting out' of their symptoms, nothing more.

The Foucauldian analysis of prison and criminality reveals a similar process of depoliticisation at work. The institution of the prison is supposed to rehabilitate offenders and return them to society as productive members. However, almost since the prison system was instituted in Europe it has been a failure. Criminality has increased rather than disappearing; offenders who are imprisoned repeatedly re-offend and return to prison. And yet the prison system continues. What purpose, then, does it serve? Foucault argues that the function of the prison system is not the apparent one of protecting society from a criminal class and reforming the character of offenders. Quite the contrary, he claims. The prison, as a social institution in the service of power, *produces* rather than controls the delinquent:

> For the observation that prison fails to eliminate crime, one should perhaps substitute the hypothesis that prison has succeeded extremely well in producing delinquency, a specific type, a politically or economically less dangerous – and, on occasion, useable – form of illegality; in producing delinquents, in an apparently marginal, but in fact centrally supervised milieu; in producing the delinquent as a pathologised subject. . . . So successful has the prison been that, after a century and a half of 'failures', the prison still exists, producing the same results, and there is the greatest reluctance to dispense with it.[123]

The prison establishes a particular category of person, about whom information is gathered, sifted and analysed. The prisoner is subject to a régime of discipline and surveillance in prison, which confirms them in their membership of this distinct group. This works for power by depoliticising a particular category and their actions. Any political voice they might have has been removed. They may safely be ignored. If they protest against their social conditions, this is no longer something we have to pay attention to: they are criminals and cannot claim a right to be heard. Its function extends beyond this group, however. It has ramifications for the control of the population as a whole. It puts in place 'a means of perpetual surveillance of the population: an apparatus that makes it possible to

[123] Michel Foucault, *Discipline and Punish: The Birth of the Prison*, trans. Alan Sheridan (London: Penguin Books, 1991), 277.

supervise, through the delinquents themselves, the whole social field'.[124] It functions as 'a political observatory'.[125]

Ruth Leys argues that while the concept of trauma may be absolutely indispensable for understanding the Nazi holocaust it becomes 'debased currency' when it is applied to relatively minor instances of harm.[126] This may well be the case. Certainly it would be hard not to wince at a discussion that placed, for example, what is now called 'talk show trauma' on the same footing as the concentration camps. However, if we take the Foucauldian example and use it here, perhaps what we have is not so much a debasement of terminology as *an extension of methods of discipline and control* that were forged in the context of post-Vietnam combat trauma to, on the one hand, the victims of reality TV, and, on the other, the survivors of the Nazi camps. These methods are now regularly applied outside the west in refugee camps and in post-conflict societies by international humanitarian agencies. They form an important part of the practices of global liberal governance. Not only can the export of western trauma treatments be culturally inappropriate, as we have seen, and detrimental to local coping strategies, it is a form of 'therapeutic governance' that pathologises and depoliticises populations.[127]

Disciplined memories

Survivors of events that we now label as traumatic have something to tell us. Specifically, they have something to tell us about how we organise ourselves with respect to power and political community in the contemporary western world. It is the intersection of trauma and political power that makes it necessary for survivors to be disciplined. If they were not, we might be able to reclaim the territory they inhabit – the last remnant beyond discipline: the soul. The processes we have been discussing are a question of 'secularising the soul',[128] or in other words, bringing the soul within the purview of the earthly power of the state. Hacking sees this as a third method of control, to set alongside those already identified by Foucault: discipline, or anatamo-politics, and biopolitics. He calls it memoro-politics. I see it not so much as the introduction of an additional pole of political control as an expression and extension of biopolitics.

As well as reflecting a form of control, the diagnosis of PTSD performs another function. As Foucault showed in *Madness and Civilisation*, the

[124] Foucault, *Discipline and Punish*, 281. [125] *Ibid.* [126] Leys, *Trauma*, 2.
[127] Vanessa Pupavac, 'Therapeutic Governance: Psycho-social Intervention and Trauma Risk Management', *Disasters*, 25, no. 4 (2001): 358–72.
[128] Hacking, *Rewriting the Soul*, 5.

mad of the seventeenth century replaced the lepers of the previous century in asylums.[129] Their function for society was to produce its boundaries, to assure the rest of the world that it was sane. They defined what sanity was. What we see today is those with PTSD being manipulated to reassure power, to put it back in place after violence. The violence of wars and revolutions is necessary to produce the state. However, the state claims to be a banding together of individuals in a peaceable fashion to secure the greater well-being of all. For this claim to be sustained, the founding violence has to be hidden. It is not only the founding violence of course, that exists and is concealed, but the violence that continues to underpin the state. In order for this charade to work, for the fantasy of the democratic state to be believable, the visions of survivors have to be hidden, ignored, or medicalised.

Viewing memory and trauma as social activities prompts us to examine them as historically and geographically situated and productive of particular temporalities. In addition, it leads us to look at a parallel question: how do social practices of memory function in terms of power relations? We have seen that the diagnosis and treatment of trauma survivors can serve to discipline their memories and render them politically powerless. However, is this all there is to it? Is there any way in which survivors can or do resist these processes of medicalisation and depoliticisation?

To address this we need to take a step back and examine the connection between power relations (in Foucauldian terms) and knowledge or 'truth'. Foucault spoke of a 'régime' of truth: '"Truth" is linked in a circular relation with systems of power which produce and sustain it, and to effects of power which it induces and which extend it.'[130] He did not regard this régime of truth as superstructural, in the way a Marxist might regard ideology as superstructural. On the contrary, the status of truth plays an economic and political role. For example, the contemporary régime of truth, based around the scientific model, 'was a condition of the formation and development of capitalism'.[131] In order to express the intimate link between régimes of truth and relations of power, Foucault coined the phrase 'power/knowledge'. As we saw in Chapter 1, Foucault's concept of power is distinct. He sees power as distributed, not centralised, and as a matter of relations of power, not its possession. Power is produced in (and produces) social relations; it is not a capacity that exists before those

[129] Michel Foucault, *Madness and Civilisation: a History of Insanity in the Age of Reason*, trans. Richard Howard (London: Routledge, 1989).

[130] Michel Foucault, 'Truth and power', in *Power/Knowledge: Selected Interviews and Other Writings 1972–1977 by Michel Foucault*, ed. Colin Gordon (Brighton: Harvester, 1980), 109–33; 133.

[131] Foucault, 'Truth and power', 133.

relationships. In addition, power is closely linked with systems of knowledge or truth, or in other words, with discursive practices. As he says: 'in a society such as ours, but basically in any society, there are manifold relations of power which permeate, characterise and constitute the social body, and these relations of power cannot themselves be established, consolidated or implemented without the production, accumulation, circulation and functioning of a discourse'.[132] The social body is produced through relations of power and the discursive practices that accompany and produce those relations of power. Once the science-based régime of truth of contemporary societies is established: 'we are subjected to the production of truth through power and we cannot exercise power except through the production of truth'.[133]

If one wanted to promote change, it would be a question of 'detaching the power of truth from the forms of hegemony, social, economic and cultural, within which it operates at the present time'.[134] This is where genealogy, as a tool of criticism and a challenge to existing hegemonies, comes in – though this is a notion of genealogy quite distinct from the rather toothless version that is often called upon by writers adopting a Foucauldian position. Foucault notes that criticism of systems of authority and power has often been most effective, surprisingly perhaps, when it has been most local and most specific. This criticism has come in part from knowledge located on the margins, knowledge that has not depended on the approval of the current hegemonic régime of truth in its production. It has involved specific, detailed, historical studies, of which Foucault's own work on penal institutions and psychoanalytic practices are good examples.[135] In part the knowledge has come from those whose voice was disqualified and whose views did not count – like prisoners and psychiatric patients. The most forceful critique seems to come from putting together these two 'subjugated knowledges', both of which, Foucault argues, are concerned with memories. These memories are the memories of past struggles that have been concealed in order to submerge conflicts and give the appearance of consensus. Foucault suggests that we call the 'painstaking rediscovery of struggles together with the rude memory of their conflicts' a genealogy:

> Let us give the term *genealogy* to the union of erudite knowledge and local memories which allows us to establish a historical knowledge of struggles and to make use of this knowledge tactically today.[136]

[132] Michel Foucault, 'Two lectures', in *Power/Knowledge*, ed. Gordon, 78–108; 93.
[133] *Ibid.*, 93. [134] Foucault, 'Truth and power', 133.
[135] Michel Foucault, *The Birth of the Clinic: an Archaeology of Medical Perception*, trans. A. M. Sheridan (London: Tavistock, 1973); *Discipline and Punish*.
[136] Foucault, 'Two lectures', 83.

Of course, once the memories of past struggles are brought to light, there is a risk that they will be re-appropriated or re-colonised.[137] We shall find numerous examples of this in later chapters as we examine memorials and practices of testimony.

So memory is central to relations of power. Dominant powers can use commemoration as a means of *forgetting* past struggles. For example, they can use accounts of heroism and sacrifice that tell a story of the founding of the state, a narrative of glorious origin. This obscures trauma. In this context practices that insist on *remembering* can be insurrectionary and counter-hegemonic. They remind us that power is provisional and contingent, and that it entails violence.[138]

Conclusion

Memory is not an object that we can abstract from social processes and that we can then study, analyse or observe. The production of memory is a performative practice, and inevitably social. The recent explosion of interest in memory in the fields of cultural studies, sociology, history, literature and politics is largely an interest in precisely this – memory as it is practised in contemporary societies.[139] This is reflected in much recent work, which, like the present book, focuses on commemoration, memorialisation and remembrance, on the one hand, and testimony, witness and survivor literature, on the other, all of which emphasise memory as a social practice. Alistair Thomson's notion of composure suggests that 'our remembering changes in relation to shifts in the particular publics in which we live, and as the general public field of representations alters'.[140] We saw this in the discussion of memories of 1914–18 at the start of the chapter. However, we are not in a position to *choose* what memories to recall and relate, as Thomson seems to imply. Not only does our remembering change, but the memories we have do too. Individuals don't compose their memories, or at least they are not entirely in control of the composition. Publics are not either. It is only the person as social being that can remember. Remembering is intensely political: part of the fight for political change is a struggle for memory. As Milan Kundera puts

[137] *Ibid.*, 86.

[138] Foucault famously inverts Clausewitz's formula 'war is politics by other means', saying 'power is war, a war continued by other means' (Foucault, 'Two lectures', 90). See also Michel Foucault, *Ethics: Subjectivity and Truth*, trans. Robert Hurley *et al.*, *Essential Works of Foucault 1954–1984*, ed. Paul Rabinow, vol. I (New York: The New Press, 1997), 60.

[139] Pierre Nora, 'Between memory and history', 7.

[140] Thomson, *Anzac Memories*, 9.

it 'the struggle of man against power is the struggle of memory against forgetting'.[141]

In the case of Vietnam veterans treated for combat stress, uncomfortable memories can be removed or invalidated – especially if that discomfort might be a threat to the state. The concept of trauma is now widely accepted, and its use has expanded from physical injury to first a few and now a range of psychic injuries. It is generally accepted that survivors of violence may suffer from post-traumatic stress disorder, and increasingly systems of care and support are put in place to help sufferers. However, this is a double-edged sword. When medical treatment is provided survivors become patients whose aim is recovery. Their anger, shame and guilt, once simply ignored and sidelined, are now turned into nothing more than the symptoms of an unfortunate disorder. We no longer need to take what they say seriously. Their memories no longer count. However, survivors resist this loss of voice, and can still evoke strong sympathy and support from people who recognise in survivors' voices their own feelings of betrayal by power relations.

When treatment is exported to parts of the world where systems based on western psychiatry are of doubtful validity, the position is even more problematic.[142] Here we find intervention by western 'experts' who diagnose and treat post-traumatic stress has a similar effect of decontextualising suffering. Agencies are able to pretend that the help they are offering is humanitarian as distinct from political. But this has the effect of depoliticising the harm and the violence of war. It proposes an individualised solution divorced from the social question of the restoration or re-building of political community in new or old forms.[143]

The view of memory as first and foremost a social activity alongside other social and political practices changes the questions we ask. We focus not on what memories we have but on how we produce them. How does this work? What are its political and social implications? What function does producing memory in these ways serve? Do practices of memory reproduce certain relations of power? Or do they foster resistance? What is at stake? We analyse the way 'memory' is produced as separate from other practices: what is it that makes us treat memory as

[141] Milan Kundera, *The Book of Laughter and Forgetting*, trans. Aaron Asher (London: Faber and Faber, 1996), 4.

[142] Patrick J. Bracken, 'Hidden agendas: deconstructing post traumatic stress disorder', in *Rethinking the Trauma of War*, ed. Patrick J. Bracken and Celia Petty (London: Free Association Books, 1998), 38–59.

[143] Derek Summerfield, 'The social experience of war and some issues for the humanitarian field', in *Rethinking the Trauma of War*, ed. Bracken and Petty, 9–37.

a distinct social practice? How does this separation function for practices of power? Does treating something as a question of memorialisation make it more or less effective politically? How does this work in practice? How does a particular social activity come to be categorised as to do with memory?

In the next chapter I look at some of these questions in the context of war memorials.

3 War memorials and remembrance: the London Cenotaph and the Vietnam Wall

'Have you news of my boy Jack?'
Not this tide
'When d'you think that he'll come back?'
Not with this wind blowing, and this tide.

'Has anyone else had word of him?'
Not this tide,
For what is sunk will hardly swim,
Not with this wind blowing and this tide.

– Rudyard Kipling[1]

Memorials and memorialisation are among the ways people confront the challenge of responding to trauma and the contending temporalities it invokes. In this chapter I look at two memorials that are exceptional in that they seem to encircle trauma rather than absorbing it in a national myth of glory and sacrifice – the Cenotaph in Whitehall, London, and the Vietnam Veterans Memorial (the Vietnam Wall) in Washington. These two memorials both show what I mean by *trauma time*, as opposed to linear narrative time. In both cases encircling and absence are key motifs.

It is important to remember that 'commemoration was and remains a business in which sculptors, artists, bureaucrats, churchmen, and ordinary people, had to strike an agreement and carry it out'.[2] There are many different and contesting objectives in the building of memorials and a whole range of views on how these could be realised. The people involved have personal as well as institutional or functional reasons for their contribution, and these strands are impossible to disentangle. A well-known example is author Rudyard Kipling and his involvement in the War Graves Commission.[3] Kipling lost his only son, Jack, whom

[1] Rudyard Kipling, 'My Boy Jack: 1914–1918', in *Rudyard Kipling: Selected Poems*, ed. Peter Keating (London: Penguin, 1993), 152.
[2] Jay Winter, *Sites of Memory, Sites of Mourning: The Great War in European Cultural History* (Cambridge University Press, 1995), 86.
[3] On Kipling, see Frank Field, *British and French Writers of the First World War* (Cambridge University Press, 1991), 153–76.

he had encouraged to enlist and who was eighteen when he was killed in September 1915. His body was not recovered and for many years Kipling refused to accept that he was dead. He is commemorated on the memorial to those missing in the battle of Loos under the words composed by his father for all the missing: 'Known Unto God'. There is continuing doubt over whether the body of Kipling's son has been found. The War Graves Commission claimed to have found his grave in 1992 in a field hospital cemetery at Loos, but this has been disputed since.[4]

We are not just talking of a struggle for memory between state authorities and the population at large, but something much more complex. All sorts of people had an input into the process of commemoration and were able in various ways to influence it, as we shall see when we examine the cases of the Cenotaph and the Wall. The power to determine what should happen was not entirely possessed by those in authority, nor was it something that could be captured by their opponents. Rather, it was dispersed. As Jay Winter and Emmanuel Sivan put it 'an ongoing process of contestation... [is] one of the permanent features of remembrance'.[5] Winter and Sivan see this as a dialogue between agents in civil society and state institutions. I shall argue that it is not so much a dialogue between 'agents' as a social and discursive practice that re-builds both people and their institutions after a period of crisis. The struggle is not just over what memorials should be built, but over the much larger issue of what form social and political institutions should take. As we saw in the last chapter, trauma involves facing the arbitrary, contingent, and ungrounded nature of authority structures. Those who fought became aware of the folly of much that they had not questioned before: the mythology surrounding the state, for example, and the limits of those who were in command. Trauma also involves an encounter with the lack of guarantees for the self as a person. Survivors have seen their friends horribly mutilated and slaughtered. Some feel they have been betrayed by the system into a pointless and futile exercise in which they are no longer in control. They are powerless. When they return they want something more than a continuation of that meaninglessness in rituals of mourning. And yet they do not want or cannot return to meanings that made sense before. They have to rebuild a different sense of personhood. The practices of remembering and remembrance are among the sites on which these various struggles take place.

[4] John Ezard, 'Discovery that keeps Kipling's soul in torment', *The Guardian*, London, 27 July 1998, 18.

[5] Jay Winter and Emmanuel Sivan, 'Setting the framework', in *War and Remembrance in the Twentieth Century*, ed. Jay Winter and Emmanuel Sivan (Cambridge University Press, 1999), 6–39; 39.

Trauma and memory can both be viewed as social practices – as things that we do – not objects that already exist in a timeless fashion but ones that we produce by our actions, as we saw in the first two chapters. Both memory and trauma play a role in the production of ourselves as persons and in the maintenance and reproduction of systems of power such as the modern state. Moreover, they are a crucial site of such processes. The memory of past struggles can also be disruptive of power. It can contest power relations. What has been forgotten – subjugated knowledges – like the memory of past traumas, returns to haunt the structures of power that instigated the violence in the first place. Trauma is that which refuses to take its place in history as done and finished with. It demands an acknowledgement of a different temporality, where the past is produced by – or even takes place in – the present. In order to avoid any 'attempt to gentrify the properly traumatic dimension of the political'[6] we need to find a way of remaining faithful to its different temporality, a way to mark or encircle the trauma.

The poem by Rudyard Kipling with which I began the chapter is an example of such a different temporality.[7] The refrain 'not this tide' that is repeated with slight variations throughout the poem, reminds us of the cycles of the tides and the waxing and waning of the moon. They reflect the endless process of mourning and the inconsolability of loss. The time evoked is repetitive and cyclical. The long-awaited news never arrives, and yet is always already known. In this sense, the poem marks the trauma without trying to recount it. And yet it moves to a resolution. As the poem progresses, the writer asks 'Oh, dear, what comfort can I find?' The response is:

> None this tide,
> Nor any tide,
> Except that he did not shame his kind –
> Not even with that wind blowing, and that tide.

and by the final stanza, the obstinate, triumphal resolution, with its overtones of sacrifice:

> Then hold your head up all the more,
> This tide,
> And every tide;
> Because he was the son you bore,
> And gave to that wind blowing and that tide!

6 Slavoj Žižek, *The Ticklish Subject: the Absent Centre of Political Ontology* (London: Verso, 1999), 190.

7 Kipling, 'My Boy Jack'.

The Cenotaph

Both the Cenotaph in London and the Vietnam Wall in Washington evoke the same temporality, the same encircling of trauma. Both are in imperial capitals and both celebrate imperial wars. One marks what has become a questionable victory: the First World War was not a war to end all wars, as had been hoped. The other marks a defeat. The Cenotaph was in place in time for the march past in July 1919, less than a year after the armistice that ended fighting in the First World War; the Vietnam Wall was not dedicated until 1982, nearly ten years after the withdrawal of US troops from Vietnam. The Vietnam Wall and the Cenotaph both had cardboard, or temporary versions, in addition to the stone monument.[8] There is a half-size, touring version of the Wall, which travels around the United States, and the London Cenotaph was initially constructed out of wood and plaster and meant to be temporary.[9]

The story of the Cenotaph begins, like that of most memorials, with a committee: the War Cabinet Committee on Peace Celebrations. This committee, chaired by Lord Curzon, was set up by the War Cabinet in June 1919 to consider arrangements for the celebration of victory, including a military parade and thanksgiving services. Prime Minister Lloyd George had been impressed by the ceremony in Paris at the Arc de Triomphe,[10] and he proposed that there be a catafalque at some point along the route of the parade in London, for troops marching past to salute the dead. Lord Curzon thought this could prove impressive, though 'it was perhaps, however, more essentially suited to the Latin temperament'.[11] Lord Curzon reported back to the War Cabinet on 4 July that there was considerable feeling against 'the French proposal' and that the King for one did not like it. If there was to be something, Curzon favoured a simple pylon – and the most suitable spot in the view of his committee was in Whitehall, almost opposite Downing Street. But the objections were 'that it was foreign to the temper and custom of the nation; that it might not be easy for the public to assume a properly reverential attitude; and, as the structure would be of a very temporary character it must be carefully safeguarded or it would be overturned and

[8] Robin Wagner-Pacifici and Barry Schwartz, 'The Vietnam Veterans Memorial: Commemorating a Difficult Past', *American Journal of Sociology*, 97, no. 2 (1991): 376–420; 413.

[9] Winter, *Sites of Memory, Sites of Mourning*, 102.

[10] Public Record Office: Office of Works and Successors: Statues and Memorials: Registered Files (WORK 20): WORK 20/139, Copy from 1914–1918, A Journal of Remembrance: The Story of the Cenotaph, told by Sir Edwin L. Lutyens.

[11] Public Record Office: War Cabinet and Cabinet: Minutes (CAB 23): CAB 23/11, 1 July 1919, War Cabinet 587, Minute 2.

trampled in the crush'.[12] The Prime Minister stressed to the Cabinet the importance of some form of tribute to the dead, and suggested that one or two well-known architects might be consulted and asked to submit designs. Despite some general scepticism and the opposition from the committee, the rest of the Cabinet agreed with Lloyd George and the proposal was accepted.

Sir Edwin Lutyens was commissioned by the Office of Works to produce a temporary shrine made out of wood and plaster. The name was changed from catafalque to Cenotaph, meaning an empty tomb. The design was of a tomb, topped by a wreath and raised on a high pedestal. It formed the centre-piece of the peace celebrations of 19 July 1919. But the success and public appeal of this temporary monument was unexpected. People laid wreaths at its base at the end of the day of celebrations, and continued to bring fresh flowers to the spot in the succeeding days (Figure 2). There was insistent public pressure beginning immediately after the peace celebrations that the temporary monument be re-erected in permanent form on the same site. Correspondence and comment in the *Times* was in support, and a petition from Members of Parliament was addressed to the First Commissioner of Works, Alfred Mond, who also did a certain amount of lobbying himself. On 30 July 1919 the War Cabinet agreed to the proposal.[13] In Lutyens' account:

> Time passed, and the plain fact emerged and grew stronger every hour that the Cenotaph was what the people wanted, and that they wanted to have the wood and plaster original replaced by an identical memorial in lasting stone. It was a mass-feeling too deep to express itself more fitly than by the piles of ever-fresh flowers which loving hands placed at the Cenotaph day by day. Thus it was decided, by the human sentiment of millions, that the Cenotaph should be as it now is, and speaking as the designer, I could wish for no greater honour, no more complete and lasting satisfaction.[14]

However, it was not quite so straightforward. There *was* considerable opposition to the decision, and in the end the fact that it went through was largely down to timing. Had the decision not been so swift, the disadvantages of the site would have become clearer, particularly to the police. The Commissioner of Police of the Metropolis had written on 23 July

[12] CAB 23/11, 4 July 1919, War Cabinet 588, Minute 1.

[13] WORK 20/139, Cenotaph: Summary account; CAB 24/84, 23 July 1919, War Cabinet 279, The Temporary Cenotaph in Whitehall, memorandum submitted by the First Commissioner of Works.

[14] WORK 20/139, Copy from 1914–1918, A Journal of Remembrance: The Story of the Cenotaph, told by Sir Edwin L. Lutyens. See also A. S. G. Butler, *The Architecture of Sir Edwin Lutyens* (London, 1950), III: 37; quoted in David Cannadine, 'War and death, grief and mourning in modern Britain', in *Mirrors of Mortality. Studies in the Social History of Death*, ed. Joachim Whaley (London: Europa, 1981), 187–242; 221.

Figure 2 The temporary Cenotaph, Whitehall, 1919 (Photo courtesy of the Public Record Office, PRO WORK 20/139)

1919 that there were no objections from a police point of view, and it was only later, after the first major test of the location on 11 November 1919, that the police began to formulate objections. In the meantime the Cabinet decision was in place.

The gathering at the Cenotaph on the first anniversary of the Armistice was in total contrast to the regimented and highly organised ceremonial that takes place today. It had been agreed that the French President would lay a wreath at the Cenotaph at 11 a.m. and that a march by about 5,000 members of the Comrades of the Great War would take place at 12.30 p.m. However, before the time arrived 'a crowd of quite unexpected proportions had collected in the vicinity',[15] and it was only with great difficulty that space was made for the carriage with the wreath to get through. All other traffic was diverted from Whitehall. The police called for reinforcements several times and by 12 noon had managed to clear a large oval space in preparation for the next wreath laying. All the time 'persons in their hundreds were continually bringing wreaths and flowers to lay at the Cenotaph'.[16] Once the Comrades of the Great War had laid their wreaths and the procession had marched off, 'the crowd again pressed on to the Cenotaph . . . Those who got near the monument would not move, consequently the majority never got to it at all. Many persons had to pass their flowers over the heads of others for the police to place them on the Cenotaph.'[17] Following this clearly unnerving experience, the police recommended that the monument be moved from Whitehall to a site in one of the parks or other open spaces. The whole question of the location of the permanent structure was re-opened. The objections stressed the risk of accidents, particularly from people crossing the street to lay flowers or to inspect those that had been placed at the foot of the monument. Mond appears to have kept *his* nerve, however, and convinced the Cabinet to keep theirs. He wrote to the Prime Minister:

The reasons that led the Cabinet to that decision are equally good today as then. The Cenotaph was not primarily instituted as a place to lay flowers, which seems to be commonly assumed. It is a historic monument, recording a great event and a great occasion in the history of the Empire. On the Peace March, it was saluted by all the Imperial and Allied Troops. Its retention is really a commemoration of that historic event.[18]

He added perhaps somewhat disengenuously, 'it is very doubtful that the deposition of flowers on the present scale will continue for any length of time – in fact it is extremely unlikely, especially when the present

15 Public Record Office: Metropolitan Police: Office of the Commissioner: Correspondence and Papers (MEPO 2): MEPO 2/1957, 14 November 1919, Metropolitan Police memorandum, Cannon Row Station.
16 MEPO 2/1957, 14 November 1919, Metropolitan Police memorandum, Cannon Row Station.
17 *Ibid.*
18 WORK 20/139, 22 December 1919, Alfred Mond to Prime Minister Lloyd George.

temporary structure is removed as it will be for an interval of a number of months'. The argument that the monument and the spot in Whitehall on which it stood had been consecrated by the salutes of soldiers in the march past was crucial. The site was now sacred, and no other would do: 'The site has become qualified by the salutes of Foch and the allied armies and by our men and their great leaders – no other site would have this.'[19] It was even stressed that since 'the ground on which the Cenotaph has been built has been consecrated . . . it would be highly undesirable to let the traffic again move over that portion of the road'.[20] In the end the Cabinet were persuaded. They adhered to their original decision and since the money had been voted, the planned work began on 19 January 1920. A scaffold was erected to conceal the removal of the Cenotaph and flowers from public view, and arrangements were made for the upper portion – the tomb itself – to be preserved and sent, together with the flags, to the Imperial War Museum, which was then at Crystal Palace.

Once it was accepted that a permanent version would be built, the question of additions or alterations was, of course, raised. When Mond wrote to Lutyens informing him of the Cabinet's decision of 30 July, he noted the general opinion that the design should be altered as little as possible – and this in the end was what happened. Suggestions for additional inscriptions were rejected, as were objections concerning the lack of Christian symbolism. An overriding concern was 'to guard against giving offence to the many non-Christian nations of the Empire who also contributed to a large extent to the Armies of His Majesty engaged in the recent conflict'.[21]

Popular demand fixed the Cenotaph permanently in place, in the middle of Whitehall, where today it is surrounded by the endless flow of traffic (Figure 3). Like the memorial to the battle of the Somme at Thiepval, it has been described as 'an embodiment of nothingness'.[22] Perhaps it works precisely because there is nothing there. The design in its simplicity provides a monument that succeeds because it does not conceal the trauma of war but yet provides a means of marking it. It attempts no narrative or interpretation. It marks something that is shared yet inexpressible in more explicit terms. What is shared, we might say, is the inexpressibility. Generally, shared or social understandings are expressed in language.

[19] WORK 20/139, 29 July 1919, Edwin Lutyens to Alfred Mond.

[20] WORK 20/139, 5 August 1919, Memorandum to Mr Russell.

[21] WORK 20/139, 15 October 1919, Alfred Mond, First Commissioner of Works, to the War Cabinet.

[22] Winter, *Sites of Memory, Sites of Mourning*, 105. The arch at Thiepval was a major influence on Maya Lin, the designer of the Vietnam Veterans Memorial. Jan C. Scruggs and Joel L. Swerdlow, *To Heal a Nation: the Vietnam Veterans Memorial* (New York: Harper Row, 1985), 77.

Figure 3 The Cenotaph, Whitehall

However, language has its limits. The sense that there are things, important things, about which we cannot speak and for which there are no words is also shared. 'Cenotaph' literally means 'empty tomb', and 'as the tomb of no one this became the tomb of all who had died in the war'.[23] But perhaps it is more than this. It represents the lack, the trauma, and its encirclement. The cenotaph is a point around which Londoners and tourists endlessly circle in the course of their daily business, which, of course, is the business not of mourning but of government, of politics. It is not tucked away in a London park or in Parliament Square Gardens where it could be forgotten, as some had wished. It is there in the middle of the traffic, as the stumbling block, the hindrance that reminds us of the impossibility of closure. It is the embodiment of the real. Jay Winter compares the Cenotaph with Maya Lin's Washington memorial – the Vietnam Wall – in the sense that both bring the dead back into the heart of the capital. As Winter puts it: 'an abstract architectural form had somehow managed to transform a victory parade, a moment of high politics, into a time when millions could contemplate the timeless, the eternal, the inexorable reality of death in war'.[24] The Cenotaph marks the site of the real, as it intrudes into what we call social reality – the myth of the nation, the glorious victory, the tale of sacrifice and the promise of fulfilment. It is uncompromising.

Lutyens' final design for the Cenotaph is composed of a series of curved surfaces of a sphere. It does not contain a single vertical or horizontal line: 'all its horizontal surfaces and planes are spherical, parts of parallel spheres 1801 feet 8 inches in diameter; and all its vertical lines converge upwards to a point some 1801 feet 8 inches above the centre of these spheres'.[25] These create an illusion of linearity. The curves were added in the final design stage and meant that the execution of the monument demanded the finest craftsmanship. Although invisible to most people, the curves are very interesting. They mean that the Cenotaph is not a free-standing, separate structure. It is a part of a larger whole – one of the pieces of a spherical shape, cut into segments the shape of the points of a star. In Chapter 1 we saw how, in psychoanalytic theory, when what we call social reality is formed something always drops out – there is always some excess, something that cannot be symbolised. The excess or gap is a stumbling block; it is what prevents the social order from becoming complete. It is called the real. In the trauma of war, people

[23] Winter, *Sites of Memory, Sites of Mourning*, 105. [24] *Ibid.*

[25] Luytens' words from Imperial War Graves Commission, 6th Report, 1926, quoted by Winter, *Sites of Memory, Sites of Mourning*, 105; see also WORK 20/139, Cenotaph: Summary account and WORK 20/139, Copy from 1914–1918, A Journal of Remembrance: The Story of the Cenotaph, told by Sir Edwin L. Lutyens.

are brought face to face with that real, which is normally hidden beneath social conventions. The Cenotaph, as a representation of the segment that has 'fallen out' of the whole, represents the real made – eventually – solid. As Winter says, it 'is a work of genius largely because of its simplicity. It says so much because it says so little. It is a form on which anyone could inscribe his or her own thoughts, reveries, sadnesses.'[26] However, I would suggest that like any work of art, its simplicity belies a complexity and it is that complexity which is the key to its success. It is not just a blank sheet on which people inscribe their own feelings. It is in tune with trauma in some distinct, anti-symbolic sense.

Flowers and wreath-laying

The popularity of the Cenotaph as a place on which to place wreaths, flowers and other mementoes continued and indeed increased after the permanent memorial was in place, contrary to Mond's prediction. Mond had argued that the laying of wreaths should be limited to one or two occasions a year, 'say 19th July, the date of the Peace Procession, and some other day such as Easter Monday'.[27] In contrast, Lutyens had welcomed the flowers, 'the ever fresh piles of flowers, which tell me the Cenotaph has passed from the domain of ceremony, however fitly impressive, into the human realm of loving remembrance'.[28] The officials of the Office of Works shared Mond's discomfort, however. They were the ones faced with the daily arrangement and removal of wreaths, and the question of what to do with the wreaths and cards afterwards. The cards and ribbons from wreaths left at the temporary Cenotaph had been collected up and kept. However, they were damp and mostly indecipherable, and although they were kept for some months in two sacks in a store, they eventually became so offensive they had to be destroyed. It was resolved to make special arrangements to preserve all cards from wreaths deposited at the new Cenotaph.[29] The proposal at the time of the unveiling ceremony in November 1920 was that the collection would be sorted at Crystal Palace, the cards inserted into albums and preserved as a record. By 11 January 1921, a total of 21,257 cards had been collected, cleaned and stacked for transmission via Crystal Palace to the Imperial War Museum. By March it had reached 30,000. The variety of shapes and sizes was causing some

[26] Winter, *Sites of Memory, Sites of Mourning*, 105.
[27] WORK 20/139, 15 October 1919, Alfred Mond, First Commissioner of Works, to the War Cabinet.
[28] WORK 20/139, Copy from 1914–1918, A Journal of Remembrance: The Story of the Cenotaph, told by Sir Edwin L. Lutyens.
[29] WORK 20/143, 25 November 1920, Memorandum to Director of Works.

difficulties, and the idea of albums was abandoned. It seems as though the curator of the Imperial War Museum was not enthusiastic about the proposed gift either, and one official shared this view, commenting: 'I cannot believe that the majority of these cards will be of the slightest interest as a museum exhibit.'[30] The museum does not house any such cards today.[31]

The question of wreaths and cards placed on the Cenotaph has been a continuing site of struggle and difficulty that has not been resolved over the years. It is recognised that private persons have a right to place wreaths in memory of relatives, and yet the state authorities feel obliged to police that activity, sometimes, perhaps unwittingly, in an unfeeling and barbaric way. Mrs S. King of Bramah Road, Brixton, placed a wreath on the Cenotaph on VE Day in 1945, in memory of her son who had been killed in the war. When she visited the Cenotaph again, she was horrified to find it gone. She wrote to the Ministry:

> I am writing to you concerning a wreath that I placed upon the Cenotaph after VE day. It should have lasted some months as it was of everlasting flowers of a mauve colour and a ribbon going up the centre also bows on the top with wire. I went to the Cenotaph today and was horrified to find it gone. It was put there for 'My Poor Dear Son' who was accidentally shot after war in Europe was ended. It was 32 shillings. I went in the home office and was given your address. I would like the wreath please. I can get it re-framed and the ribbon can be washed. It is sacred to 'My Poor Dear Son's memory.' I await your reply . . .[32]

The reply she received may not have been very helpful. The wreath in question was reported as destroyed, being in 'a very shabby condition, presumably having been damaged during VJ celebrations'.[33] But she was offered a spare frame as a replacement:

> Madam
> 1. I am directed by the Minister of Works to say that the delay in answering your letter of 12th September is regretted.
> 2. The wreath which you laid on the Cenotaph has, unfortunately, been destroyed. I am to explain that, after remaining on the Cenotaph for some months, it was removed on 10th September as it had become rather shabby . . .
> 3. I am also to explain that, owing to the number of wreaths which have to be removed in this way, it is not possible to preserve them. . . . Consequently, your wreath was destroyed in the normal way. This is greatly regretted.

[30] WORK 20/143, 3 March 1921, Annotated Memorandum to Chief Architect.
[31] Discussions with Gill Smith, Imperial War Museum, May 2001.
[32] WORK 20/255, 12 September 1945, Letter from Mrs S. King. (Spelling and punctuation standardised.)
[33] WORK 20/255, 24 September 1945, Superintendent of Works to Mr Clouting, Architect.

4. You may, however, care to have a spare circular frame which could possibly be recovered. This frame can be obtained from Mr. C. A. Ward, Superintendent of Works . . .[34]

It's a pity they couldn't find a replacement son for Mrs King while they were about it.

The type of wreaths placed by the public had caused official unease from the start, leading to questions being asked in the House of Commons. In 1922 the First Commissioner of Works, the official in charge of the Cenotaph, came to a decision that restrictions were needed in regard to permanent wreaths. In response to a question in the House, he stated that 'the practice of placing permanent memorials – bronze tablets, metal wreaths, and glazed artificial flowers – seems inappropriate, as such objects are unbecoming in themselves and prevent the display of humbler and more transitory tributes of affection'.[35] In internal memoranda in the Office of Works the feelings of revulsion against 'unbecoming' objects becomes plain. Artificial wreaths and glass domes are 'hideous sophistications like the things which disfigure French cemeteries . . . glazed horrors'. The latest abomination was of another character – a portrait – described as 'a very commonplace bronze relief, apparently connected with an American'.[36] These strictures were, however, extended to units of the fighting forces, on the grounds that if units were allowed permanent memorials there would be no room left for private wreaths, 'one of the principal objects of the Cenotaph'.[37] The solution was to have a quiet word with those who arranged the new flowers and remove the old ones to the effect that 'no memorial has any prescriptive right of position or prominence, just because it is made of permanent material'.[38]

The question of overt or implied political motivations for placing wreaths has been a concern, again since the Cenotaph was erected. Although there was a reluctance to act as 'censor of inscriptions, which might raise delicate issues', nevertheless general instructions had been put in place in 1922 'to safeguard the use of the Cenotaph', and the hope was expressed that 'public sentiment as a whole' would support efforts to maintain the Cenotaph's 'original object and character . . . as a direct memorial to those who lost their lives in connexion with the

[34] WORK 20/255, 3 October 1945, Letter to Mrs S. King.
[35] 'The Cenotaph', *The Times*, London, 27 July 1922.
[36] WORK 20/255, 15 June 1922, Memorandum No. 154.
[37] WORK 20/255, 23 November 1922, Letter to Private Secretary, Secretary of State for Air.
[38] WORK 20/255, 15 June 1922, Memorandum No. 154.

Great War'.[39] Public sentiment and the judgement calls of officials again did not always coincide, though ways of reconciling the two were on occasions found. In May 1933, a wreath was laid at the Cenotaph by a representative of German Chancellor Adolf Hitler, Dr Rosenberg, who was visiting Britain to gauge the attitude to the new régime in Germany.[40] Some people saw this wreath-laying as a desecration. During the night the card and swastika were removed from the wreath.[41] The following day Captain James Edmonds Sears, an estate developer and prospective parliamentary candidate, removed the entire wreath from the Cenotaph as 'a deliberate protest against the desecration of our national war memorial by placing on it a wreath by Hitler's emissary, especially in view of the fact that the Hitler Government are contriving to do those very things and foster those feelings which occurred in Germany before the war, for which many of our fellows suffered and lost their lives'.[42] Captain Sears immediately gave himself up to the police and was charged with theft and wilful damage. The charge of theft was dismissed, but the magistrate said that 'most people would agree that whatever the defendant's private opinions were, it was an improper and unmanly thing to do'.[43] Sears was fined forty shillings for wilful damage.

Some commentators, while sympathising with Captain Sears' motives, saw the *removal* of the wreath as a desecration and thought the sentence should have been more severe. The Cenotaph was sacred, and should not be 'the demonstration ground for the clash of sentiments', however reasonable.[44] It was not an appropriate place to express contentious sentiments: 'to whatever heights of fierceness political animosities may rise in this country, they ought never to be allowed to touch the memories enshrined in the Cenotaph in Whitehall'.[45] Most people deplored Sear's action, at least in public. However, some of the Yorkshire press were more forthright. The incident 'should at least convince Herr Rosenberg of the strong feeling that exists in this country as the result of Nazi outrages'. And if he had any illusions the north of England thought any differently from the south, the *Yorkshire Evening News* informed him, 'he should be speedily corrected. Fascism of any kind falls on stony ground up here,

[39] 'The Cenotaph', *The Times*, London, 27 July 1922.
[40] 'Herr Hitler's wreath', *Leeds Mercury*, 12 May 1933.
[41] WORK 20/255, 11 May 1933, Memorandum Secretary 22C.
[42] 'Hitler wreath thrown in the Thames: Cenotaph protest by ex-Captain: "Desecration" of memorial', *Daily Telegraph*, London, 12 May 1933.
[43] 'Dr. Rosenberg's wreath: removal from Cenotaph: protest against desecration', *The Times*, London, 12 May 1933.
[44] 'Keep it sacred: the Cenotaph is no place for demonstrations', *Daily Sketch*, 13 May 1933.
[45] 'Herr Hitler's wreath', *Leeds Mercury*, 12 May 1933.

and the spate of protest meetings against Jew-baiting shows that the reaction to the particular brand adopted by Herr Hitler is even less likely to command respect and admiration.' The *Yorkshire Post* pointed to the final fate of the wreath. It had been thrown into the Thames by Sears' associates, but was recovered by the Thames police. After the case in court, a representative of the Office of Works was called to the police station to sign for the wreath, which the police were originally intending to return to the Cenotaph. However, when he arrived, the wreath was still at the station. It was never in fact replaced on the memorial. Another official later reported that the wreath 'was so damaged by being thrown into the river, that it was unfit to be replaced on the Cenotaph... it is to be disposed of with other dead wreaths'.[46] Hitler's tribute had been officially yet quietly consigned to the rubbish bin.[47]

A two-minute silence in memory of the fallen was instituted on 11 November 1919. This was 'as total as it was effective', and provided, like the Cenotaph and local war memorials and ceremonies, an opportunity, according to David Cannadine, to make 'public and corporate those unassuageable feelings of grief and sorrow which otherwise must remain forever private and individual'.[48] During the original two-minute silences nothing moved, anywhere: time itself was suspended. The two-minute silence combined with the reiteration of 'We will remember them' served as 'a concentrated appeal to memory by literally breaking a temporal continuity'.[49] The flow of traffic halted, all work stopped, shops ceased trading, and people stood very still, so that, in the words of the King's message 'in perfect stillness, the thoughts of everyone may be concentrated on reverent remembrance of the Glorious Dead'.[50]

Over the week following the unveiling of the permanent Cenotaph and the burial of the body of the Unknown Soldier[51] in Westminster Abbey on Armistice Day 1920, over one million people visited the Cenotaph and the grave and 100,000 wreaths were laid, a public response the remarkable extent of which again surprised the authorities.[52] In Britain

[46] WORK 20/255, 12 May 1933, hand-written memorandum.

[47] 'End of the wreath', *Yorkshire Post*, 12 May 1933.

[48] Cannadine, 'War and death', 222.

[49] Pierre Nora, 'Between Memory and History: *Les lieux de mémoire*', *Representations*, 26 (1989): 7–25, quoted in Catherine Moriarty, 'Private grief and public remembrance: British First World War memorials', in *War and Memory in the Twentieth Century*, ed. Martin Evans and Ken Lunn (Oxford: Berg, 1997), 125–42; 137.

[50] Public Record Office: Board of Education and Predecessors: Private Office: Papers (Series 1) (ED 24): ED 24/2035, King's message on first anniversary of Armistice.

[51] Ken Inglis, 'Entombing Unknown Soldiers: from London and Paris to Baghdad', *History and Memory*, 5 (1993): 7–31.

[52] Cannadine, 'War and death', 224. The parallels with the mourning of Diana Princess of Wales in 1997 are obvious. Cannadine notes that the popularity of Remembrance Day

the key ceremonies still take place not around the tomb of the Unknown Soldier in Westminster Abbey, but around the Cenotaph as symbol of the 'empty tomb'. Over the years the form of the ceremonial has changed. The event is now highly scripted: the informality of crowding around the Cenotaph, passing wreaths over the heads of the people in front, is no more. Present-day ceremonies seem an attempt to tame the Cenotaph; they re-introduce the elements of myth and glory that the monument itself so carefully side-stepped. The ceremony begins, after the two-minute silence, with the laying of wreaths by the Queen and members of the royal family, UK government ministers and opposition leaders, ambassadors of Commonwealth countries and chiefs of the armed services. A short service conducted by Christian religious leaders is followed by the British national anthem, after which the royal family leave. Only then are wreaths laid by the representatives of the soldiers themselves – the Royal British Legion. There follows a regimented march past of veterans, and wreaths are discretely taken from the leaders of each group as they pass. In 2000 for the first time civilian groups – the Bevan Boys, the Women's Land Army, Evacuees Returning Association, members of the Post Office, the merchant navy, firefighters, members of the actors' union, Equity, and others – were included in an attempt to widen participation.[53] Relatives of those shot for alleged cowardice joined the march past for the first time in the same year under the banner of the First World War Pardon Association.[54] However, this latter change was more by chance than intention, an accident of timing. It was a result of the way Remembrance Sunday fell in 2000. The Association normally holds its own ceremony at the Cenotaph on the Saturday before Remembrance Sunday. But in 2000 this was 11 November, a day already taken by the Western Front Association for their ceremony. So representatives of those 'shot at dawn' were allowed to join the main parade instead.[55]

(transferred to the preceding Sunday in 1946) declined from the 1950s onwards. It is interesting to note the move in the late 1990s to reinstate remembrance on the anniversary itself, rather than the nearest Sunday, which began in 1995, gained momentum due again to public action not to government decree. See Chapter 1.

[53] Tania Branigan, 'Poppy day marches into a new century', *The Guardian*, London, 13 November 2000, 7.

[54] In 2001 a statue in memory of those 'shot at dawn' was unveiled at the National Memorial Arboretum, near Litchfield in Staffordshire. A campaign for posthumous pardons for those executed has been unsuccessful. Kim Sengupta, '"Tragic" statue for the Great War's executed soldiers', *The Independent*, 22 June 2001, 6.

[55] David Ward, 'Battle for recognition: shamed soldiers acknowledged', *The Guardian*, London, 10 November 2000, 5; Bryan Appleyard, 'The troops we chose to forget', *The Sunday Times*, London, 12 November 2000, 6.

The Vietnam Wall

Much of the debate in the case of the Vietnam Wall focuses on the way the memorial commemorates a defeat – not a victory nor a popular war – and hence appears to call for different, more ambiguous forms of commemoration.[56] As Robin Wagner-Pacifici and Barry Schwartz put it: 'suppose a society is divided over the very event it selects for commemoration. Suppose that event constitutes a painful moment for society, such as a military defeat or an era of domestic oppression ... How is commemoration without consensus, or without pride, possible?'[57] But was the First World War a popular war? The lack of consensus is perhaps more obvious in the case of Vietnam, but to the extent that any war marks a more than painful moment – a trauma – there will be controversial aspects to commemoration. The task is not just (or even at all) that which Wagner-Pacifici and Schwartz identify for Vietnam: 'incorporating painful events into the collective memory'.[58] As we have seen, some events resist incorporation into narratives of collective memory of the standard form. While this resistance is clearly uncomfortable or even painful for some, for others, including many survivors, incorporation is not in any case something to be desired. Survivors often want to remember traumatic events in all their affront to meaning and to sense and are unwilling to see them encapsulated in common platitudes.

In the US the controversy was not at first around what form the memorial should take but the very thought of building a memorial at all. This is not dissimilar to London after the First World War, where there was originally to be no specific commemoration of the dead, just a victory parade. The proposal for a Vietnam memorial came from an individual veteran of the war, Jan Scruggs.[59] In 1979 he was inspired by the film *The Deer Hunter* to think that it was time that the war should be publicly remembered – time for healing. With fellow veteran Robert Doubek, he established the Vietnam Veterans Memorial Fund.[60] Initial responses

[56] Wagner-Pacifici and Schwartz, 'The Vietnam Veterans Memorial', 410. See also James M. Mayo, *War Memorials as Political Landscape: the American Experience and Beyond* (New York: Praeger, 1988), which has separate chapters on monuments to 'Victory as Justice', 'Victory as Manifest Destiny', and 'Defeat'.

[57] Robin Wagner-Pacifici and Barry Schwartz, 'The Vietnam Veterans Memorial: Commemorating a Difficult Past', *American Journal of Sociology*, 97, no. 2 (1991): 376–420; 379.

[58] *Ibid.*, 381.

[59] Scruggs and Swerdlow, *To Heal a Nation.*

[60] 'Vietnam Veterans Memorial Wall Replica', http://thevietnamwall.com/thestory.html, 26 December 1998.

from the public were not encouraging; the fund organisers, though determined, were not powerful or influential.[61] A month after the launch at a press conference on 28 May 1979, the fund had collected only $144.50, despite a steady flow of letters.[62] But they persevered. Eventually they attracted the support of veterans in Washington and others with useful contacts who were able to bring them more substantial support and more donations. The decision had been taken by Scruggs and his fellow fund organisers that they would build the memorial entirely from private contributions. Other key decisions 'that determined a great deal about the character of the memorial and the kind of community that it rebuilt' were taken at that early stage.[63] It was to list all those killed, missing or still held as prisoners of war. What was imagined was a *veterans* memorial, not a *war* memorial. And they wanted it built on the Mall in Washington to give the project the national recognition the veterans needed. When the original proposals were put forward 'political neutrality was a condition for . . . support' and the very name 'the Vietnam Veterans Memorial' rather than Vietnam War Memorial reflected the narrowness of the area of agreement.[64] Kristin Hass emphasises the need to make alliances and find common ground with people who were likely opponents and in the end many of these were, with some difficulty, persuaded to support the fund. This was a result of being careful to 'negotiate a public memory without either celebrating or explicitly renouncing the war'.[65] Building a public community of support through the contributions to the fund was central, and was to prove even more so as controversies arose later in the process. The campaign for the memorial also built a community of veterans.

There was an open contest for the design itself, with a jury of architects, sculptors and critics. The veterans committee set four major criteria: the memorial had to be reflective and contemplative in character; it had to harmonise with its surroundings, especially the neighbouring national memorials, the Washington Monument and the Lincoln Memorial; it should contain the names of all who died or remained missing; and, finally, it should make no political statement about the war.[66] These requirements are inconsistent: the alignment of the memorial, and indeed its very location, defines Vietnam as a national event, putting the wall in

[61] Kristin Ann Hass, *Carried to the Wall: American Memory and the Vietnam Veterans Memorial* (Berkeley: University of California Press, 1998), 10.
[62] 'Vietnam Veterans Memorial Wall Replica'. [63] Hass, *Carried to the Wall*.
[64] Wagner-Pacifici and Schwartz, 'The Vietnam Veterans Memorial', 392.
[65] Hass, *Carried to the Wall*, 11.
[66] *Vietnam: Echoes from the Wall*. The Teachers Guide: Module 5 Appendix, URL: http://www.teachvietnam.org/teachers/guide/html/module_5_appendix.htm, 18 January 2003.

the context of the Lincoln and Washington memorials. The Lincoln and Washington monuments are in a sense seen as 'surrogates for the national flag' so that there was no absence of politics.[67] The listing of names in itself is a political move, ironically only possible because the death toll of 58,000 is so comparatively low that all the names could be listed on one monument. Of course, it was only American casualties who were to be included. In that sense it was to be a standard war memorial. A wall carved with the names of all the Vietnamese victims of the war would be sixty-nine times the size and would stretch the whole distance between the Washington and Lincoln monuments.[68]

A site was requested and secured – two acres at the western end of Constitution Gardens on the Mall – and an open competition was held to select the design for the monument. This turned into the largest competition of its kind in the US, with 2,573 registrants and 1,421 designs submitted.[69] The winning design was for two long retaining walls built of polished black marble and set into the ground. Each nearly 250 feet long, the walls meet each other at a wide angle, like open arms. Each is shaped like an elongated triangle and slopes downwards into the earth. They are set into the ground, below the level of the surrounding lawn, and a path leads the visitors from the start of the wall, where it is a few inches high, to the meeting point of the two, where the depth is some ten feet. The alignment of the two walls is designed such that looking along one, you see the high column of the Washington Monument and along the other the white marble palisades of the Lincoln Memorial. The marble is highly polished like a mirror, and reflects the surrounding area – monuments, trees and visitors (Figure 4). The site is south-facing and sunny. The walls carry the names of those lost or missing in the war. They are carved into the shiny marble filling the panels, which increase in height towards the apex of the memorial. The shortest panels have one line of names, the tallest 137 lines.[70] The names follow each other, running from line to line like words on the pages of a book (Figure 5). The paths that lead alongside the walls are plain flags and cobbles, with lights set in them to illuminate the walls at night, and they widen gently towards the centre where the walls are at their highest. The designer, Maya Ying Lin, saw the memorial as creating a serene area, quiet but not enclosing:

[67] Wagner-Pacifici and Schwartz, 'The Vietnam Veterans Memorial', 407.

[68] Hass, *Carried to the Wall*, 129.

[69] Vietnam Veterans Memorial Fund, 'The Wall – The Design: The Memorial's History', http://www.vvmf.org/wall/history.htm, 27 December 1998, no longer active.

[70] Vietnam Veterans Memorial Fund, 'The Wall that Heals: About the Vietnam Veterans Memorial', http://www.vvmf.org/wall/wall.htm, 27 December 1998, no longer active.

Figure 4 Visitors to the Vietnam Veterans Memorial, Washington DC

Figure 5 The names on the Vietnam Wall

Walking through this park-like area, the memorial appears as a rift in the earth, a long, polished, black stone wall, emerging from and receding into the earth. Approaching the memorial, the ground slopes gently downward and the low walls emerging on either side, growing out of the earth, extend and converge at a point below and ahead. Walking into this grassy site contained by the walls of the memorial we can barely make out the carved names upon the memorial's walls. These names, seemingly infinite in number, convey the sense of overwhelming numbers, while unifying these individuals into a whole.[71]

The adjudicators' selection of this design proved controversial, for a variety of reasons, including its use of black marble, the absence of any symbol of the nation, whether flag or statue, the way the monument is placed within the earth – and the fact that the winner, Maya Ying Lin, was a young architecture student from Yale, a Chinese-American woman. The criticism was vituperative, sexist and racist. The design was seen as an example of an elitist, modernist trend to minimalism in art – an 'abstract form that the public would find difficult to interpret'.[72] It was described as 'a perfect piece of sculptural orthodoxy for the early 1980s. . . . elemental, even banal . . . comprised solely of straight lines and flat planes'.[73] Before it was built, some veterans condemned the memorial as insulting to those who fought: 'If Americans allow that black trench to be dug, future generations will understand clearly what America thought of its Vietnam veterans.'[74] It was variously described as ' "the black gash of shame and sorrow," a "degrading ditch," a "tombstone," a "slap in the face," and "a wailing wall for draft dodgers and New Lefters of the future" '.[75] It seemed that the identity of the designer – as a woman and a Chinese-American – and the non-traditional form of the memorial led to the design being read as a political statement:[76] 'Many saw its black walls as evoking shame, sorrow and dishonor and perceived its refusal to rise above the earth as indicative of defeat. . . . A racially coded reading of the colour black was combined with a reading of a feminised earth as connoting a lack of power.' The question of blackness was resolved when General George Price spoke out at a meeting about the memorial: 'Black is not the color of shame. I am tired of hearing it called such by you.

[71] By Maya Ying Lin, statement as part of her competition submission, March 1981. Available in *Vietnam: Echoes from the Wall*. The Teachers Guide: Module 5 URL: http://www.teachvietnam.org/teachers/guide/html/module_5.htm, 18 January 2003.

[72] Marita Sturken, *Tangled Memories: the Vietnam War, the AIDS Epidemic, and the Politics of Remembering* (Berkeley: University of California Press, 1997), 49.

[73] Tom Wolfe, 'Art disputes war', *Washington Post*, 13 October 1982, B4, quoted in Sturken, *Tangled Memories*, 48–9.

[74] Tom Carhart, 'Insulting Vietnam vets', *New York Times*, 24 October 1981, quoted in Sturken, *Tangled Memories*, 52.

[75] Sturken, *Tangled Memories*, 51. [76] *Ibid.*, 52.

Figure 6 Figurative sculpture overlooking the Vietnam Veterans Memorial

Color meant nothing on the battlefields of Korea and Vietnam. We are all equal in combat. Color should mean nothing now.'[77]

The other controversies were addressed in a number of ways, and the monument as it now stands is a reflection of these compromises. The original design did not contain any reference to Vietnam, or to the fact that these were soldiers that died. An inscription was later added. The memorial was supplemented by a figurative element in the form of a statue of three combatants, and later, another statue of women combatants and nurses. The male statue was commissioned from a traditional sculptor who had won third place in the original competition. It stands, ironically enough, in the tree line, the three figures facing the memorial (Figure 6). Visiting veterans often stand there too, watching from a distance before they can summon up the courage to visit the memorial itself. The women's memorial was not added until much later, in 1993, and it was a response to the figurative representation of men. Neither of these statues, nor the flag which was added, intrudes into the space of the wall itself. In a sense the supplementation of the monument is appropriate. It emphasises the original design's message of the complete yet incomplete, contested nature of the war it commemorates. And crucial features survived: the

[77] Quoted in Scruggs and Swerdlow, *To Heal a Nation*, 100.

reflective black marble was retained, as was the placing of the wall within the earth.

Like the Cenotaph in London, one of the striking things about the Vietnam memorial, after all the controversy, was the public's 'extraordinary and unexpected reaction'.[78] Once the wall was in place 'the debate about aesthetics and remembrance surrounding its design simply disappeared.... The experience of viewing Lin's work was so powerful for the general public that criticism of its design vanished.'[79] People were moved by it. As Maya Lin predicted, people cry when they visit. Her aim was to bring home the reality of death. The troops in Vietnam died: 'You have to accept that fact before you can really truly recognise and remember them. I just wanted to be honest with people.... I wanted something that would just simply say, "They can never come back. They should be remembered".'[80] In her design statement she put it even more plainly:

> We the living are brought to a concrete realisation of these deaths. Brought to a sharp awareness of such a loss, it is up to each individual to resolve or come to terms with this loss. For death is in the end a personal and private matter, and the area contained within this memorial is a quiet place, meant for personal reflection and private reckoning.... This memorial is for those who died, and for us to remember them.[81]

Visitors to the memorial are responsive to this message. This is from one note left at the Wall:

> I could feel pulled toward this black wall and yet my feet didn't want to move. I was so scared. I was afraid I would find your name on this wall and yet I was afraid that some mistake had been made and the name was left out. Then I saw it. My heart seemed to stop. I seemed to tremble. I shook as though I was freezing. My teeth chattered. I felt as though I couldn't get my breath. How it hurt. From the wall, like a mirror reflecting through my blurry tears, I seemed to see faces. Then I realised it was not the faces of the ones who had died, but of the living, who were here, like me, to find the name of a loved one.[82]

The Wall attracts large gatherings of people. It 'has become an object of emotion. This is not the case for the Memorial site as a whole, just for the wall and its names. The names on the wall are touched, their letters traced by the moving finger. The names are caressed. The names are reproduced

[78] Wagner-Pacifici and Schwartz, 'The Vietnam Veterans Memorial', 380.
[79] Sturken, *Tangled Memories*, 58.
[80] See also P. McCombs, 'Maya Lin and the Great Call of China', *Washington Post*, 3 January 1982, Section F, 9, quoted in John D. Bee, 'Eros and Thanatos: an analysis of the Vietnam Memorial', in *Vietnam Images: War and Representation*, ed. Jeffrey Walsh and James Aulich (London: Macmillan, 1989), 196–204; 198–9.
[81] Lin, Statement. http://www.vvmf.org/wall/design.htm, 27 December 1998.
[82] Scruggs and Swerdlow, *To Heal a Nation*, 134.

on paper by pencil rubbing and taken home. And something is left from home itself – a material object bearing special significance to the deceased or a written statement by the visitor or mourner.'[83] This produces a collective act of mourning, where, like the Cenotaph, private grief can find public support. Or, rather, where the private/public distinction can be overcome in an act of communal mourning. It makes the memorial populist: despite the controversy, the memorial Wall has in Jay Winter's sense turned out to be exactly a traditional war memorial, one that is not simply a 'tool of state power'.[84]

The Vietnam Wall's blackness, its placing within rather than on the earth, at the entry to 'the realm of darkness and earth',[85] the underworld, seems to represent an encircling of the trauma, a remembering of the real and the actuality of mortality and death. Its non-phallic, reflective character is important. When Maya Ying Lin was asked whether she thought that the memorial showed a female sensibility, she replied:

> In a world of phallic memorials that rise upward it certainly does. I didn't set out to conquer the earth, or overpower it in the way Western man usually does. I don't think I've made a passive piece, but neither is it a memorial to the idea of war.[86]

Whereas an uplifting, triumphal, phallic monument might be seen as reinstating the social fantasy of completion and sovereignty, a monument that encircles the earth does not conceal the lack revealed by death and trauma. It does not cover over the problematic nature of certainty and social power. It marks the trauma and enables us to recognise it. This is not an easy or unproblematic process, of course, and the re-erection of the phallic order could be much more comforting in some senses. Marita Sturken read the debate around the memorial as having 'a disconcerting subtext . . . in which the memorial is seen as implicitly invoking castration. The V of the two black granite walls, it seems, is read as a female V. The "gash" is not only a wound, it is slang for the female genitals. . . . To its critics, this antiphallus symbolised the open wound of this country's castration in an unsuccessful war, a war that "emasculated" the United States.'[87] However, in psychoanalytic theory, castration stands in for a more all-embracing notion of loss.[88] Loss is only figured exclusively in

[83] Wagner-Pacifici and Schwartz, 'The Vietnam Veterans Memorial', 403.
[84] Jay Winter's analysis of memorials is discussed in more detail below.
[85] Wagner-Pacifici and Schwartz, 'The Vietnam Veterans Memorial', 398.
[86] Maya Ying Lin, quoted in Wagner-Pacifici and Schwartz, 'The Vietnam Veterans Memorial', 397.
[87] Sturken, *Tangled Memories*, 53.
[88] Bruce Fink, *The Lacanian Subject: Between Language and Jouissance* (Princeton University Press, 1995), 99–101.

terms of castration in a highly patriarchal social order. Indeed this whole discourse depends on a particular articulation of feminine and masculine that is culturally specific. A memorial that successfully deals with much wider issues of lack and loss, issues that lie at the heart of the human condition, inevitably lays itself open to the link with castration that was made, explicitly or implicitly, by its critics. That is not to say that these connections are irrelevant either – they will be shared by many visitors. But the aim of Lin's memorial is not to heal (or rather, conceal) the wound or the lack by a reimposition of masculinity and triumphalism, but to enable a recognition of loss and an acceptance of the scarring. The openness that this entails is undoubtedly a vulnerability and an exposure to an articulation as feminine.

The black marble is central to the way the Wall is designed as a mirror, reflecting the visitors and their surroundings. Maya Lin saw the design as a circle, the final part of which is the living person who visits.[89] In her design submission she wrote: 'The memorial is composed not as an unchanging monument, but as a moving composition to be understood as we move into and out of it.'[90] It has to be engaged with, approached. It can't be seen from a distance: 'Unlike the other memorials, you can't see the Wall from a car. You have to approach it. Enter its domain.'[91] Its meaning is infinitely flexible, varying with the visitor and the time of day. Maya Lin again: 'It is a living park, a symbol of life – the life of the returning veteran, who sees himself reflected within the time, within the names.'[92] Visitors see themselves and others reflected in the Wall as they examine or photograph the names (Figure 7). More than this though, the names appear as if 'etched enduringly upon the sky'.[93]

Its spatial configuration is different – antiphallic, if you like – but the Vietnam memorial also evokes and represents a different temporality. The reflection of the faces of the living upon the names of the dead is one aspect of this. Another is the names. The memorial lists the dead soldiers in the order of the date of their death. This could be seen as perhaps a key example of the authority of stone producing a sequence in time, a temporal sequence. It makes it difficult to find a particular name, but it is an integral part of the design concept, which makes the wall read 'like an epic Greek poem': those who served together are brought together in the panels of the Wall. It is rather like the military cemeteries

[89] Scruggs and Swerdlow, *To Heal a Nation*, 77. [90] Lin, Statement.
[91] Cara Sutherland, 'Preface', in *Hunger of the Heart: Communion at the Wall*, ed. Larry Powell (Dubuque, Iowa: Islewest, 1995), ix–xi; x.
[92] Maya Ying Lin, quoted in Scruggs and Swerdlow, *To Heal a Nation*, 132–3.
[93] Scruggs and Swerdlow, *To Heal a Nation*, 130.

Figure 7 Reflections in the Vietnam Wall

on First World War battlefields. Finding a name then becomes rather like finding a body on the battlefield. As in the military cemeteries of the Commonwealth War Graves Commission, there are index books available on the site for visitors to consult to locate a name on the Wall (Figure 8).[94] But then, quite stunningly, all this temporality is overturned: the Wall brings together alpha and omega, the beginning and the end. The first and last deaths of the war appear together at the intersection of the two walls, the focal point of the monument (Figure 9). This is not what people expect, and many visitors assume that the Wall represents a temporal sequence showing the increase in deaths at the height of the war, during the middle years. This is not so. What it does is to bring together the beginning and the end and make both uniquely atemporal. The name of the first death sits side by side with the last. In Maya Lin's original design statement she describes how the memorial works as a 'moving composition', in more senses than one:

[94] The names are listed in Scruggs and Swerdlow, *To Heal a Nation*, 177–414. The status of some of the names on the Wall was provisional. When a person was confirmed dead, the symbol next to their name was a diamond (◆). For those missing in action at the end of the war the symbol was a cross (✦). When a death was confirmed, the diamond was superimposed on the cross. If a person had returned alive a circle on the cross would form a symbol of life.

Figure 8 Visitors check the indexes to locate names on the Vietnam Wall

The passage itself is gradual; the descent to the origin slow, but it is at the origin that the memorial is to be fully understood. At the intersection of these walls, on the right side, is carved the date of the first death. It is followed by the names of those who died in the war, in chronological order. These names continue on this wall appearing to recede into the earth at the wall's end. The names resume on the left wall as the wall emerges from the earth, continuing back to the origin where the date of the last death is carved at the bottom of this wall. Thus the war's beginning and end meet; the war is 'complete,' coming full-circle, yet broken by the earth that bounds the angle's open side, and continued within the earth itself.[95]

This feature of the denial of the temporal sequence is, of course, what all memorials do in some sense. References to time in memorial poetry reflect this also: 'At the going down of the sun and in the morning we

[95] Lin, Statement.

Figure 9 The intersection at the focal point of the Vietnam Wall

will remember them.' The controversy about the two-minute silence in the first years of commemoration of the First World War is instructive here. Many thought that to set aside two minutes for remembrance was inappropriate when for the bereaved at least their loss was always present. However, this view betrays a misunderstanding of the meaning of this act of remembrance. It is not relevant that for the bereaved, memories take place all the time, not just during moments of silence. What the two-minute silence does is different. By stopping all 'everyday' activity, by halting the flow of traffic, the flow of time itself is stopped. 'Time stands still': and we are open to the 'moment'. This is the ethical moment, the moment of decision, the moment of the political, which is outside (and escapes) politics. Everything 'is' in the present: *there is only one time*, and that is now. Remembering and testifying to that is what memorials and commemoration are all about.[96]

The 'things'

A similar aspect of the temporality of the Wall is the way people bring messages and artefacts to it as their communication with the dead, with

[96] I am indebted to Véronique Pin-Fat for discussions that clarified for me this point and others relating to radical notions of time.

Figure 10 Vietnam Veterans Memorial exhibit, National Museum of American History

other visitors and with the state. These messages treat time as absent, the dead soldiers as present. But then, interestingly enough, the park authorities remove these artefacts (called 'things') daily, and catalogue them – place them sequentially in time. They are stored in the Vietnam Veterans Memorial Collection, Museum and Archaeological Regional Storage Facility (MARS).[97] This restores the order of time and imposes on these messages (which deny time) the dead hand of the museum.[98] Items such as flowers and the American flag are no longer kept, unless the flags have writing on them. Everything else is carefully entered in records, which show when and at which panel it was left. Exhibits are organised to display selections from the collection, which in 1998 had reached some 53,000 things, including a now permanent exhibition at the Smithsonian's National Museum of American History in Washington, a short walk from the Wall (Figure 10). Almost a third of the items

[97] Wagner-Pacifici and Schwartz, 'The Vietnam Veterans Memorial', 404.

[98] There is not space here for a discussion of museums as memorials – and how this relates examples of imposing a linear temporality and denying the political moment. Famine and Holocaust museums locate 'today' in a temporal sequence separate from 'yesterday'. There was a museum in Aberystwyth called 'All our yesterdays', a private collection of memorabilia, which remained open to the feeling that the past is our present. I discuss museums more fully in the next chapter.

are military – patches, insignias, parts of uniforms, medals, certificates. Letters, poems and statements left at the Wall carry on the debate about the war. More than half are ambivalent or negative.[99] Kristin Hass argues that the things that people leave at the memorial are part of a continuing conversation about 'the relationship of individuals and bodies to nations and to patriotism and nationalism'.[100] This conversation marks a shift in the understanding of these relationships. It also shows people taking responsibility for contributing to the memory of the war and taking part in a debate about the shape of the nation. She argues that far from being an indication that the nation has become irrelevant, these very personal memories, because they are brought to the Wall and not taken to cemeteries where the fallen are buried, indicate an intense desire to reconstitute the nation: 'Americans making memory with their things are too intensely involved in negotiations with the nation to have abandoned it; they are trying to recover a useable idea of the nation in the face of the betrayals and contradictions of Vietnam.'[101]

There is another interpretation. If we examine closely what is happening, we could argue that the Wall represents not the nation – America – but a community of veterans, or even a wider community of those that visit the memorial. The things are seen not by the state, except in the persons of the curators of the Vietnam Memorial Collection. Some are seen by no one – the sealed letters that are left for example are never opened. Other things left without explanation are so personal that their meaning would be entirely opaque to anyone other than the person who left them and the one they were meant for. They are, however, often things of intense personal significance: mementoes or souvenirs that are completely irreplaceable. They are objects that encapsulate memories and often things that have outlived their original owners. Sometimes people bring things to Washington only to find themselves unable to part with them.[102] Once left at the Wall they cannot be retrieved. Perhaps what is happening here is that people are giving precious objects to their dead friends or relatives as a way of 'giving' their friend to death, a way of recognising the real of death and the fact that the friend is truly 'gone'. This 'turns the memento – and the language of the memento – into an act, not of a symbolic return or wish for possession, but of an ability to give the dead something that can never, now be returned'.[103] The gift is not only a memento of the

[99] Wagner-Pacifici and Schwartz, 'The Vietnam Veterans Memorial', 405.
[100] Hass, *Carried to the Wall.* [101] *Ibid.*, 102.
[102] Museum Resource Centre Facility: Vietnam Memorial Collection Narrative. Collection overview. http://www.nps.gov/mrc/vvmc/vvmc.htm, 29 December 1998.
[103] Cathy Caruth, 'Parting Words: Trauma, Silence and Survival', *Cultural Values*, 5, no. 1 (January 2001): 7–26.

dead person for the living, but of the living for the dead. This produces a separation that is a creative act, and is itself a form of memorialisation. As an act of bearing witness to the friend's death it produces a drive for life, 'a life that is not simply possessed, but given, in some sense, and received, as a gift from the dead'.[104] This type of giving is reflected in some of the letters left at the Wall:

> Barnett, my brother of war, our skin was not the same but our hearts were. I've missed you soul brother.... This ten pack is on me. I've come to have one last smooth one with you.[105]

> My dearest Ben, I miss you and think of you so much.... I'm bringing 'Teddy Bear' and a picture of your loved race car. I realise they can't stay here long, but they're yours and I want them to be with you. In time, I hope we can all be together.[106]

> Oh, Eugene, my friend, how I remember the good days when we were all young.... I left you my crew hat and my jungle shirt. Just look at it and 'member me, cause brother, I remember you. 'Til we meet again, broman.[107]

Laura Palmer spent several months in 1986 travelling around the US interviewing people who had left things at the Wall – relatives and friends of the names. She talked to them about their experiences and their feelings. A former nurse describes it this way: 'There's no explanation, there's no marker, there's just a hole they fell into.... There are fifty-eight thousand men who just fell into a hole in eternity, and I saw it and no one wants to listen.'[108] Another veteran who is now a psychologist running a centre for veterans: 'We've met our maker at least once, sometimes many times, and lived to walk away from it. That's an experience most people don't have in their lives; they meet their maker once and that's it. So what sets us apart from other people is that we've already been to the end of the road and come back.'[109] Wagner-Pacifici and Schwartz argue that 'effective commemorative tools check ambivalence....The memorial... expresses the contradictions of society'.[110] On the contrary, effective memorials, in reflecting the real or encircling the trauma, express the impossibility of closure and the inevitable contradictions of any society. Memorials such as the Wall and the Cenotaph are exceptional in that they occasion 'solidarity in the absence of common beliefs',[111] or, in other words, by providing space for that which is unsymbolisable they

[104] Caruth, 'Parting Words', 14.
[105] Laura Palmer, *Shrapnel in the Heart: Letters and Remembrances from the Vietnam Veterans Memorial* (New York: Vintage House, 1987), 34.
[106] Palmer, *Shrapnel in the Heart*, 22. [107] *Ibid.*, 85.
[108] *Ibid.*, 130. [109] *Ibid.*, 73.
[110] Wagner-Pacifici and Schwartz, 'The Vietnam Veterans Memorial', 407.
[111] *Ibid.*, 408.

encompass the realm of the real. If we examine some of the letters left at the Wall we find a certain rawness.[112] This example is addressed 'An open letter to my brothers' and signed Glen:

> This marks the second year I have come to the wall. I have seen the names of those I know and yes, I have cried. My problem is I don't know the names of those I tried to help only to have them die in my arms. In my sleep I hear their cries and see their faces.... I wish I knew your names so I could touch your names in the black stone. But I don't and I'm sorry.[113]

And this one, addressed 'Dear Smitty':

> Perhaps now I can bury you; at least in my soul. Perhaps, now, I won't again see you night after night when the war reappears and we are once more amidst the myriad hells that Vietnam engulfed us in.... You got a bronze star, a silver star, survived eighteen months of one demon hell after another, only to walk into a booby trapped bunker and all of a sudden you had no face or chest. I never cried. My chest becomes unbearably painful and my throat tightens so I can't even croak, but I haven't cried. I wanted to, just couldn't. I think I can today. Damn, I'm crying now. 'Bye Smitty, Get some rest.[114]

These letters to the Wall show a desire for narrative closure, but alongside a clear acceptance of openness. Narrative, in Hayden White's account, is related to the imaginary, or at least to a notion of imaginary wholeness: the 'value attached to narrativity in the representation of real events arises out of a desire to have real events display the coherence, integrity, fullness, and closure of an image of life that is and can only be imaginary'.[115] We have already come across this desire. It is similar to that found in what is called in psychoanalytic theory the mirror phase. This is the point at which the very young child first sees its own image in a mirror. At this point in its life the infant has little co-ordination and no sense of itself as a separate being. The mirror presents an image of wholeness and completeness: the child gleefully sees itself as separate and experiences a sense of control and mastery as it sees the image move in response to its own movements. It recognises itself, but this is a misrecognition. The child is not more capable than it was before of controlling its world. It is no more whole. Although it is an impossible fantasy, in the west we continue to strive for this imaginary wholeness and sovereignty throughout life. White's notion of the role of narrative is similar to the reflection in the mirror: it gives us a sense of imaginary wholeness, imaginary closure. It is a fantasy, but a comforting one. Of course nations, whose narratives are often invoked in relation to deaths in war, are, as Benedict Anderson has

[112] Palmer, *Shrapnel in the Heart*. [113] *Ibid.*, 25. [114] *Ibid.*, 27.
[115] Hayden White, *The Content of the Form: Narrative Discourse and Historical Representation* (Baltimore: Johns Hopkins University Press, 1987), 24.

argued, imagined communities, 'imagined as both inherently limited and sovereign'.[116] The nation is limited, because 'even the largest of them... has finite, if elastic, boundaries, beyond which lie other nations'.[117] It is imagined as sovereign because coming after the age that dreamt of a universal religion, 'nations dream of being free, and, if under God, directly so'.[118] Finally it is imagined as a community, 'a deep horizontal comradeship'.[119] The Vietnam Wall, as a mirror, taps into and invokes the imaginary. But the imaginary wholeness that we see in the mirror is interrupted by the real of the names: 'Looking at the Wall, we see the world reflected: sun, moon, clouds, the trees in the distance, the people standing next to us. Finally, we see ourselves on its surface. These reflections remind us that the Wall is as much about the present as the past. We see our world mirrored in the names we find there and realise that the slightest movement changes the view. No image is permanent on the Wall. Only the names are eternal.'[120] We realise the mistake, the misrecognition.

There are two sites in Washington that pay homage to the Vietnam Wall through imitation: the Korean War Memorial and the National Memorial to Law Enforcement Officers. Both these mimic specific features of the Wall, but in doing so highlight how the Wall itself is unique. The Law Enforcement Officers Memorial is situated to one side of the Mall. It comprises a series of low curved walls, on which the names of officers killed in the course of duty are inscribed. The walls are white, encircling lawned areas and a pool. This area is a thoroughfare between two blocks, and passers-by do not pause to view the memorial but walk straight through. Lions guard the walls, and indexes are provided, as with the Vietnam Wall, for visitors to locate names. Slips of paper and pencils are also provided, for those who wish to take rubbings of names. The memorial to the fallen of the Korean war occupies a site on the opposite side of the Reflecting Pool and the Lincoln Memorial to the Vietnam Wall. Its site is mundane in contrast with the magical feel of the Vietnam memorial although the scale and the setting are apparently similar. The Korean memorial is above ground and dramatic. Larger-than-life-sized figures of soldiers as if on patrol in a paddy-field walk towards a US flag (Figure 11). To one side is a wall – black marble, no longer a problematic colour since the Vietnam Wall, but there are no names, just faces and figures etched on the marble. Visitors do not study the wall; they do not see their own faces reflected in it. On the contrary, they stand with their backs to it. The

[116] Benedict Anderson, *Imagined Communities: Reflections on the Origin and Spread of Nationalism*, revised edn (London: Verso, 1991), 6.

[117] Anderson, *Imagined Communities*, 7. [118] *Ibid*.

[119] *Ibid*. [120] Sutherland, 'Preface', x.

Figure 11 Korean War Memorial, Washington DC

wall stands proud of the ground. Approaching it, the visitor is walking upwards towards the flag. The inscription reads:

> OUR NATION HONORS
> HER SONS AND DAUGHTERS
> WHO ANSWERED THE CALL
> TO DEFEND A COUNTRY
> THEY NEVER KNEW
> AND A PEOPLE
> THEY NEVER MET

The original design for the Vietnam Wall had no inscription: nothing but the names. This was changed in response to criticism, and there are now two inscriptions. At the start:

> IN HONOR OF THE MEN AND WOMEN OF THE ARMED FORCES OF THE UNITED STATES WHO SERVED IN THE VIETNAM WAR. THE NAMES OF THOSE WHO GAVE THEIR LIVES AND OF THOSE WHO REMAIN MISSING ARE INSCRIBED IN THE ORDER THEY WERE TAKEN FROM US.

And at the end of the sequence (Figure 12):

> OUR NATION HONORS THE COURAGE, SACRIFICE AND DEVOTION TO DUTY AND COUNTRY OF ITS VIETNAM VETERANS. THIS MEMORIAL WAS BUILT WITH PRIVATE CONTRIBUTIONS FROM THE AMERICAN PEOPLE.
> NOVEMBER 11, 1982

Figure 12 Inscription on the Vietnam Wall

though, of course, both inscriptions appear in the centre of the memorial where the first and last names meet. This concession risks reinstating an imaginary narrative, that of the nation and sacrifice. I shall consider how these narratives work, and to whose benefit, in the final section of the chapter.

Sacrificial memory – bodies of state

We have examined two very unusual memorials to the fallen of war, the Cenotaph and the Vietnam Wall. I want to finish now by looking at some of the general issues about more traditional memorials, instances where there *is* closure, where the debate *is* captured by the state, where a narrative of the nation *is* reinforced. These are quite possibly much more common, though even in these instances, contestation is not absent and consensus cannot be assumed. I examine how the state co-opts the bodies of the fallen in its search for closure, and how narratives of sacrifice in particular help in this capture. Of course, a more recent example of how the state can capture the debate, reinforce the narrative of the nation and produce closure is to be found in the practices of remembrance following the events of September 11 in New York and Washington, and in the final part of the chapter I briefly examine these practices and their relation to the rhetoric of war in the aftermath of 9/11. I will also look at how they have been contested, and discuss how the acts of memory here relate to those discussed earlier in the chapter.

In the literature on forms of memorial and commemoration, there is a split between those who see memorials as primarily a response to the popular need to mourn the dead and those who regard them as a tool of nation building. Jay Winter's recurring theme is 'the powerful, perhaps essential, tendency of ordinary people, of many faiths and of none, to face together the emptiness, the nothingness of loss in war'.[121] Winter sees the process as a search for meaning, which, as we have seen, implies an attempt to narrativise the trauma of war and loss, to locate trauma within a logocentric framework, to enable 'life to go on'. He contrasts the situation after the First World War with that after the second, and the different forms of monument he sees as reflecting this: 'The search for meaning after the Somme and Verdun was hard enough; but after Auschwitz and Hiroshima that search became infinitely more difficult.'[122] Apocalyptic visions – drawing on images of the end of the world, revelation and divine justice – predominated in the wake of the First World War, as Winter recounts it. There was still a belief in 'progress' then; after the Second World War, there wasn't. After the Second World War and Hiroshima, universal annihilation became a real possibility rather than an apocalyptic image and Auschwitz questioned the possibility of the divine justice upon which apocalyptic notions are founded. As Winter puts it: 'After 1945 those visions, these literary sites of memory, seemed to fade away, leaving abstraction and silence in their wake.'[123]

Winter stresses the function of war memorials and ceremonial as places (and times) where the bereaved could mourn.[124] The reaction to war is part of the process of bereavement, a process of separation: 'of forgetting as much as remembering'.[125] The inclusion of the names of the dead and the localised, distributed war memorials in Europe reflect their 'sombre, existential purpose' and 'ritual significance'.[126] Cannadine, too, argues that 'the Armistice day ritual, far from being a piece of consensual ceremonial, cynically imposed on a divided and war-weary nation by a cabinet afraid of unrest and revolution, was more of a requiem demanded of the politicians by the public. It was not so much a matter of patriotism as

[121] Winter, *Sites of Memory, Sites of Mourning*, 53. [122] *Ibid.*, 228. [123] *Ibid.*, 203.

[124] *Ibid.*, 93. See also Moriarty, 'Private grief and public remembrance', 125–42; 136, where the author cites messages left by those grieving. James M. Mayo interestingly notes the role of the home as a site for memorials. James M. Mayo, *War Memorials as Political Landscape: the American Experience and Beyond* (New York: Praeger, 1988). See also James M. Mayo, 'War Memorials as Political Memory', *Geographical Review*, 78, no. 1 (1988): 62–75.

[125] Winter, *Sites of Memory, Sites of Mourning*, 224. [126] *Ibid.*, 94.

"a display of bereavement".'[127] This becomes apparent in the story of the Cenotaph, as we saw above, where the public action of laying wreaths prompted a response by politicians.

While Winter sees the remembering of the First World War through memorials as part of a personal process of mourning that called up traditional symbolism to enable families and communities to come to terms with their bereavement, George Mosse sees the process much more as the creation of a nationalist myth of war, through military cemeteries, war memorials and commemorative ceremonies.[128] He points to the separation of the dead into cemeteries for each nationality, with a particular concern to distinguish victor and vanquished, and the creation of national ceremonial around the tomb of the Unknown Soldier. Mosse links the inclusion of names of all those killed, not just officers, on war memorials with this notion of the tomb of the Unknown Soldier: both reflect the view of war as a battle involving the nation as a democratic community. The creation of a myth of the war experience led to what Mosse calls 'the domestication of modern war, its acceptance as a natural part of political and social life'.[129]

After the First World War, Mosse tells us, remembrance was of central importance. The war had been different in a number of ways from previous conflicts, specifically in the vast number of people killed, and the fact that the soldiers were no longer mercenaries or professionals but volunteers – in other words, citizens. But changes in warfare had begun before the First World War and Mosse argues that they led to the myth of glorious death in war as a sacrifice for the nation. First, the scale of slaughter made it more necessary than before to provide some account or justification of it. The second change was that mercenaries were replaced, after the French Revolution, by largely volunteer citizen-armies. A lot of these new soldiers were literate and educated and all were respectable members of the community, not semi-outcasts as mercenaries had been. This meant that many of those serving could write about their experiences, and all would have relatives who cared what became of them. Volunteers saw war as an opportunity for 'camaraderie . . . and meaningful relationships in an ever more abstract and impersonal society' and a transcendent, sacrificial mission.[130] One volunteer, blessed in church before going to fight in the First World War, said 'Now we are made sacred.'[131] In this context, military cemeteries and war memorials

[127] Cannadine, 'War and death', 219.
[128] George L. Mosse, *Fallen Soldiers: Reshaping the Memory of the World Wars* (Oxford University Press, 1990).
[129] Mosse, *Fallen Soldiers*, 11. [130] *Ibid.*, 24.
[131] Quoted in *ibid.*, 25.

became new sacred spaces and 'the burial and commemoration of the war dead were analogous to the construction of a church for the nation'.[132] It was not until towards the end of the nineteenth century that soldiers were buried individually in Europe, though military cemeteries had already been established in the United States during the Civil War. It only became standard during the First World War. Again Mosse argues that the scale of mass death made this practice necessary.[133]

However, it is impossible to determine which is more central to processes of commemoration, the myth of nation or the question of personal loss and bereavement. Not only is it impossible to say which is prior or predominant, to attempt to do so is to miss the point. Commemoration reflects the way in which personal and social existence are inseparable. It is not simply a case of whether grieving should be private or national, and *whose* story should be told, but a question of how to negotiate the necessary relation between them. There is a struggle for both relatives, as individuals, and their representatives, as figures of state. It is a struggle over whether to tell the story as part of a linear narrative or whether to mark the trauma without compromise. For Jay Winter, the purpose of commemoration is as much forgetting as remembering. Memorial practices help bereaved relatives to forget the trauma of war undergone by those who served and to come to terms with what happened. Mourning can follow its 'natural' course and life-histories be re-woven. For George Mosse, the myth of nation provides a justification for the appalling slaughter of war and the notion of noble sacrifice a reason for the individual deaths. The nation, born or strengthened in warfare, provides an account in which the event of war is no longer traumatic. It rewrites it into a narrative of origin. For both, memorial practices cover over the trauma by reinstating what we call social reality, the comforting collective fantasy that provides answers where there are none. Time plays a role in this mutual constitution of community and person. The question of a particular, imposed notion of time, the time of the state and the time of modernity, is important here.

Benedict Anderson argues that the coming into being of the modern nation-state in the eighteenth and nineteenth centuries – which he sees incidentally as having been initiated by 'Creole pioneers' in the new American states of Brazil, the USA and the former colonies of Spain – would not have been possible without an alteration in the imagining of time. In mediaeval ways of thinking events were linked not causally nor temporally but by reference to a divine providence. This is similar to what Walter Benjamin calls Messianic time, and means, according to Anderson, 'a simultaneity of past and future in an instantaneous

[132] Mosse, *Fallen Soldiers*, 32–3. [133] *Ibid.*, 46.

present'.[134] It is replaced in modern times by an idea of 'homogeneous, empty time', a concept of time that is necessary for any view of history as a progression.[135] This notion of time is also necessary for any concept of the nation. Homogeneous, empty time is what I called earlier in the book linear, narrative time. In this form of time simultaneity is not, as in mediaeval time, marked 'by prefiguring and fulfilment, but by temporal coincidence, and measured by clock and calendar'.[136] The reason that this form of time is so necessary for the birth of nationalism is related to the structure of the nation as an 'imagined community'. The modern nation is a sovereign body that exists in parallel with and alongside other nations. This form of co-existence or simultaneity requires and produces a notion of homogeneous empty time.[137] We saw that the modern individual or subject is produced in the mirror phase, according to psychoanalytic theory, as having a mistaken wholeness or completeness: an identity. The same is the case with the social or symbolic order of the nation-state in modernity: 'As with modern persons, so it is with nations. Awareness of being embedded in secular, serial time, with all its implications of continuity, yet of "forgetting" the experience of this continuity... engenders the need for a narrative of "identity".'[138] This narrative is produced retrospectively, starting from an originary present. Deaths are retrospectively claimed by the nation. From the 'remorselessly accumulating cemeteries... the nation's biography snatches, against the going mortality rate, exemplary suicides, poignant martyrdoms, assassinations, executions, wars, and holocausts. But to serve the narrative purpose, these violent deaths must be remembered/forgotten as "our own".'[139] The nation must co-opt the dead into its own narratives. The rupture of war, its trauma, must be forgotten.

The co-opting of the dead into national narratives sometimes takes a very literal form. Fallen soldiers remain the property of the state. Having been sanctified or made sacred, they are no longer 'ordinary' people. They do not die in the same sense. Their bodies are remains that belong to the state, or in other words, they are the remains of the state. These bodies are what is left over, the surplus that arises when the state is made or re-made, the remainder. How and where they are buried is for the state to decide. The question of the burial of the First World War dead

[134] Anderson, *Imagined Communities*, 24.
[135] Walter Benjamin, *Illuminations*, trans. Harry Zohn (London: Fontana, 1992), 252.
[136] Anderson, *Imagined Communities*, 24. Of course, this clock time, and the associated view of work, was essential for the capitalist mode of production where time is money and can be wasted. (Max Weber, *The Protestant Ethic and the Spirit of Capitalism*, trans. Talcott Parsons (London: Unwin, 1930), 157–8).
[137] Anderson, *Imagined Communities*, 187–8. [138] *Ibid.*, 205. [139] *Ibid.*, 206.

was as controversial and difficult as the building of war memorials. The overwhelming desire of the bereaved in France was to bring the bodies home: 'although they are dead, we want to remove them from those accursed places in the battlefields ... To abandon them there is to condemn them to eternal torment', wrote one father.[140] At first this was denied by the French authorities. Some people, those who could afford it, had the bodies exhumed secretly, by entrepreneurs doing it for a fee. Eventually, since this illegal traffic continued, the government gave in, and families were given the right to reclaim the bodies of their relatives, starting in the summer of 1922. This was for French soldiers only: British, German and, to some extent, United States authorities all ruled it out.[141] Richard Holmes argues that the majority of soldiers would prefer to remain buried where they fell: not returned to their homes or repatriated, nor exhumed and reburied in the regimented rows of military cemeteries, but where they were buried on the battlefield by their comrades.[142] When the reinterment took place, 2,000 of the crosses that had marked the (temporary) battlefield graves during the First World War were returned home to some confusion: no one knew what to do with them.[143] A collection of these battlefield crosses is displayed on the wall of St Mary's Church, Byfleet, and some 300 of around 2,000 that were returned to Britain survive altogether.[144] The remaining hundreds of thousands not claimed by relatives were burned and the ashes scattered in the war cemeteries.[145]

In contemporary US practice, the bodies of fallen soldiers are brought home with ceremony for burial either in local cemeteries, in the case of Vietnam casualties, or in Arlington National Cemetery in Washington (Figure 13). In Arlington, the biopolitics of 'showing' the military buried in one place becomes obvious; even the families of the slain are co-opted into this demonstration: the wives of serving officers are commemorated on the reverse of the soldier's gravestone. After Vietnam, the return of missing bodies became somewhat of an obsession. On a visit to Vietnam in 2000 President Bill Clinton visited a site where a huge excavation involving the sifting of many tonnes of earth was underway – all to retrieve

[140] Winter, *Sites of Memory, Sites of Mourning*, 25.

[141] Though in the case of US soldiers, 70 per cent were repatriated. (Thomas W. Laqueur, 'Memory and naming in the Great War', in *Commemorations: the Politics of National Identity*, ed. John R. Gillis (Princeton University Press, 1994), 150–67; 162.)

[142] Richard Holmes, *Acts of War: The Behaviour of Men in Battle* (New York: Free Press, 1986), 200–1.

[143] Mosse, *Fallen Soldiers*, 91.

[144] According to the UK National Inventory of War Memorials held by the Imperial War Museum in London.

[145] The UK National Inventory of War Memorials, 'History of memorialisation', November 2001, 4. http://www.iwm.org.uk/collections/niwm/history_memorials.pdf, 25 July 2002.

Figure 13 Arlington National Cemetery

the remains of a single American casualty. The returning body bags have become symbolic of US failure abroad to the extent that missions are not undertaken if the risk in US lives is considered too great.

The symbolic return of the Unknown Soldier is a ceremonial that seems to fill the gap by providing not only a grave for those who had none, but a place of mourning for those whose relatives were buried overseas. The first instance of this was the burial of an Unknown Soldier in Paris and London after the First World War, but this gesture was copied in nearly all the countries involved, both the victorious and the defeated, over the next ten years.[146] For Anderson, cenotaphs and the tombs of Unknown Soldiers are 'arresting emblems of the modern culture of nationalism... saturated with ghostly *national* imaginings'.[147] It is interesting that in London the Cenotaph has been much more the focus of ceremonial and private mourning than the tomb of the Unknown Soldier. The Unknown Soldier was chosen by a process designed to ensure anonymity. This form of selection, varying in detail but generally similar each time, was carried out by other nations adopting this form of commemoration. Three or four corpses were disinterred from different battlefields and brought to a location where either a high-ranking soldier or a representative of the ranks made the final selection between them. The chosen body was then returned to the home country with high ceremony for interment. However, this is not entirely the democratic, inclusive process that it seems. The body chosen does not stand in for all those others buried anonymously on the battlefields. Rather, it reminds us of the extent to which the state commands both the living body of the soldier, his bare life, and his dead corpse. The Unknown Soldier from Vietnam buried in Arlington Cemetery in Washington has now been identified. The remains are those of Air Force 1st Lt. Michael Joseph Blassie, shot down near An Loc in 1972. The identification, made by mitochondrial DNA testing, was announced on 30 June 1998 but is under review.[148] The embarrassment has yet to be resolved. The problem with the Vietnam war was the absence of any unidentified remains. This, and perhaps the general procrastination in recognition of Vietnam servicemen and women, delayed for some years the interment of an Unknown.[149] Now even that has not settled the matter. It seems that the Vietnam war stubbornly refuses to be remembered like any other ordinary war.

[146] Inglis, 'Entombing Unknown Soldiers', 7.
[147] Anderson, *Imagined Communities*, 9.
[148] US Army Military District of Washington, Public Affairs Office, 'Tomb of the Unknowns at Arlington National Cemetery'. *MDW Fact Sheet*, FS-A04, http://www.mdw.army.mil/FS-A04.HTM, 26 December 1998.
[149] Mayo, *War Memorials as Political Landscape*, 205.

The significance of tombs of Unknown Soldiers and cenotaphs indicates, Benedict Anderson claims, the concern of the nationalist imagining with death and immortality, and its strong affinity with religious imaginings.[150] Nationalism has not exactly replaced religion, but it arose as religions declined and provides alternative responses to questions about human existence, according to Anderson. Religion is in any case only an expression of the existence of the social order. As Emile Durkheim puts it, people 'are not mistaken when they believe in the existence of a moral power to which they are subject and from which they receive what is best in themselves. That power exists and it is society. . . . Religion is first and foremost a system of ideas by means of which individuals imagine the society of which they are members and the obscure yet intimate relations they have with it.'[151]

The link between nationalism and religion, between sovereignty and the sacred, can be seen in the use of the notion of sacrifice to describe the deaths of soldiers fighting for their country. The concept of sacrifice is complex and is linked with the idea of the victim of sacrifice – the person or animal killed – as 'sacred'. In early anthropological work and in Durkheim's sociology, the concept of the sacred is regarded as ambiguous. Something that is sacred must not be touched, because it is holy and to touch it would be to bring it back into the realm of the profane, or to dirty it. On the other hand, there are things that are untouchable because to touch them renders the person doing the touching unclean. These things, which are taboo, resemble in their untouchability things that are sacred. Hence the notion of sacred is regarded as ambiguous: 'The pure and the impure are not two separate genera but two varieties of the same genus that includes all sacred things. There are two sorts of sacred, lucky and unlucky.'[152] There is no radical discontinuity between the two forms, and the same object can pass from one to the other. This constitutes the ambiguity of the sacred. However, as Giorgio Agamben points out, this ascription of ambiguity is not an explanation of the sacred but rather is itself what is in need of explanation.[153] This ambiguity extends to the rite of sacrifice, which appears to have two aspects. In one light it is seen as a criminal act, a murder, and in another as a sacred obligation which must be obeyed. To explain this the sacred character of the victim is adduced: 'because the victim is sacred, it is criminal to kill him – but the victim is

[150] Anderson, *Imagined Communities*, 10.
[151] Emile Durkheim, *The Elementary Forms of the Religious Life*, trans. Karen E. Fields (New York: The Free Press, 1995), 226–7.
[152] Durkheim, *Elementary Forms*, 415.
[153] Giorgio Agamben, *Homo Sacer: Sovereign Power and Bare Life*, trans. Daniel Heller-Roazen (Stanford University Press, 1998), 80.

sacred only because he is to be killed'.[154] This circularity leads back to the notion of ambiguity. But again to speak of ambivalence or ambiguity, as René Girard notes, is only to point out a problem that has yet to be solved. Girard suggests that sacrifice is primarily a method of dealing with violence. It does not require any notion of a deity to operate but it does require a concealment or misunderstanding of its purpose, and the role of a deity can be helpful here. Violence can spiral, as one act is avenged by another. The system of sacrifice seeks to avoid this escalation by the substitution of a victim who can be killed without the need for vengeance. Girard argues that human violence cannot be obliterated but it can be diverted to a victim who is similar to the intended target of the violence, vulnerable to attack, but, crucially, whose death or injury will not prompt revenge: 'Society is seeking to deflect upon a relatively indifferent victim, a "sacrificable" victim, the violence that would otherwise be vented on its own members, the people it most desires to protect.'[155] The success of this sacrificial substitution depends on a concealment of the displacement of violence – but this must produce only a partial misunderstanding, otherwise the sacrifice would have no effect. As a process then, sacrifice 'serves to protect the entire community from its own violence; it prompts the entire community to choose victims outside itself.... The purpose of the sacrifice is to restore harmony to the community, to reinforce the social fabric.'[156]

Sacrificial rites are one measure against violence, one that takes place, according to Girard, in primitive societies or those without centralised authority. Another is curative measures that cut violence short, for example, the reconciliation and mutual compensation measures common in Islamic societies, or ritualised forms of armed encounter like a duel. In modern societies there are, according to Girard, no sacrificial rites. The vicious circle of vengeance has been broken in such well-policed societies by the judicial system, where 'the system does not suppress vengeance; rather, it limits it to a single act of reprisal, enacted by a sovereign authority specialising in this particular function'.[157] This 'monopoly on the means of revenge' can only exist 'in conjunction with a firmly established political power'. This is, of course, reminiscent of the Hobbesian claim that only by subjecting ourselves to a centralised or sovereign power can we avoid the escalating cycle of violence in a state of nature. However, it is not just primitive religion that 'postulates a strange mixture of violence and non-violence'. Our own judicial system does not avoid violence either.

[154] René Girard, *Violence and the Sacred*, trans. Patrick Gregory (Baltimore: The Johns Hopkins University Press, 1977), 1.

[155] Girard, *Violence and the Sacred*, 4. [156] *Ibid.*, 8. [157] *Ibid.*, 15.

The law has to be 'enforced', potentially through violence.[158] A particularly graphic example is where, under the rule of law, people starve to death in front of well-stocked and well-policed food shops, as happened in Bengal in the 1940s.[159] Girard leaves the role of sovereign power in the judicial system unexamined. He ignores the link that Agamben later makes between *sovereign power* and *bare life*, or *homo sacer*. Agamben argues that sovereign power is characterised by the production of *homo sacer* or sacred life, 'life that cannot be sacrificed and yet may be killed'.[160] Its political space is constituted by the production of sacred life: '*The sovereign sphere is the sphere in which it is permitted to kill without committing homicide and without celebrating sacrifice, and sacred life – that is, life which can be killed but not sacrificed – is the life that has been captured in this sphere.*'[161] The idea of the sacredness of life, which is invoked as an individual right against the political power of the state, in fact expresses how, in contemporary political communities, life is subjected to the power of the sovereign over life and death. The link between sovereignty and the sacred, or between nation and religion that Anderson remarked on, is not just a residue of the religious character of secular power or an attempt to give it a religious basis. The link is much more significant than that: 'sacredness is instead the originary form of the inclusion of bare life in the judicial order'. It is the way in which human life is included in the sovereign nation-state. We shall return to this later, in Chapter 5.

As well as neglecting to discuss the specificity of sovereign power and the judicial system, Girard does not examine either how the selection of sacrificial victim defines, indeed produces, the community itself. The sacrificial victim must bear 'a sharp resemblance' to the original object of violence, but there must also be 'a degree of difference that forbids all possible confusion'.[162] The resemblance that forms the basis of substitution is physical resemblance, and 'in some societies whole categories of human beings are systematically reserved for sacrificial purposes in order to protect other categories'.[163] This has clear overtones of racialisation. Thus although the role of sacrifice is to 'unite society and establish order',[164] it works only through the production of forms of exclusion or racial categorisation that distinguish sacrificial victims from the remainder of the population. In the First World War we could hypothesise that

158 Jacques Derrida, 'Force of law: the "mystical foundation of authority"', in *Deconstruction and the Possibility of Justice*, ed. David Gray Carlson, Drucilla Cornell, and Michel Rosenfeld (New York: Routledge, 1992), 3–67.
159 Jenny Edkins, 'Legality with a Vengeance: Famines and Humanitarian Intervention in "Complex Emergencies"', *Millennium*, 25, no. 3 (1996): 547–75.
160 Agamben, *Homo Sacer*, 82. 161 *Ibid.*, 83.
162 Girard, *Violence and the Sacred*, 12. 163 *Ibid.*, 11. 164 *Ibid.*, 8.

the working classes were seen as outsiders to the political order and hence 'sacred' and able to be sacrificed. The 'Tommy' who went like a sheep to the slaughter would be an archetypal victim. To claim this as a sacrifice, on memorials and in commemorations, has several results. In one sense it belittles the actions of the servicemen and women, picturing them as victims who had no control over their fate and no motivation for acting as they did. Lyn MacDonald takes the view that this degrades those who served, as we saw in Chapter 2. In another sense, it covers up the role of sovereign power in sending them to their deaths. As 'bare life', with no political say in the war, they could not have been sacrificed, only killed. Yet the state claims not only that they were sacrificed, but that this was a self-sacrifice. This is an inversion of what happened: 'Whilst they appear to have made the sacrifice, it is in fact the nation that has sacrificed them.'[165] In the case of the persecution of the Jews in Nazi Germany, the notion of sacrifice is strongly repudiated by survivors. They insist instead on adequate compensation and on the persecution of war criminals as a recognition that the Jews were not sacrificable victims but deserved some form of recompense or revenge. If a death is a sacrifice, then vengeance is not demanded.

In the aftermath of the events of September 11 in New York, there were immediate moves by the state to take control in terms of memorialisation.[166] President George W. Bush was visiting a school in Florida as the events in New York were taking place. He was told of the first impact before entering the school, but the visit went ahead as planned. Some minutes later, during a classroom session, a presidential aide, Chief of Staff Andrew Card, came up to Bush and whispered in his ear the news of the second plane's impact on Tower Two of the World Trade Centre. The visit was suspended as the President consulted hastily with his staff, both those to hand and others in the White House and elsewhere by telephone. He later told the press that as soon as he heard of the second collision his thoughts were 'this is war'. At a hastily convened press conference held at the school Bush made a short speech, ending by asking the audience to join with him in a moment's silence to remember the victims and their families. His final words were 'May God bless the victims, their families and America'.[167]

[165] Michael Rowlands, 'Memory, Sacrifice and the Nation', *New Formations*, no. 30 (Winter 1996): 8–17; 13.

[166] For a more detailed discussion of practices of memorialisation after September 11, see Jenny Edkins, 'September 11 and the timing of memory', Paper presented at the International Studies Association Annual Convention, New Orleans, March 2002.

[167] Scott Cummings, 'World Trade Center and Pentagon Attacks: Presidential Speeches', Emma Booker Elementary School, Sarasota Florida, September 11, 2001, 9.30 a.m. EDT. http://www.patriotresource.com/wtc/president/address1.html, 8 March 2002.

At the point when this speech was made, roughly 9.30 a.m. on a morning when the chronology was not the only thing that was confused, both towers of the World Trade Centre were still standing. That they might collapse was at that point inconceivable. The third aircraft had not yet crashed into the Pentagon: this did not take place until seven minutes after Bush's speech. And it was still unimaginable that the US air force might be forced to shoot down a US airliner full of civilian passengers. At that point there was no talk in the media of third, fourth, fifth or sixth planes, attacks on Capitol Hill or the White House. And yet here was a head of state calling already for a moment's silence in memory of the victims. This was premature, to say the least. During the silence, people in the Trade Centre towers were calling relatives on their mobile phones; firefighters were streaming up the staircases to rescue those trapped; aircrew on other hijacked planes and their passengers were attempting to alert people to what was happening to them. The traumatic events of that day had only just begun to unfold, and yet there was already a rush to memorialisation by the state. This can be seen as an attempt, ill-judged and premature perhaps, to secure the authority of the state, reinforce the narrative of the nation and produce closure in the face of events that had thrown all three into question.

Later, the link between the rush to memorialisation and the rhetoric of war that the state chose to pursue became clearer. Although the usual order was reversed – in a sense the victims of war preceded the war itself – the federal government chose to use the deaths in New York as a reason for what it called the 'war on terrorism', or later simply the 'war on terror'. By the time the six-month anniversary of that September morning arrived, state remembrance was already ritualised and relegated to a subsidiary but vital supporting role on occasions of state. In a ceremony on the White House lawn on 11 March 2002, the coalition of nations supporting the war on terror was celebrated, with the flags of each nation flown on the lawn behind the President and other representatives.[168] The victims of September 11 and their 'loved ones' were mentioned, but the flags were not flown at half mast: by then the nations had been reinstated as protectors and guarantors of security to their peoples. Bush ended his speech 'May God bless our coalition'.[169]

The rhetoric of war promulgated by the state was only one of a variety of possible responses, and it did not go uncontested.[170] Right from the

[168] Rupert Cornwell, 'Bush maps out global strategy against enemies'. *The Independent*, 12 March 2002, 4.

[169] CNN, 'Bush: America will not forget', http://europe.cnn.com/2002/US/03/11/gen.bush.speech/index.html, 8 March 2002.

[170] Jenny Edkins, 'Forget Trauma? Responses to September 11', *International Relations*, 16, no. 2 (2002): 243–56.

start there were people, some among those most closely affected by the trauma of 9/11, who disputed the use of victims as motivation for the war. There was a direct fight against the link that had been forged by the state between the victims and their sacrifice and the move for revenge. Widow Amber Amundson insisted that her husband's name no longer be used by the government in relation to the campaign. In the *Chicago Tribune* on 25 September she wrote: 'My anguish is compounded exponentially by the fear that his death will be used to justify new violence against other innocent victims.' Craig Scott Amundson, a twenty-eight-year-old enlisted specialist in the US army, was killed at the Pentagon. His widow addressed 'our nation's leaders', some of whom had advised 'a heavy dose of revenge and punishment', and she continued: 'To those leaders, I would like to make it clear that my family and I take no comfort in your words of rage. If you choose to respond to this incomprehensible brutality by perpetuating violence against other innocent human beings, you may not do so in the name of justice for my husband.'[171] In New York a performance took place where protesters, each wearing around their necks placards with the wording 'Our grief is not a cry for war!', stood silently holding hands in Union Square. People had been gathering in Union Square since the evening of the 11th to talk and grieve. The 100 artists, wearing black and with dust masks covering their mouths, stood in a semicircle for an hour. The performance was repeated in Times Square on two occasions.[172] The protesters took on the status of sacrificial victim in Girard's sense – in the sense that they wanted themselves and their own loss viewed as the end of the cycle, not its beginning. They did not deny the trauma or gentrify it; they silently encircled it, displaying their grief. The use of dust masks by the artists to render themselves speechless was significant. It drew attention to the way in which witnesses to trauma are silenced: they cannot speak of trauma in language but have to find another way.

There was also a search for different forms of memorialisation, and some were forms that did not reinstate the narrative of the state as the source of security. In the course of this search, mourners were able to call on a wide range of forms developed not only in relation to war memorials but also to Aids victims and survivors of genocides and famines. Flowers, poems, pictures, candles, ribbons, flags and scarves were used at impromptu memorials or street shrines that appeared around the city – outside firehouses, in parks, on railings, and on the temporary barriers

[171] Amber Amundson, 'A widow's plea for non-violence', *Chicago Tribune*, 25 September 2001. I am indebted to Helle Rytkonen for this reference.

[172] Artists Network of Refuse and Resist, 'Artists performance in New York City "Our grief is not a cry for war!"' http://www.artistsnetwork.org/news/news14.html, 1 August 2002.

erected around the inappropriately named Ground Zero.[173] In the period immediately after the collapse of the towers in New York there was no need for a special memorial: the site itself provided the main focus in the early days. Although it was visited by both New Yorkers and others, some saw the fascination with the location of trauma as voyeuristic and kept away. Others found the disruption it caused objectionable. But Salman Rushdie claimed it was not voyeurism but rather a 'graver, more honourable compulsion to bear witness' that drew people to the site.[174] One visitor wrote, on the wall of the viewing platform at Fulton Street, 'We all lost you all, and mourn together. We are not "sightseers".'[175] Rushdie described how he 'spent a long sad afternoon prowling around the perimeter of the smoking ruins of the World Trade Centre, trying to take in the horror of what I was seeing, exchanging numb civilities with equally shell-shocked strangers. . . . I walked for hours, looking in people's eyes for the answers none of us had.'

The visit to Ground Zero did seem for people who came to be a solemn occasion. It was very much an act of witness, an encircling of the trauma, both in an attempt to acknowledge what had happened, and an act of marking it in all its horror. People were happy to queue for several hours to obtain tickets and then queue again for admission to the viewing platforms, even though once they reached the point where they overlooked the site of the destruction, people were rationed to two minutes. It seemed to be not those moments so much as the whole process of coming and joining in with others that was important. Others circled the site, following the contours of the safety fencing (Figure 14). A map produced by Laura Kurgan as an act of memory itself showed a suggested path and marked the sites of temporary memorials and viewing platforms.[176] The site was brilliantly illuminated at night – to enable the work to carry on twenty-four hours a day – and from the air it looked like the open wound that it was. Six months after the events, a temporary memorial was installed in the form of two huge banks of lights shining upwards into the sky, mimicking the missing towers. And at night the endless circling of visitors around Ground Zero continued.

[173] 'Ground Zero' is the technical term for the point on the surface of the ground immediately below or immediately above the detonation point of an atomic weapon. It is familiar from Cold War discussions of the material effects of nuclear explosions and is correctly used in relation to Hiroshima and Nagasaki. Its use in connection with 9/11 is a regrettable exaggeration of the destruction caused.

[174] Salman Rushdie, 'Reach for the sky', *The Guardian Review*, London, 27 July 2002, 3.

[175] Message written on the viewing platform at Fulton Street, signed Mariette and dated 26 January 2002.

[176] Laura Kurgan, 'Around Ground Zero: February/March 2002', New York New Visions Coalition for the Rebuilding of Lower Manhattan. Folded map, 2002, http://www.aroundgroundzero.net.

Figure 14 Visitors at the site of the World Trade Centre, New York

Bringing things to the temporary shrines, reminiscent in its way of the 'things' brought to the Vietnam Wall, began first in the areas that were the closest people could get to the Trade Centre site – for example, in Union Square. Later, as people were allowed back into the areas below 14th Street, to the perimeter of Ground Zero itself, similar shrines grew up at shifting points on the fences or church railings (Figure 15). Later still, when official viewing platforms were constructed and ticketing controlled the flow of visitors, semi-official lists of victims were placed on the slopes leading to the platforms as temporary memorials. Visitors, enjoined not to deface these lists, left their messages on the plywood of the temporary platforms to mark their visit and to exchange their thoughts with others. The relatives of the killed did add their thoughts to the printed lists, despite the notices. These temporary shrines moved from place to place as the work of clearing around Ground Zero proceeded and the trucks removing the debris took different routes to and from the site. Some complained that these memorials, and others throughout the city, had been removed too quickly, often by those concerned to preserve them for posterity in museum collections.

An unusual aspect of the process was the urge to document the mourning activities: this was apparent from the start. People were photographing

Figure 15 Temporary shrine at Broadway and Cedar Street, New York

not only the destruction, but also the posters of the missing, the memorial offerings and fellow mourners. In part this was a form of resistance to the dominance of the official narrative and the newspaper images. People needed their own images of what they thought important. Several collections were set up to which the public at large could donate photographs. One, called The September 11 Photo Project, 'began as a grassroots project to collect material from anyone who wished to participate... allowing people to bear witness to the expression and pain of others'[177] and another, entitled Here is New York: a Democracy of Photographs, again displayed images submitted 'by anyone and everybody' and stipulated only that 'all pictures must relate to the events of 9/11/2001, in the broadest and yet most intimate sense'.[178] In both of these a large number of the photos showed the memorialisation of the events rather than the events themselves. They were pictures not of the destruction that had caused the grief, but of people showing their grief. One of the most famous photographs of all from the immediate aftermath, of course, is that

[177] Michael Feldschuh, ed., *The September 11 Photo Project* (New York: Regan Books, HarperCollins, 2002).

[178] Publicity flyer, Here is New York: A Democracy of Photographs, March 2002, www.hereisnewyork.org

of a group of firemen engaged, not in a rescue attempt, but in the raising of the US flag over the ruins of Ground Zero. In a configuration reminiscent of the Iwo Jima memorial that stands next to Arlington Cemetery in Washington, itself taken from a staged photograph taken in the Second World War, the four firemen hoist the stars and stripes over the rubble. It is almost as if people were very self-conscious. They were drawing on the full range of memorial tropes at their disposal, and they wanted to get it right. It somehow seems that after the outpouring of grief over the events of 9/11, the practices of memory that were developed during the twentieth century have almost been exhausted too. They no longer work on their own. We have to record ourselves doing the remembering. As we shall see in the next chapter, sometimes it seems almost as if a memorial does the remembering for us, in our place. And, in the case of memorials to horrors such as the Nazi genocide, sometimes it seems enough to have a debate about the form a memorial should take but never build one. Now, perhaps, we need the photograph of us remembering to prove that we do remember. Or perhaps it is just that after 9/11, when the buildings and those they contained completely vanished in a plume of smoke, people just needed something to hold on to, something to mark the passing moment.

Conclusion

It remains to be seen what form a permanent memorial to the events of September 11 will take. The two memorials with which we began this chapter – the Cenotaph and the Vietnam Wall – are both exceptional in that they seem to respond to some desire other than the need to celebrate and re-narrate national glory in the aftermath of trauma. They seemed to provide, at least when they were first built, memorials that responded to the trauma of war in a rather particular way. Both were originally controversial – seemingly unlike what would be expected of a more traditional war memorial – and yet both became the focus for public emotion of a particular sort. I have argued that these two memorials can be seen as reflecting, in the case of the Wall, or marking, in the case of the Cenotaph, what I have called trauma time. They refuse to be readily incorporated into the national myth of glory and sacrifice for king or country. Instead they provide a site where relatives of the dead or fellow combatants can come to remember their loss, not to forget it. The Cenotaph takes the form of a stumbling block, standing in the middle of the regular flow of the London traffic at its busiest. It is not tucked away in some park or quiet square, providing romantic ideas of heroism and sacrifice. It is located where the troops march past, on the occasion of the peace march in 1919 and at Armistice Days since, providing a continuing marker across the generations. The Wall mirrors the faces of its visitors, refusing to allow them to forget their own existence, their own survival. It gives no easy answers, yet it is a spot that prompts acceptance of the reality of death rather than the myth of sacrifice, as its designer intended it should.

Neither of these memorials is for ever. When I visited the Vietnam Wall in February 1999, I was struck by a group of young American high school students. They were clearly on some sort of organised visit to the Wall. But they strolled past it without so much as a sideways glance at the names – names of those their own age only a bare generation ago – engrossed in their own conversations, listening to their own music. In London a year later a group of young people involved in an anti-capitalist May Day protest daubed the Cenotaph with paint. For them it was nothing but a signifier of imperialism, a celebration of nationalism and an expression of centralised authority. European school parties visiting concentration camp sites share the same insouciance. Of course, at one level, the reaction is to want to drum home the horror of what happened – to make them respond. On the other, however, it is good that the present generation has not had to face these traumas. One would certainly not wish it on them.

Memorials in stone are not permanent, and their intended message – whatever it is – can change as it is seen by different generations or co-opted into new purposes. The intentions of those that built them are forgotten. As James Young puts it 'monuments seem to remember everything but their own past, their own creation', and eventually they 'assume the polished, finished veneer of a death mask, unreflective of current memory, unresponsive to contemporary issues'.[179] However, what memorials like the Vietnam Wall and the Cenotaph remind us is that the nation-state itself is not a natural or unchanging feature of our lives. It is one that has to be continually reproduced, often through wars and their remembrance, always through violence. We ourselves are implicated in that violence – this is what the trauma of war tells us. We need the myth of the state and are tempted by its narratives of security and belonging. But the state as sovereign power produces its obverse, the bare life of the citizen-soldier trapped in the battlefields of the Somme or Vietnam. It also produces, in return for our sense of belonging, the excluded – within as well as outside

[179] James E. Young, *The Texture of Memory: Holocaust Memorials and Meaning* (New Haven: Yale University Press, 1993), 14.

the boundaries of the state. In the next chapter I turn to examine memorials to holocausts, genocides and famines, where the state turns not on its own citizens, but those it considers do not belong, those it excludes. In these cases there seem to be no narratives that will retrospectively encompass the horrors involved and we are left, at least in the beginning, with silence.

4 Concentration camp memorials and museums: Dachau and the US Holocaust Memorial Museum

> It was impossible to bridge the gap we discovered opening up between the words at our disposal and that experience.... And then, even to us, what we had to tell would start to seem *unimaginable.*[1]
>
> – Robert Antelme

If memorials to commemorate wars are difficult, commemoration of the horrors of famines and genocides is even more so. The political stakes are equally high – and for survivors and relatives the trauma is too great. Survivors find that they have no words for what happened. Robert Antelme recounts the encounter between American soldiers and former inmates in newly liberated Dachau concentration camp in Germany at the end of the Second World War. The soldiers are, of course, appalled by what they see. But they are unwilling or unable to listen to the prisoners' accounts of what happened, satisfied instead with the verdict 'frightful'. It doesn't take long for the soldiers to become accustomed to the horror and devastation that they have uncovered. It turns out that 'most consciences are satisfied quickly enough, and need only a few words in order to reach a definitive opinion of the unknowable'.[2] For the inmates it is more difficult. The encounter with the liberator is their first taste of how difficult telling the story will be for those who know that there is more to it than that. The inmate 'senses welling up within him a feeling that he is from now on going to be prey to a kind of infinite, untransmittable knowledge'.[3] This difficulty can be traced to the way in which the traumatic event lies outside the boundaries of experience. It is not encompassed within language. It is the real: in other words it is precisely that which lies outside the linguistic or symbolic order that circumscribes what we call social reality.

In Hiroshima, the A-bomb (or Genbaku) Dome stands alongside the Peace Park – a mute reminder of the first use of atomic weapons and

[1] Robert Antelme, *The Human Race*, trans. Jeffrey Haight and Annie Mahler (Evanston, Illinois: The Marlboro Press/Northwestern, 1992).

[2] Antelme, *The Human Race*, 289. [3] *Ibid.*

Figure 16 Genbaku Dome: Hiroshima Peace Memorial (Photo courtesy of Steve Smith)

the huge destruction that was produced[4] (Figure 16). It symbolises what cannot be told in the museums, with their photographs of people horribly burned and their displays of objects scarred in the blast. The Dome is also a remnant, an excess: like something that is left over in the process of symbolisation, something that is outside the symbolic. It is not part of the new, rebuilt Hiroshima, unlike the Peace Park next to which it stands. Much of the emphasis in the reconstruction of the city was the removal of sites that might bring back the rawness of memories.[5] The debate was whether the ruin should be preserved or whether it should be allowed to decay in the course of time.[6] As a remainder of the bombing, the Dome serves memory when attempts at symbolisation fail. In the film *Hiroshima Mon Amour*, a Japanese man and his French lover are talking about what she has seen in her visit to the city.[7] She insists: 'I saw

[4] The City of Hiroshima and the Hiroshima Peace Culture Foundation, *Hiroshima Peace Memorial (Genbaku Dome)*, (Hiroshima: Sanko, 1997). I am indebted to Steve Smith for a copy of this publication.

[5] Lisa Yoneyama, *Hiroshima Traces: Time, Space and the Dialectics of Memory* (Berkeley: University of California Press, 1999), 66.

[6] James M. Mayo, *War Memorials as Political Landscape: the American Experience and Beyond* (New York: Praeger, 1988), 214.

[7] *Hiroshima Mon Amour*, director, Alain Renais, script, Marguerite Duras (Argos Films, Como Films, Pathé Overseas, Paris, Daiei Motion Picture Co Ltd, France/Japan, 1959).

everything. Everything.' ('*J'ai tout vu. Tout.*')[8] She visited the museum four times: she watched people looking pensively at the photographs, the reconstructions, and the explanations and looked at them pensively herself. She visited the hospital, stood under the epicentre of the explosion. But he insists: 'You saw nothing in Hiroshima. Nothing.' ('*Tu n'as rien vu à Hiroshima. Rien.*') It is not simply a question of the places she has actually visited, but rather, 'the problem with the woman's sight is not what she does not perceive, but *that* she perceives, precisely, a *what*'.[9] She sees 'Hiroshima', the emblem, the symbol – not the reality of the event. The traumatic event cannot be captured in the realm of sight nor in the explanatory texts that situate the photographs, artefacts and locations of memory. Somehow it exceeds them. The 'scandal' of the film is that 'nothing is unforgettable'.[10] Producing a narrative is a form of forgetting. What the film explores is 'how one can be fully alive under the burden of a history that is not a stranger to trauma but that has not fully domesticated the traumatic'.[11] For Michael Roth 'to make the past into a narrative is to confront the past with the forces of forgetting. If something is unforgettable, this is, paradoxically, because it cannot be remembered or recounted.' This is to oversimplify the concept of narrative, and to assume it takes the form of an account from a single point and within a linear temporality,[12] but there is nonetheless a way in which narrative domesticates, 'hides the "primitive terror" behind us, obscuring the possibility that a "non-sense" lurks behind all "sense"'.[13]

Antelme argues that despite the difficulties, indeed the impossibility of imagining the unimaginable, that attempt must be undertaken since 'only through that self-same imagining could there be any attempting to tell something about it'.[14] And this has indeed taken place since the Nazi persecutions, for example, as it has also in the case of other genocides, famines and destructions. Initially there has often been silence. Though witnesses of the Nazi era such as Robert Antelme and Primo Levi produced accounts very soon after liberation, other witness accounts were to remain submerged until much later. In the case of the Irish famine of the

[8] Marguerite Duras, *Hiroshima Mon Amour* (Paris: Gallimard, 1960), 6.
[9] Cathy Caruth, *Unclaimed Experience: Trauma, Narrative, and History* (Baltimore: Johns Hopkins University Press, 1996), 28.
[10] Michael S. Roth, 'Hiroshima Mon Amour: you must remember this', in *Revisioning History: Film and the Construction of a New Past*, ed. Robert A. Rothenstone (Princeton University Press, 1995), 91–101; 98.
[11] Roth, '*Hiroshima Mon Amour*', 99.
[12] I am indebted to Annick Wibben for this point and for many useful conversations about narratives.
[13] Hans Kellner, 'Beautifying the Nightmare: the Aesthetics of Post-modern History', *Strategies*, 4, no. 5 (1991): 292–3, quoted in Roth, '*Hiroshima Mon Amour*', 99.
[14] Antelme, *The Human Race*, 4.

1840s, it seemed to be only after 150 years had passed that people were able to think of widespread commemoration. In the immediate aftermath it was not so much the unspeakability of the horror that led to silence – nor the abstract guilt of the survivors who felt they should have shared the fate of those who perished – but the way that survivors had often profited at the expense of those who died or were evicted from their land.[15] But in 1995 the political climate in Ireland was different. The peace process was beginning, and attitudes were shifting in tandem with the new political situation. British officials were promoting the idea of moving forward, forgetting the past and moving into the future, a future where reconciliation was central. There was a need to draw a line under what had been, and one of the ways this was accomplished was through the erection of memorials and the establishment of a Famine Museum at Strokestown Park House, County Roscommon.[16] Apologising for the suffering caused is a contemporary response to the victims of trauma from states or governments considered responsible. The British government's admission of 'policy failure' – not a formal apology – in relation to the Irish famine, was voiced during the commemoration of the 150th anniversary.[17] What does this apologising, and the sudden rash of memorials do? Does it acknowledge the voices of the victims? Or does it perhaps deny the trauma, by gentrifying it? The commemoration concert in Millstreet in 1997 was seen as a chance to look to the future: time must now start to move onwards. In this way, apologies can be seen as part of a re-narrativisation that reinstates normal time and forgets what I have called 'trauma time'.

Accounts of American slavery remain muted and poorly recognised even now, with cities in Europe that benefited from the proceeds of the slave trade only just having begun in the last years of the twentieth century to recognise their own history and complicity.[18] In places such as Bristol in the south-west of England, a port whose wealth derived in large part from its involvement in the eighteenth century in the triangular trade with the West Indies, the connection of this wealth to the slave trade is finally

[15] Jenny Edkins, *Whose Hunger? Concepts of Famine, Practices of Aid* (Minneapolis: University of Minnesota Press, 2000), 11.

[16] Stephen J. Campbell, *The Great Irish Famine: Words and Images from the Famine Museum, Strokestown Park, County Roscommon* (Strokestown: The Famine Museum, 1994); for a discussion of the museum, see Niall O'Ciosáin, 'Hungry Grass', *Circa Art Magazine*, no. 68 (Summer 1994): 24–7.

[17] Rachel Donnelly, 'Blair admits famine policy failure by British', *The Irish Times*, 2 June 1997, 1. http://www.ireland.com/newspaper/front/1997/0602/archive.97060200004.html, 18 January 2003.

[18] David Richardson, 'The Bristol Slave Traders: a Collective Portrait' (Bristol Branch of the Historical Association, The University, Bristol, 1997), 31.

being acknowledged through exhibitions and tourist trails.[19] The link has long been recorded in street names such as 'Whiteladies Road' and 'Blackboy Hill', but only recently has the history of plantation-owning families who built many of the city's elegant Georgian houses been made part of the local narrative. In the United States, testimony of former slaves is inhibited by the shame and humiliation that is still felt, as expressed in Toni Morrison's novels,[20] and accounts that acknowledge the complexity of slavery in American history and the inter-relationships of slave-owning families and their slaves are rare.[21] Memorials in the United States are either confined to a portrayal of the heroic liberator and the kneeling slave (Figure 17)[22] or, more often, as in the Lincoln Memorial in Washington, they fail to deal with the issue of slavery at all. That monument's focus is on Lincoln as saviour of the Union. Monuments can be re-appropriated, however, as when Martin Luther King, Jr., made the Lincoln Memorial the setting for his civil rights speech.[23]

In war memorials, as we saw in the last chapter, the contrast is often drawn between personal mourning and the imposition of national myths through memorialisation. However, the two are not opposed, though finding meaning to personal tragedy in nationalism is problematic. This is not only because of the imaginary nature of the national community but because it is often that very community that has demanded the deaths that are being mourned. Citizen-soldiers have been 'sacrificed' ostensibly to preserve one nation but in reality to secure the order of nation-states. It is in part this betrayal of people by the sovereign state structures in which they are implicated that makes the suffering traumatic.

In the case of a famine or other genocide it is plain to see that the nation, often as an imperial power, has turned on a section of its own community. Redefining those who saw themselves as its citizens, or identifying an 'enemy within', it proceeds to slaughter them or starve them to

[19] 'A Respectable Trade? Bristol and Transatlantic Slavery', Bristol City Museum and Art Gallery exhibition, 6 March–1 September 1999; Bristol Museums and Art Gallery, 'Slave Trade Trail Around Central Bristol', Bristol City Council with sponsorship from The Society of Merchant Venturers, 1998.

[20] Toni Morrison, *Beloved* (New York: Plume, 1987); J. Brooks Bouson, *Quiet as it's Kept: Shame, Trauma and Race in the Novels of Toni Morrison* (Albany: State University of New York Press, 2000).

[21] A recent example is Edward Ball, *Slaves in the Family* (New York: Ballantine Books, 1998). There is a collection of testimonies in Ira Berlin, Marc Favreau and Steven F. Miller, eds., *Remembering Slavery: African Americans Talk about their Personal Experiences of Slavery and Freedom* (New York: The New Press, 1998).

[22] Kirk Savage, *Standing Soldiers, Kneeling Slaves: Race, War and Monument in Nineteenth Century America* (Princeton University Press, 1997).

[23] Kirk Savage, 'The politics of memory: black emancipation and the Civil War Monument', in *Commemorations: the Politics of National Identity*, ed. John R. Gillis (Princeton University Press, 1994), 127–49; 143.

Figure 17 Emancipation Monument, Boston, Massachusetts

death. There is no possibility afterwards of survivors claiming that those who died sacrificed themselves for some greater cause. In the last chapter we saw that the common narrative of sacrifice in war precisely 'makes sense' in this way. We discussed two memorials where the narrative was not imposed – the Vietnam Wall and the London Cenotaph. In these two cases (and no doubt in other examples) the notion of a redeeming sacrifice was not in the foreground. In the instance of famines and genocides there is on the whole no story in which the loss 'makes sense' in any ordinary way. Memorialisation has to look for other forms. One answer in Jewish communities was the Yizkor Bikher or memorial books. The narratives in these books remember the destruction of communities and their lives and act as substitute graves: the writers hoped that they would turn the site of reading into a memorial space.[24] The memorial to the Holocaust by British artist Rachel Whiteread unveiled in 2000 in Vienna's Judenplatz uses books cast in stone to evoke lost lives, bringing this symbolism full circle. The question that is raised forcefully in the case of the Nazi genocides is whether representation is to be sought, or avoided. To what extent is there a type of 'truth' that is beyond telling, beyond narrative, that a straightforward linear narrative or an objective historical account misses? When does memory shade into a form of forgetting? When what is to be remembered is so extreme that everything else can be remembered but not 'the horror, the horror'? Aharon Appelfeld warns that 'anyone who underwent the Holocaust will be as wary of memory as of fire. It was impossible to live after the Holocaust except by silencing memory.'[25]

However, despite these distinctions between wars and genocides, as long as memories are organised in a framework of nations and states there will always be attempts to recount even genocides and famines as triumphs and their victims as having sacrificed their lives for future generations. The deaths of Jews in Nazi persecutions are redeemed for some by the birth of the Israeli state, for example. Indeed, the way that memory of the Nazi persecutions has developed, both at sites in Europe and in Israel, it has been difficult to find an inclusive form of memory. Ironically, different groups have been remembered separately, following the distinctions that the Nazis themselves operated with: Jew, Poles, gypsies, homosexuals and so forth. Camp sites such as Buchenwald in Germany and

[24] James E. Young, *The Texture of Memory: Holocaust Memorials and Meaning* (New Haven: Yale University Press, 1993), 7.

[25] Aharon Appelfeld, *Beyond Despair: Three Lectures and a Conversation with Philip Roth* (New York: Fromm International, 1994), ix, quoted in Geoffrey H. Hartman, *The Longest Shadow: in the Aftermath of the Holocaust* (Bloomington and Indianapolis: Indiana University Press, 1996), 154.

Mauthausen in Austria have been divided into memorials to the different national groups – and Jews are now seen as one of these groups – as I discuss below. In Israel, a way has been found both to remember the victims of the Nazis as the founding martyrs of the Israeli state and to distinguish modern Israelis, who see themselves as self-reliant state builders and defenders, from their predecessors, the diasporic Jews, seen by Israelis as weak victims.[26] Immediately after the founding of the state, the survivors and their narratives of the persecutions and the camps were ignored in favour of new Zionism. It was only in the 1960s after the Eichmann trial that survivors were recognised and later assimilated to the new state: 'the victims are memorable primarily for the ways they demonstrate the need for fighters, who, in turn, are remembered for their part in the state's founding'.[27] The era of the Holocaust 'actually emerged as an era of heroism, of triumph over past passivity'.[28] The memorial narratives of Israel today combine martyrs and heroes in an effective story that supports the militarism of the state. It is not a single story, however, it still has both a religious and a secular thread.

The story of the Irish famine has in the past been incorporated by republicans into a romance of resistance to British imperialism. More strangely perhaps, it has been co-opted into the narrative of the American dream. A recent addition to the cityscape of Boston, Massachusetts, located on the city's Freedom Trail, is a memorial to the victims of the Irish famine. Standing in front of Borders bookstore, and surrounded by seats on which workers and tourists gather at lunchtime to eat and talk, the memorial comprises two groups of three figures. Recent monuments in Ireland, such as the Famine Memorial by Rowan Gillespie on Custom House Quay in Dublin or the National Famine Memorial in the form of a 'Coffin Ship' at Murrisk, County Mayo, adopt sketchy or even a semi-abstract approach to the task of conveying the victims of famine.[29] Emaciated figures are presented schematically or semi-symbolically, and sometimes, as in the memorial in a Belfast park, it is difficult to make the figures out.[30] The Boston Irish Famine Memorial does not have the same approach. It comprises two family groups, each of three figures

[26] See, for example, Yaron Ezrahi, *Rubber Bullets: Power and Conscience in Modern Israel* (Berkeley: University of California Press, 1997).

[27] Young, *Texture of Memory*, 212. [28] *Ibid.*, 213.

[29] Both are the responsibility of the Office of Public Works. For the Custom House Quay memorial see 'Famine', The Office of Public Works, 1997. For the Coffin Ship, see Fr Colm Kilcoyne, 'A reek of famine memories', *Sunday Tribune*, Dublin, 27 July 1997. I am obliged to project architect Mary MacKenna for information on the Murrisk memorial. The Custom House Quay memorial is reminiscent of the Korean War Memorial in Washington: it shares the image of a group of semi-realistic figures, placed separately yet all walking in the same direction, roughly life-size.

[30] I am indebted to Annick Wibben for access to her photographs of this Belfast memorial.

presented realistically: three figures shown 'before' and another three 'after'. The first group represents a family in the agonies of starvation before they set out on their desperate journey from Ireland (Figure 18). The second shows another family. The gender of the child has changed: the starving girl has become a confident boy. The family is prosperous, striding out into the future, with new clothes, re-styled hair, and a confident demeanour (Figure 19). The first group represents 'a family leaving Ireland's shores, impoverished and desperate', and the second 'a family arriving in Boston, filled with hope and determination' as they encounter the American dream.[31]

The Boston Irish Famine Memorial is part of a recent proliferation of memorials on both sides of the Atlantic. Another is planned for Penn's Landing, Philadelphia, 'to serve as testimony', not to the suffering of people in the famine, but 'to the rich heritage of the Irish-American people who proudly claim their Irish legacy'. Its design emphasises the 'indefatigable spirit of the Irish' and the transition from 'anxious immigrant' to a 'future of freedom and opportunity' amongst 'the challenges of a new world'.[32] A memorial planned for Chicago has similar aims: 'In the face of Despair, Hope arose and Triumph succeeded!' the information proclaims. This proposal does at least acknowledge the 'prejudice and bigotry' that faced immigrants on their arrival in the United States.[33] This is forgotten, or rather erased, at other locations. At another landing site, Grosse le, in Canada, there has been an Irish cemetery since 1832, when the disease prevalent among Irish immigrants was cholera. In 1847 because of the number of deaths from typhus, individual burials were abandoned and mass graves dug. There have been memorials at the site since 1853, when a monument to physicians was built. This was followed in 1905 by a Celtic-style cross to commemorate the typhus victims. But in 1998, a further memorial was built, commissioned by Parks Canada. This memorial 'leads visitors into the earth, a symbol of darkness, before emerging into the light, in an area where the names of those who died were engraved.... A symbolic voyage, making the visitor relive the emotions provoked by the anxiety of a trying crossing, the conclusion of a merciless famine, and by the desire and hope of discovering a new land.'[34] The guide talks as if it were possible or desirable to relive the

[31] 'The Boston Irish Famine Memorial: The Sculpture', Boston Irish Famine Memorial Project, http://www.boston.com/famine/resources.stm

[32] 'The Irish Memorial, a National Monument at Penn's Landing, Philadelphia: The Memorial', http://www.irishmemorial.org/memorial.html, 15 July 2000.

[33] 'The An Gorta Mor Memorial Monument', http://www.irishfamine.com/memorial.htm, 15 July 2000, no longer active.

[34] Parks Canada, 'Grosse le and the Irish Memorial National Historic Site, Quebec, Canada: Grosse le at a Glance', 9 May 2000, 3, http://parcscanada.risq.qc.ca/grosse_ile/glance_e.html, 15 July 2000, no longer active.

Figure 18 Famine Memorial, Boston: famine group

Figure 19 Famine Memorial, Boston: the American dream

trauma without trivialising the suffering. In contrast, the Irish inscription on the 1909 cross translates as 'Children of the Gael died in their thousands on this island having fled from the laws of foreign tyrants and an artificial famine in the years 1847–8. God's blessing on them. Let this monument be a token to their name and honour from the Gaels of America. God Save Ireland.'[35] Grosse le was twinned with the National Famine Museum of Strokestown in 1997.[36] The new monuments not only promote Irish-American identity, they provide a foundational myth for white America. Perhaps the most explicit statement of how the famine has been hijacked to promote American nationalism is in relation to the Western New York Irish Famine Commemoration in Buffalo, where the language of sacrifice re-appears. There is a monument on the Buffalo waterfront in the form of a stone circle, and supporters can purchase a commemorative stone plaque to be inscribed with names of their Irish ancestors, 'the people who, through their courage and sacrifice, gave us the opportunity to become Americans'.[37]

This rash of monuments and memorials signals perhaps a time of forgetting – or at least forgetting the rawness of trauma. Survivors have built new lives, whether in Ireland or overseas, and the new generations that they have raised need to look back on the famine without guilt or anger. They can register their connection with it through donations or the purchase of inscribed plaques on websites and then move on. As with Ben in Anne Michaels' *Fugitive Pieces*, they need to feel their own sorrows, rather than be responsible for the sufferings of their ancestors.[38] Ben is an example of the response of the second generation. It is not until the end of the novel that he is able to tell us: 'I know the elation of ordinary sorrow. At last my unhappiness is my own.' In this process of laying the ghosts of the past to rest, new generations read back into the famine a

[35] Michael Quigley, 'Grosse le: "The most important and evocative Great Famine site outside of Ireland"', in *The Hungry Stream: Essays on Emigration and Famine*, ed. E. Margaret Crawford (Belfast: The Institute of Irish Studies, The Queen's University of Belfast, and the Centre for Emigration Studies at the Ulster-American Folk Park, 1997), 36–7.

[36] Minister visits Grosse le, Quebec, Ministry for Foreign Affairs, Ireland, Press section, 3 December 1997. At the twinning ceremony, the speech of the Irish Minister for Foreign Affairs emphasised not the new life that a minority of the immigrants found in Canada, but the strength of present-day Ireland and its responsibilities to famine victims in the rest of the world. (Speech by the Minister for Foreign Affairs David Andrews, TD, at a ceremony to mark the twinning of the National Famine Museum, Strokestown Park, Co. Roscommon, with the Grosse le and the Irish Memorial National Historic Site, Québec, Canada.)

[37] 'The Western New York Irish Famine Commemoration: Memorial to the Victims of Ireland's Great Hunger', http://www.webt.com/jneville/, 15 July 2000, no longer active.

[38] Anne Michaels, *Fugitive Pieces* (Toronto, 1998), 292.

heroism and a courage that was not found in the bitterness, hostility and humiliation of the event itself.

The situation has perhaps changed in the latest case. The most recent in the line of monuments to the Irish famine placed in the landing sites of Irish immigrants is one dedicated in Battery Park, New York, on 16 July 2002. At the lower tip of Manhattan Island, it overlooks the Hudson River, the Statue of Liberty and Ellis Island, where immigrants disembarked, locating the memorial in a landscape of patriotic symbolism. This memorial, designed by New York sculptor Brian Tolle, is itself a landscape – a quarter-acre of the Irish countryside recreated on a concrete slab that is raised and tilted on a wedge-shaped base. It is 'a walk-in relic of a distant time and place tenderly inserted into the modern world almost as if it were an offering'.[39] Visitors enter through a reconstructed fieldstone cottage from County Mayo and can walk through a replica of a ruined Irish peasant holding of the nineteenth century planted with Irish wildflowers and grasses.[40] Like the museum in Strokestown, this memorial is designed not only as a monument to a particular famine, but rather as a call to action against hunger in the contemporary world. Texts place facts about the Irish famine alongside statistics about hunger today.

Although a monument to the Irish famine in New York had been under consideration for several decades, planning for the Battery Park memorial began in March 2000 and the groundbreaking took place on 15 March 2001. The site chosen was just two blocks from where the World Trade Centre stood. The events of September 11, 2001 intervened when the memorial was half completed, and the equipment in use in its construction was commandeered for the rescue effort after the collapse of the two World Trade Centre towers. Although the memorial was designed to commemorate events of 150 years ago, by the time of its dedication in July 2002 – less than one year after September 11 – it was being seen as, in some senses, a memorial to those events too, one that, strangely, was already half-completed when the destruction of 2001 took place. Certainly any complacency in the descendants of the Irish immigrants was shattered with the deaths of so many, including Irish-Americans, in the WTC collapse. As Roberta Smith noted, writing in the *New York Times*, 'the memorial has arrived at a time when Americans, especially young Americans, have a deeper understanding of tragedy and grief, of fate's capriciousness and of the complexities of power'.[41]

[39] Roberta Smith, 'A memorial remembers the hungry', *New York Times*, 16 July 2002.
[40] 'Governor Pataki dedicates permanent "Irish Hunger Memorial"', Press Release, Office of the Governor of New York State, 16 July 2002, http://www.state.ny.us/governor/press/year02/july16_2_02.htm, 19 July 2002.
[41] Smith, 'A memorial remembers the hungry'.

In the case of the catastrophe and loss of the Nazi period, several commentators in the USA and Britain argue so many attempts have now been made to acknowledge and remember the time that we have a veritable 'Holocaust Industry'.[42] Public memorials to the Nazi persecutions have taken on a more pedagogic function as the distance from the events commemorated increases. It is no longer sufficient to evoke a recognised narrative symbolically: the story has to be explicitly told. In Boston the New England Holocaust Memorial itself almost blends into the cityscape of downtown Boston. It is situated opposite governmental buildings and just off the main tourist route, the Freedom Trail. With the licence of both geographic and temporal distance, the symbols used can be more explicit and graphic than might have been possible earlier, without being offensive. The memorial comprises six towers or chimneys of glass on which are etched six million numbers. The tall glass chimneys each represent a particular extermination camp. At the base of the tower is a shallow well covered by a metal grid, across which visitors walk (Figure 20). Beneath the grid are smouldering coals, and smoke or steam rises through the grid and up the chimney: a rather literal representation of the camp crematoria. At night the chimneys are illuminated. A printed guide available at the site lists the quotations and poems from famous survivors that are engraved on the glass. Also engraved on the memorial is information about the Nazi period. According to the pamphlet, in order 'to encourage a universal understanding... factual statements about the Holocaust, its many victims and heroes, are inscribed in the granite walkway'.[43] In addition, a granite slab is inscribed with a brief historical statement of what happened in the Nazi period, with a timeline underneath. In 1990s USA, monuments seemed increasingly to commemorate not only the 'victims' but also the sponsors of the monument itself: the contemporary equivalent perhaps of an intercessory mass for the soul of the departed or the dedication of a chapel in a cathedral as a penance for riches in mediaeval times. The Boston memorial gives a prominent space, adjacent to the memorial itself, to the names of its sponsors. The park in which it stands was renamed 'Carmen Park... in recognition of William Carmen's... vision and leadership in creating the

[42] Tim Cole, *Images of the Holocaust: the Myth of the 'Shoah Business'* (London: Duckworth, 1999); Peter Novick, *The Holocaust and Collective Memory: the American Experience* (London: Bloomsbury, 1999); Norman Finkelstein, *The Holocaust Industry: the Abuse of Jewish Victims* (London: Verso, 2000). This question is also discussed outside the Anglo-American context; see, for example, Richard Chaim Schneider, *Fetisch Holocaust: Die Judenvernichtung–verdrängt und vermarktet* (Munich: Kindler Verlag GmbH, 1997).

[43] *The New England Holocaust Memorial* (Boston: Friends of the New England Holocaust Memorial, supported by Bank Boston, 2000), brochure, 6pp.

Figure 20 New England Holocaust Memorial

New England Holocaust Memorial'. At one end of the memorial pathway stands a vertical granite slab carrying a version of Martin Niemöller's 'First, they came for . . .'[44] At the other end, is the slab carrying a history of the Nazi period. Separated from the glass chimneys that form the memorial itself, two larger slabs stand facing each other. The first is engraved with the history of the memorial, and carries the names of those who donated money towards its construction. On the other slab, under the inscription 'I will give them an everlasting name' and the dedication to the 'six million', is a list of the names of the great and the good involved in the memorial: the designer, the chairs of the various committees and the committee members.

The proliferation of museums and memorials in this case also seems to promote forgetting – or at least to commercialise and hence trivialise remembering. I return to this question later. First I want to examine the variety of ways in which the reluctance to represent and commemorate the unimaginable horrors of the Nazi era was overcome in the post-war years in Europe and consider what sort of memorials, monuments and museums were established. A number of distinct forms of monument or genres of artistic interpretation have emerged. Their use has changed over the post-war decades and is specific to their various national settings. Concentration camp sites and places of mass executions have also become memorials, and are often the location of commissioned monuments. I look at the response of visitors, particularly young visitors, to these 'tourist' memorial sites, taking the Concentration Camp Memorial at Dachau outside Munich as an example. Particularly affecting at other sites like Auschwitz are the displays of personal belongings – suitcases, shoes, prosthetic limbs – taken from deportees before they were gassed. I ask why this is so.

Latterly, at around fifty years from the liberation of the camps, a number of monuments and narrative museums had been set up in the US. I examine the Holocaust Memorial Museum in Washington, opened in 1993. This museum set the benchmark for a series of other projects and, rather strangely, it is even being considered the model to emulate by museum designers at concentration camp sites such as Dachau in Germany.

The charges of commercialisation and trivialisation made in the US have reverberated in the UK. In London at the turn of the twentieth century a new exhibit opened at the Imperial War Museum, a Holocaust Memorial Day was instituted, and the Irving-Lipstadt libel case took

[44] The 'original' version is cited in Novick, *The Holocaust and Collective Memory*, 221. Novick points out that in Boston, Catholics are added to Niemöller's list.

place amid accusations that charges of commercialisation are tantamount to Holocaust denial.

'Holocaust' memorials

Despite the acknowledged difficulties, there are many attempts to find some way of memorialising the mass murders carried out under the Nazis.[45] The absence of a language adequate to the witnessing of trauma has led survivors to express their testimony in other forms: Elsa Pollak says: 'I feel obligated to leave something of all the suffering. . . . Man created these horrors, but did not invent a language in which to describe them. The memories stayed alive and urged me on without respite. And thus I arrived at sculpture.'[46] A number of people who are not directly survivors produce works that carry on these attempts to 'voice the void' whether in art or literature.[47] Examples in the visual arts include Christian Boltanski's assemblages of projections and reflections of haunting black and white images of nameless people, with spotlights and wires, and Rebecca Horn's installations of mechanical hammers and shattered mirrors.[48]

In order to evoke trauma without seeking to represent it, some monuments convey a sense of a blank space, an enclosure where unspeakable (but not unimaginable) horror took place. One work that attempts this is Boltanski's *Missing House* in Berlin. This is a permanent memorial to absence: an installation at the site of a house that was destroyed by Allied bombing in 1945. The house was originally inhabited by Jews, but when they were deported, it was taken over by Germans, and it was they who were killed in the bombing raid. The empty space where the house stood forms the Boltanski installation. Plates on the rebuilt walls on each side

[45] For two surveys of monuments and sites, see Young, *The Texture of Memory*; and Sybil Milton and Ira Nowinski, *In Fitting Memory: the Art and Politics of Holocaust Memorials* (Detroit: Wayne State University Press, 1991). The former covers monuments in Germany, Poland, Israel and America, the latter also extends to Austria, France, the Netherlands, Italy, the Soviet Union, Canada, Japan and South Africa. See also the detailed, historical discussion of monuments and camp sites in Paris and in Germany in Caroline Wiedmer, *The Claims of Memory: Representations of the Holocaust in Contemporary Germany and France* (Ithaca: Cornell University Press, 1999).

[46] Elsa Pollak, quoted in Milton and Nowinski, *In Fitting Memory*, 268. Käthe Kollwitz' work *Die Eltern* in Roggevelde German War Cemetery, Vladslo, Belgium, is a testimony in sculpture from a parent to a child killed in the First World War. See Jay Winter, *Sites of Memory, Sites of Mourning: the Great War in European Cultural History* (Cambridge University Press, 1995), 114.

[47] Sara R. Horowitz, *Voicing the Void: Muteness and Memory in Holocaust Fiction* (Albany: State University of New York Press, 1997).

[48] Works from these artists were shown at *Between Cinema and a Hard Place*, Tate Modern, London, 12 May–31 December 2000.

give the names of those living in the various apartments when the building was destroyed. They don't indicate the fate of the previous tenants, however.[49]

In its largely abstract form, the Paris Mémorial de la Déportation near Notre Dame seems to appeal to blankness and absence in a similar way. While the tomb of the Unknown Soldier is under the Arc de Triomphe, at the centre of the monumental streets and architectural alignments that celebrate victory, the monument to those deported from France to the concentration camps is tucked away right at the tip of the Île de la Cité, a short walk from Notre Dame cathedral. It is dedicated to 'the 200,000 French martyrs killed in the camps and deportations, 1940–1945'.[50] A long flight of steps leads steeply downwards from an elegant formal garden into the centre of the monument, an austere space surrounded by high concrete walls that screen out the surrounding buildings. On one side is a striking cast-iron sculpture; beneath, through a portcullis, there is a glimpse of the waters of the river Seine. On the other side, between two tall stone blocks, is a narrow entrance just wide enough to walk through. This leads into the chamber of the memorial, an enclosed space with small side lobbies and passages. Two contain in their walls small triangular alcoves bearing the names of concentration camps; the third is a long corridor illuminated by light shining through 200,000 tiny quartz pebbles representing those killed. At the head of this corridor stands the tomb of an unknown deportee. At its end is an eternal flame. There is little by the way of explanation: only the dedication, a few poems and quotations etched on the internal walls, and the inscription on the tomb.

For some visitors 'the low ceilings in this crypt, iron bars and long corridors evoke a sense of confinement and menace'.[51] However, although undoubtedly solemn and enclosed, it hardly even hints at the horrors of the transports or the gas chambers. The surfaces and forms are clean, simple and aesthetically pleasing, and the sculpture of 'black metal stakes with small jutting metal triangles [which] resemble barbed pikes' does not convey anything more than a slight hint of aggression (Figure 21).[52] Although in the centre of Paris it is invisible except to those who seek it out. It is definitely there, at the heart of the oldest part of the city, but at the same time it is hidden. It is a memorial that does its job of remembering unobtrusively. What's more, it goes along with the idea, noted by Antelme, that to recognise the unimaginable nature of the horrors is

[49] Abigail Solomon-Godeau, 'Mourning or Melancholia: Christian Boltanski's *Missing House*', *Oxford Art Journal*, 21, no. 2 (1998): 1–20.
[50] Milton and Nowinski, *In Fitting Memory*, 204.
[51] *Ibid.*, 210. [52] *Ibid.*, 206.

Figure 21 Mémorial de la Déportation, Paris

sufficient. We need go no further. We can take refuge – this time in the beauty and pathos of abstraction.

This memorial was one of those built in the 1960s under Général de Gaulle. As Caroline Wiedmer points out, by this period the official memory of the war in France had crystallised 'around a dominant myth, that of French "*résistancialisme*"' which divided the country neatly 'into a mass of résistants and a mere handful of collaborationists and traitors'.[53] The memorials built at that time reflected this version of history. The Île de la Cité memorial was dedicated by de Gaulle on 12 April 1962. Like the other Paris monuments erected in the late 1950s and early 1960s, it comprises a series of motifs that evoke an eternal, supposedly permanent vocabulary of memory: the everlasting flame, the poems or religious quotations, the tomb of an unknown to represent – and claim for the narrative – the bodies of all the murdered, the imposing monumental dedication, and the symbolic sculpture evoking suffering and despair. They install a singular version of national memory, one that does not acknowledge ambiguity or plurality. In the case of the French memorials of this period, there is no reference to the shared responsibility for the mass deportations or to French collaboration with Germany.[54] They make concrete a particular reading of events that has little to do with living memory but rather replaces it, as Pierre Nora argues.[55] As products of an official, state-led commemoration, 'rather than encouraging active remembering on the part of the community, these memorials remember for the community'.[56] Unlike the sites that evoke a popular response, like the Cenotaph or the Vietnam Wall, these monuments stand as evidence of a problem solved. We visit, ponder a while, and then turn our backs: 'under the illusion that our memorial edifices will always be there to remind us, we take leave of them and return only at our convenience'.[57] In some senses, we don't even have to visit. The Île de la Cité memorial is almost hidden from view although it is in the centre of one of the busiest tourist areas of Paris. It does not need to attract attention. It is not there to be visited, except on days of national ceremonial. It is enough, for the national conscience, that it is there.

Another place in Paris was for many years the location for purely private commemorations by survivors and their families. The Vélodrome d'Hiver was the site where Jewish immigrants arrested by the French police in July 1942 were held awaiting deportation to Auschwitz. Some

[53] Wiedmer, *Claims of Memory*, 33. [54] *Ibid.*, 35.
[55] Pierre Nora, 'General introduction: between memory and history', in *Realms of Memory: Rethinking the French Past*, ed. Pierre Nora and Lawrence D. Kritzman (New York: Columbia University Press, 1996), 1–20; 2.
[56] Wiedmer, *Claims of Memory*, 36. [57] Young, *Texture of Memory*, 5.

8,160 people, including over 4,000 children, many separated from their parents, were held in appalling conditions. The children were deported at the request of the French police, not on the orders of the Nazi occupiers. The developments in the way these events were commemorated mirrored the evolving French understanding of the Vichy period and the eventual acknowledgement of the extent of French collaboration.[58] The original stone plaque erected in 1949 on a street near the Eiffel Tower where the now demolished stadium once stood made no mention of the involvement of the French in the deportation, indicating only that the Jews were held 'by order of the Nazi occupier'.[59] In 1986 under Jacques Chirac (then Mayor of Paris) this plaque was replaced by another that does mention the police, although it still leaves the extent of their role unspecified. For many years, relatives and survivors held an annual ceremony in front of the plaque. Government ministers were not even invited to take part until 1982. Ten years later senior officials including the President, François Mitterand, took part in the ceremony in an attempt to allay the controversy that had been provoked by Mitterand's practice of laying a wreath at Pétain's tomb. The attempt was disastrous: the President was booed by the crowd.[60] Mitterand went on to make the day of commemoration an official one, and to order the erection of a new monument. The first official commemoration was held in 1993, with a carefully planned programme, invited guests and selected participants – and, of course, crowd barriers and security officers. Effectively this was a take over of the previous private gathering by the organs of the state. Survivors' responses were not entirely positive. One is quoted as saying 'Of course it was good. They're finally recognising what they did. But in my heart of hearts I preferred it before. It was just us. There we were every year. Nobody clapped. It was dignified. And then above all, there weren't all those barriers to channel the people. Barriers, here, they don't realise what that reminds us of.'[61] What had been important to the survivors, the annual gathering as a communal act of memory, was replaced by a self-congratulatory, orchestrated ceremony devoid of simple dignity. Ironically, in the new ceremony uniformed French police officers stood each side of the memorial plaque throughout the proceedings, a task previously performed by survivors dressed in their camp uniforms. In the following years, speeches by succeeding President Chirac and Prime Minister Lionel Jospin acknowledged France's complicity. Jospin's 1997 speech invoked and co-opted the language of memory. By then the ceremonial had become more elaborate and the guest list more extensive. And 'the fact that the wreath laying by the various survivors' associations

[58] Wiedmer, *Claims of Memory*, 38–57. [59] *Ibid.*, 44. [60] *Ibid.*, 214. [61] *Ibid.*, 52.

was relegated to last place in the order of events [made] the sense of displacement of the old crowd first aired... at the 1993 ceremony... complete'.[62] There are echoes here of the formalisation of the ceremonies at the Cenotaph in London. In the course of time the changing and private practice of memory had been replaced by a fixed official narrative, presented by the authorities for consumption by the populace at large.

As we have seen it does not seem to be necessary to visit a memorial: it is sufficient that the memorial exists. Sometimes even it seems to be enough just to have a *plan* for a memorial.[63] As time passed after the end of the Second World War, the impetus to build memorials increased but so did the difficulties that seemed to surround their design and construction. Controversy over what was eventually called the Memorial for the Murdered Jews of Europe planned for Berlin was symptomatic of the problems involved more generally in Europe, but it also reflected specifically German debates. The demand that a memorial be built was first made by journalist Leah Rosh in 1988, but despite two competitions, in 1995 and 1997, by 2000 there was still no decision as to what, if anything, would be built. The former Gestapo area in Berlin was the site first suggested but later ruled out. This site had already been the location of inconclusive debates over memorialisation in the late 1970s and early 1980s and a design competition in 1984.[64] After the fall of the Berlin Wall and re-unification, the site of the former Ministergärten was chosen. Controversy shifted from where the memorial should be built to two central issues: first, who should be commemorated, and, second, the combined question of who was erecting the monument and who it was to address: what was the audience. The first issue was, of course, highly controversial. Many people were in favour of a memorial, but would not support the erection in Berlin of a monument that commemorated only one of the many groups of Nazi victims. The Jewish claim to a unique memorial reflected claims to the uniqueness of the Holocaust itself; the argument of Perspective Berlin (a group founded by Rosh) was that 'no other victim group had been persecuted as massively or as fervently as the Jews and that anti-Semitism had been Hitler's central and indeed programmatic mode'.[65] On the other hand, if Jewish groups rejected the idea of a common memorial, the alternative, that of memorials for each

62 *Ibid.*, 56.
63 Philipp Blom, 'The impossible monument', *The Independent Friday Review*, London, 4 September 1998, 13; Denis Staunton, 'The art of remembrance: haunted still', *The Guardian*, G2, London, 12 August 1998, 1–3.
64 Young, *Texture of Memory*, 81–90. Objections to the chosen design led to the decision not to act on the selection and nothing was built.
65 Wiedmer, *Claims of Memory*, 144.

separate group – the Roma or Sinti, homosexuals, the mentally deficient, Jehovah's Witnesses, Soviet prisoners of war – would be equally unacceptable. The sorting and selections of the Nazis would be being repeated: we would have 'the differently coloured triangles of the camp prisoners return[ing] after 50 years as memorials' as historian Reinhart Kosellack noted.[66]

The second question, alongside the issue of *who* should be commemorated, was *why* they were to be commemorated and *by whom*. In many senses this debate was the more revealing. In the initial demand for a memorial Leah Rosh said, 'I demand of this country of perpetrators a memorial... a site of remembrance, something that recalls THIS DEED.'[67] Again, in an advertisement published in 1989 and 'directed specifically at Germany's non-Jewish population', Perspective Berlin said that the lack of a memorial 'that remembers the victims' was shameful 'in the country of the perpetrator' and called on 'all Germans in East and West' to honour their 'obligation'.[68] In other words what was planned was not a memorial to mourn the victims, such as would have been appropriately placed by survivors or relatives – or by the state in Israel perhaps – but one which would 'symbiotically combine mourning, shock and respect with remembrance in shame and guilt'.[69] This requirement for a memorial erected by 'the Germans' – whoever they might be: many young Germans 'reject the notion of collective guilt reaching them across generations'[70] – sits uneasily with the notion of a monument purely to Jewish victims. Do we mean those victims defined as Jewish by 'the Germans'? In any case, weren't the Jews Germans until the Nuremberg Laws? What of 'another sore spot in the debate, the tendency of the Germans to identify with the victim'?[71] The call for Germans to erect a memorial to their victims recalls the purging of guilt through buying indulgences. This point was made particularly strongly in connection with one of the designs that called for the engraving of the names of the 4.2 million Jews already identified by Yad Vashem as murdered by the Nazis. The money available would not allow for the inscription of all 4.2 million names at the start; it was suggested that names be added as additional money was subscribed by the public.

Writing in 1993 in a study that focuses on changing processes of memory rather than static memorials, James Young suggests that 'were the competition [to design a memorial for Berlin] to be extended indefinitely, its proposals collected, displayed, and perpetually debated, the

[66] Quoted in *ibid.*, 148. [67] *Ibid.*, 142. [68] Wiedmer, *Claims of Memory*, 143.
[69] Quotation from the project brief (Wiedmer, *Claims of Memory*, 150).
[70] Wiedmer, *Claims of Memory*, 151. [71] *Ibid.*, 155.

entire process might recommend itself as an exemplary, ever-expanding memorial text... comprised not by material space and ruins, but by memory-work itself'.[72] As it turns out this almost indefinite extension of the debate is what seems to have happened.

Perhaps it is just that Germany seems to specialise in 'the perpetually unfinished monument'.[73] German public debate on memory is sophisticated and the dangers of a memorial being an obstacle to memory rather than an aid to it are by now well recognised. One form of memorial that has grown out of these concerns is the counter-monument. Here the visitor is invited to take an active role in the process of memory, sometimes by adding their voice to the monument, sometimes by 'being' the monument itself. The monument is often designed to be buried or sunk, leaving a trace of its presence. One example of this is the 'negative-form' monument designed by Horst Hoheisel to the *Aschrott-Brunnen* (Aschrott Fountain) in Kassel. The original fountain was donated to the city by Sigmund Aschrott, a Jew, and destroyed by Nazi activists in April 1939.[74] The monument is designed as a hollow concrete mirror image of the old fountain, sunk beneath the pavement of the square. The water flows through canals in the square into the depths of the inverted fountain, leaving visible only the 'visitors themselves standing in remembrance, looking inward for memory'.[75] Another example is the Gerzes' counter-monument in Hamburg.[76] This Monument Against Fascism is a pillar that was designed to be sunk into the ground in stages over a period of five years, each time with a photographic record of the event. Visitors had to sign their names on the part of the memorial just above ground prior to each sinking. The inscriptions, which included swastikas and slogans like 'Foreigners get out' as well as names and signatures, reflected back to the community its own memories and its reactions to them. It reminded visitors of their shared responsibility. Counter-monuments are the inversion of phallic victory monuments: they are monuments to defeat, in a sense, not monuments to the genocide. We have seen how monuments *do not need to be visited*, how indeed they *do not need to be built*: planning to build a monument is sufficient and this is an apt solution to the insoluble problem of design. In the case of the German counter-monuments, it is sufficient for the monument to have been built, once. We can visit the site of the monument, and remember not what was commemorated but the pure fact of commemoration. These monuments *do not need to be permanent*. We remember that there was a monument. We remember only that we have remembered.

[72] Young, *Texture of Memory*, 89–90. [73] *Ibid.*, 40. [74] *Ibid.*, 43.
[75] *Ibid.*, 46. [76] *Ibid.*, 28–37.

This takes us even further from the business of memory itself. In this I disagree with Young's analysis. In a sense it might be argued, as Young does, that the debates over memorialisation constitute a 'memory-work'. But on the other hand these debates are not so much concerned with the difficulty of representing a horror beyond the imagination but with *who* gets to mourn, in what way and with what political outcomes. The contest is a tug-of-war between victim groups, or those who wish to identify with them. The result is an enhancement of precisely those aspects of exclusion and separation that memory under the guise of 'never again' is trying to avoid. Even 'the Germans' are constituted in this way, by their claim to be thoroughly and deeply engaged in the question of memory. As perpetrators, or descendants of perpetrators, current generations demand a particular, unique place in the memory of the horror. In one sense, then, the debates refuse closure by forestalling the literal setting in stone of a particular linear narrative of events. This does acknowledge the contested nature of memory. However, in another way the agenda they set for debate is unacceptably narrow. What we have is a struggle for adequate acknowledgement between various groups that consider themselves representative of victims. This obliterates the need to search for ways of remembering that could be 'true' to the trauma that was experienced. Survivors report a grey area in the camps – an area of indistinction between perpetrator and victim – and the horror of this is lost if victims are regarded as unproblematically distinct. The current 'memory wars' are amnesiac about the origins of the persecutions. The Nazis did not attack pre-existing groups of people; they first produced the groups they were then to murder. Memorials risk doing nothing more than perpetuating the distinctions the Nazis introduced while glossing over the horror of what happened next.

Dachau concentration camp memorial

The historical site as a site of remembrance is recognised as possibly more valuable than any attempt at the construction of a monument, although how such sites should be presented remains problematic.[77] Visitors to the remnants of the camps at Majdanek and Auschwitz find that 'guard towers, barbed wire, barracks and crematoria – mythologised elsewhere – here stand palpably intact... [collapsing] the distinction between themselves and what they evoke. In the rhetoric of their ruins, these memorial sites seem not merely to gesture towards past events but to suggest

[77] The battle of the crosses at Auschwitz is an extreme example of this. Neil Bowdler, 'Faith and rage at Auschwitz', *The Guardian*, London, 2 September 1998, 8.

themselves as fragments of events, inviting us to mistake the debris of history for history itself.'[78] Hamburg citizens in 1984 demanded landmark status for the remains of Neuengamme concentration camp: a 'private initiative' called for 'because the city of Hamburg has not deemed it necessary to preserve this place of martyrdom by protecting this site'.[79] Such sites do more than commemorate: they fuse the actions of remembrance and witness. There is a memorial in France that takes the form of the preserved site of the massacre of a village, at Oradour-sur-Glane. Here, 'visitors... have explicit roles to play', they 'become actors recapturing the scenes of a tragedy'.[80] At the entrance to the site, the key instruction is 'remember', and the visitor becomes a witness to what took place. The same thing happens at concentration camp sites.

James Young's account of the memorialisation of the camps at Buchenwald and Mauthausen is interesting, however. He demonstrates how even a camp site could be made into a national monument. In the case of Buchenwald, the German Democratic Republic turned the camp ground into a memorial to the foundation of the new communist state, scripted as the anti-fascist struggle. The camp had been the site of imprisonment of German communists during the Hitler era and thousands died there. The monuments celebrated the liberation of the camp by its political inmates shortly before the arrival of the American troops in 1945. These are more triumphal than commemorative of suffering, and Jews are included, Young remarks interestingly, only as political activists, not as a religious or ethnic group. What was studiously forgotten in this, however, was not only the memory of Jews shipped to Buchenwald from the east later in the war, but also the post-war use of the camp by the Soviet régime for victims of Stalinist purges, as well as those rounded up in post-war de-Nazification. After re-unification in 1991, the story of the camp was again re-processed, to include not only the German victims of Nazism but those of Stalin as well. As Young concludes bitterly, the camp site is again in danger of being co-opted into the German national memory as 'with the introduction of further German victims into its memorial landscape, Germany's normalisation proceeds apace'.[81] Mauthausen in Austria became the site for monuments to the heroes of twenty nation-states from which political prisoners, criminals and prisoners of war were taken in the Nazi era. The Jewish monument is just one of the twenty national sculptures.[82] Each of the victorious Allied powers has adopted into its own national memory the names of the camps liberated by its

[78] Young, *Texture of Memory*, 120–1. [79] Milton and Nowinski, *In Fitting Memory*, 38
[80] Mayo, *War Memorials as Political Landscape*, 232–6.
[81] Young, *Texture of Memory*, 79. [82] *Ibid.*, 95.

own advancing troops: Bergen-Belsen by the British, for example, and Dachau by the Americans.[83]

The camp at Dachau, just outside the boundaries of the city of Munich, claims the dubious distinction of being the first Nazi concentration camp. It was set up by Heinrich Himmler, Chief of Police of Munich, just two months after the new régime took power in January 1933.[84] Originally Dachau was intended for German political internees – opponents of the régime such as communists, social democrats, trade unionists, conservatives and monarchists – and German Jews were imprisoned there only after Kristallnacht in November 1938. Once the war started this changed and people from all the occupied countries were sent to Dachau, including members of resistance groups, Jews and clergymen. Catholic priests made up 2,579 of the 2,720 clergy held in the special section according to statistics taken from SS records.[85] Over the twelve years it was in operation 206,206 prisoners were registered as arriving at Dachau.[86] Although it was not chiefly an extermination camp and the actual number of deaths is not known, some 31,951 deaths were recorded. From 1942, at least 3,166 of the weak and ill at Dachau were transported to Hartheim castle near Linz, where they were gassed.[87] In addition, mass shootings of Soviet prisoners of war took place at firing ranges near to the camp in 1941 and 1942. Towards the end of the war Dachau became the destination for prisoners evacuated from camps further east in the face of the advancing Russian troops. Two days before the Americans reached the camp, some 7,000 prisoners had been forced to march south under SS guard. Many died. Dachau was finally liberated on 29 April 1945.

Over the twelve years from 1933 to 1945 Dachau had changed from an internment camp for political prisoners to a final destination for thousands evacuated hurriedly from death camps in the east. It was the horrific sight of corpses in cattle cars and starving inmates that greeted the American liberators in 1945. As with other concentration camps, the history of the Dachau site did not stop with liberation.[88] In the first few days and

[83] Tony Kushner. 'The Memory of Belsen', *New Formations*, no. 30 (1996–7): 18–32; 20.

[84] Barbara Distel, *Dachau Concentration Camp* (Comité International de Dachau, 1972). See also Barbara Distel and Wolfgang Benz, *Das Konzentrationslager Dachau 1933–1945: Geschichte und Bedeutung* (München: Bayerische Landeszentrale Für Politische Bildungsarbeit, 1994).

[85] Barbara Distel and Ruth Jakusch, *Concentration Camp Dachau 1933–1945*, trans. Jennifer Vernon (Munich: Comité International de Dachau, Brussels and Lipp GmbH, 1978), 60.

[86] Distel and Jakusch, *Concentration Camp Dachau*, 212. [87] *Ibid.*, 165.

[88] For an account (published after this chapter was written) that traces the history of the Dachau camp from 1933 through its various uses as a memorial in parallel with a discussion of the changing attitudes of succeeding German generations, see Harold Marcuse, *Legacies of Dachau: the Uses and Abuses of a Concentration Camp, 1933–2001* (Cambridge University Press, 2001).

weeks many more prisoners died; the camp was quarantined by a typhus epidemic. And once released, inmates faced a painful, slow recovery. The camp itself became first an internment camp for SS officers awaiting trial, and from 1948 when the trials had finished, a refugee camp for Germans expelled from the Sudetenland. As a refugee camp with the barracks divided into family accommodation, Dachau accommodated 5,000 people from 1948 to 1960. A section of the camp was at that time used by the Americans as a food-processing centre for troops stationed in Germany and Austria.[89] On the tenth anniversary of liberation in 1955 a meeting of former prisoners of all nationalities took place. Appalled by the state of the site, they decided to re-establish the Comité International de Dachau, the former resistance organisation within the camp, this time to lobby for a decent memorial. The first result was the setting up of a provisional display in the crematorium building, and the memorial site, with a new museum, was re-opened in 1965.[90] This was in spite of considerable opposition from local inhabitants.[91] In the interim, Catholic clergy had campaigned for a monument in the grounds. This initiative was led by the Catholic auxiliary bishop of Munich, Johannes Neuhäusler, and was more acceptable to local people. A memorial chapel was built and dedicated on 5 August 1960.[92] Further religious memorials were built later: a Carmelite convent in 1964, a Jewish Memorial Chapel and a Protestant Memorial Church in 1965, and a Russian-Orthodox Chapel in 1995.[93]

The extensive and complex history of the site makes its status as a memorial problematic. Among visitors today there is a demand for historical accuracy: they want to see things as they were during the Nazi period. They want to see 'the concentration camp'. Yet there are two problems with this. First, many of the buildings from the period 1933–45 were modified or demolished in the immediate aftermath of the war, when the camp was used for refugees. Second, even during the twelve years of the camp's notoriety, it existed in a number of configurations. Which version would the visitor like to see? The barracks where each prisoner had his own bed, with a shelf for belongings and a hook for their cap? Surely not, this looks far too civilised, by no means horrific enough. Or the stripped-down version, where each bed was home to four or five prisoners and the details such as personal wardrobe space had almost disappeared? Still

[89] Young, *Texture of Memory*, 61–26.
[90] Distel and Jakusch, *Concentration Camp Dachau*, 4.
[91] Young, *Texture of Memory*, 64.
[92] Johannes Neuhäusler, *What was it Like at the Concentration Camp at Dachau? An Attempt to Come Closer to the Truth*, 29th edn (Dachau: Trustees for the Monument of Atonement in the Concentration Camp at Dachau, 2000), 71.
[93] 'Dachau Concentration Camp Memorial Site', Small guide, c.2001, 4pp.

not horrific enough for you? How about the final layout of the barracks, where all semblance of separate beds (even to be shared by five) had disappeared? They were replaced by sleeping platforms, in three layers, where the lack of divisions meant that more prisoners – no doubt thinner prisoners by then too – could be accommodated. These certainly look as though they might be more uncomfortable. In fact, what we are offered in Dachau is a reconstructed barracks or *Wohnbaracken* that contains examples of all three types of accommodation and visitors are conducted from one to another. There remains a feeling of unreality. These are reconstructions. The wood is clean and new. There is no sign of the filth or the horror of life in close proximity. Four hundred people, we are told, ate together in this room – a room impossibly small for such a purpose. It seems crowded with the tour group of fifty or so well-fed and well-dressed visitors. And yet, despite what is almost a sense of disappointment, there is no doubt that this is real: this is the very spot where all this took place.[94] But the ghosts have long since departed.

The site at Dachau is stripped bare. Apart from the two reconstructed barracks and the administration block, and a reconstructed section of barbed wire and ditch, the whole area is laid out with concrete rectangles filled with pebbles to represent the foundations of the other barracks (Figure 22).[95] It is a park-like environment, with trees and gravel, and visitors wander across the vast expanse of the site somewhat uncomfortably. There is something missing. The monument by Nandor Glid above the International Memorial, with its elongated, skeletal figures intertwined in agony, provides the only real intimation of what the camp was about. From a distance, their outstretched fingers make them look like a section of barbed wire (Figure 23). Apart from this monument, even the gatehouse or *Jourhaus*, with its inscription '*Arbeit Macht Frei*', fails to instil a sense of foreboding. The gatehouse is currently blocked off from the outside, so that people can no longer enter the camp from that direction. Under a proposed redesign, it will once again form the main entrance. Just the other side of the gatehouse, outside the camp and screened by a mound and a few trees, stands what used to be the SS quarters, which was, we are told, a luxurious setting with its own casino. At present these buildings are not open to the public. They are still in use – incredibly – as a training centre for Germany's riot police. Visitors looking for evidence of mass executions are disappointed too. The yard where these took place

[94] Actually, it's not. The reconstructed barracks is on the site of the infirmary barracks or *Wirtschaftsgebäude*, museum leaflet.

[95] This information now appears at 'Dachau Concentration Camp Memorial Site, the History of the Concentration Camp', http://www.kz-gedenkstaette-dachau.de/english/frame/idx gese.htm, 2 February 2003.

Figure 22 Reconstructed barbed wire at Dachau concentration camp

Figure 23 Monument by Nandor Glid, Dachau

is still there, but the wall itself is unmarked. Again, we are told, the original wall is still there, but covered up now by a facing put in place by the Americans. Just outside the fence at this point, about six feet outside and within a stone's throw of the yard, is a newly built detached house with a balcony looking directly into the camp. Clearly part of a smart modern development, it can't be more than a few years old. Who, visitors ask themselves, could possibly live *there*?

The administrative block or *Wirtschaftsgebäude* is at present the site of the Dachau museum. There was a museum there in the days of the Nazis too – containing 'plaster images of prisoners [with] bodily defects or particular characteristics'.[96] But the museum opened on 9 May 1965 was different. It took up almost the whole of what had been the building housing the kitchen, the laundry, storage rooms for prisoners' clothing, and the shower baths or punishment rooms where prisoners were tortured. The exhibition told the story of the camp, beginning with displays recounting the rise of National Socialism in Germany and then following the history of the camp through from 1933 to liberation in 1945. A 250-seater theatre showing *KZ Dachau 1933–1945*, a film of the rise of Nazism and the concentration camps with a focus on Dachau, was part of the museum. The administration building also housed the camp archives and library, as well as offices that dealt with enquiries and organised visits from all over the world.

One small room in the museum was set aside for a rather strange display. This room contained an eclectic collection of mementoes, reminiscent in many ways of the objects left at the Vietnam Wall in Washington. The items ranged from substantial stone carvings or marble headstones dedicated to groups of prisoners, to stone tablets, photographs and other objects left in memory of individuals. These were displayed on shelves or mounted on the walls of the room, and the whole exhibit was behind glass. Numerically the most preponderant were pennants and fringed silk bands bearing woven texts and emblems. These were hung together around the upper and lower parts of the walls. This memorial room was the place where objects left at the memorial site by visiting survivors and relatives were kept. Often a group wanting to memorialise members killed at Dachau would arrange in advance with the camp authorities to place a small memorial in this room. Wreaths are often left outside at monuments on the site, such as the statue of a camp prisoner by Fritz Koelle, with its inscription '*Den Toten zur ehr den Lebenden zur Mahnung*' (Figure 24) or the tomb of the unknown prisoner that forms part of the International Memorial. These wreaths are removed regularly. If they bear ribbons

[96] Neuhäusler, *What was it Like at the Concentration Camp at Dachau?*, 12.

Figure 24 Monument by Fritz Koelle, Dachau

with a dedication, these are kept and placed in the memorial room in the museum. Some groups place wreaths every year on the anniversary of liberation, when a commemorative ceremony is held. Often they use the same ribbon each year, returning it to the memorial room in between.

The memorial room was set up as part of an attempt to satisfy conflicting demands on the memorial site.[97] Over the years a compromise has been found. Former prisoners or prisoners' relatives wanted to set up places around the site where they could come to mourn their loss. They wanted to mark these spots with memorial stones or small monuments. But this wouldn't tie in with the demand from the general public for historical accuracy and the presentation of the camp in as authentic a way as possible. So eventually, when individuals or groups expressed a desire for a memorial, they were gently persuaded by the administrative staff that they should use the memorial room in the museum as somewhere to place their memorial object. Or, as an alternative, they could place a headstone at one of the two mass graves in the town of Dachau rather than in the camp.

This conflict between history and memory arose again in connection with the restructuring and reorganisation of the Dachau Memorial Site exhibition that was underway in 2001. The original plan was for a more up-to-date display, making use of all the contemporary museum techniques and taking up the whole of the central area and west wing of the administration building. Plans had to be changed, however, when it was discovered that the west wing of the building, formerly the entry point for prisoners going through the dehumanising reception process, was still largely intact in its original form. It was here that new prisoners were stripped of their belongings, and underwent the process of admission to the camp. This process was horrendous, involving abuse and physical violence as well as the degrading ordeal of being photographed, shaved, bathed and issued with camp uniform and clogs. For former prisoners and their relatives this makes the building a site of particular significance. Those responsible for the reorganisation of the museum agreed that the area uncovered would no longer form part of the main museum but would be opened to visitors in as authentic and sensitive way as possible. There was a dilemma over what to do. The need to explain to those unaware of the historical background clashed with the need for 'authenticity': the need to retain the building in its original form. The concern of present-day visitors is to know what is 'original' and what is not: a concern for historical accuracy. In the past this was not the chief concern of visitors.

[97] This and the subsequent paragraphs draw on conversations with staff of the Dachau Memorial site, archive and library, 10 April 2001.

Survivors knew what had happened there, and their concern was for a place to mourn. This expressed itself in their attempts to set up gravestones or memorials for lost friends and relatives. Not only is there a conflict between authenticity and remembrance, there is also a problem when it comes to retaining as much of the original atmosphere as possible whilst at the same time making it clear to present-day visitors – who often have little knowledge of the background – what exactly went on in these buildings. As a compromise the reception area will be kept as authentic as possible, but unobtrusive explanatory notices will be added for those ignorant of the history.

Another result of the reorganisation and restructuring will be the displacement of the small memorial room. In line with the trends in other places, such as the US Holocaust Memorial Museum in Washington, a hall will be provided for remembrance. There will also be rooms that can be used by groups. However, these spaces are unlikely to provide for the type of personal mementoes that are kept at present. It will no doubt be a solemn, impersonal ecumenical space designed to encourage visitors to reflect on their experiences at Dachau, and to take certain lessons home. In a sense, while the expansion of the remit of the museum from a purely historical account to a more contemplative form of remembering is to be welcomed, it will mean a moulding of the diverse personal reflections into a standardised, suitably formalised context. The success of the Vietnam Wall is that it does allow specific mourning. At Dachau the person is abstracted and rendered nameless and faceless even in death.

A plain bound book is available in the memorial room at the end of the museum visit for people to write comments or enter their names. These books, like books of condolence, are kept in the Dachau archive. The responses of current visitors to Dachau reflect an enormously disparate set of attitudes and reflections. A lot of the entries are by schoolchildren on group visits. Occasionally there is nothing more than the equivalent of 'We were here.' On 7 February 2001, for example, Class 9a of Hauptschule Leck wrote '*Wir waren hier*' and then all inscribed their names.[98] Some books consist of nothing more than a series of more or less identical entries, with visitors creating their own columns in the blank book provided for their names, where they are from and the date of visit.[99] Even in these books, some people will go against the general pattern and add a comment: one anonymous visitor from India added on 26 September 1999,

[98] Dachau Concentration Camp Memorial Site, visitors' books: book 563, 2–24 February 2001, Dachau archive.

[99] See, for example, book 544, 18 September–07 October 1999, and book 556, 22 July–15 August 2000.

'Did God exist?'[100] In other books the layout becomes quite different, with people taking the space to make extensive comments, or even in some cases using a whole page for a drawing or a crude sketch. If the comments go beyond what the camp authorities think is acceptable – by including swastikas or fascist slogans, for example – the particular book will be removed and replaced with a fresh one. The offending book will still be kept in the archive, however.

Some of the comments are along fairly predictable lines. People express in various ways the need to ensure such things never happen again. An Australian writes, 'I feel very sorry that so much pain was given to so many people. I pray that we never let this happen again.'[101] And an American also calls on God: 'May God bless us and watch over us in order to prevent the same repercussions.'[102] For other writers it is a question of individual responsibility: 'Let each of us resolve that we would not let this happen again'; and 'We must work to love and understand each other'.[103] Or a question of teaching future generations: Barbara Stephens brought her grandson here 'to learn about the atrocities and hope his generation will never let this happen again'.[104] And one visitor signs himself 'Grandson of an American liberator returning to ensure the memories are never forgotten'.[105] Once a theme is started, subsequent writers take it up. The comment 'I hope this will never happen again in the whole world', is followed by '*Wir hoffen auch, dass so etwas nie wieder geschieht*! (We also hope that this never happens again)'.[106] Another similar theme is that, of course, such events are still taking place: 'Look now to what's going on today. Let us not need the benefit of hindsight to open our eyes to atrocities we'd rather ignore,' writes Simon Cercoran, and 'Thank God that this ended . . . if only other countries would follow', is the contribution from Christana Kinecz-Shamrock and Robert Shamrock from the USA.[107] Several writers make the link between genocide in the 1940s and events in Rwanda, Kosovo or Bosnia.

A few see redemption in the events themselves. Aloha and Warren Werksman from Sydney, Australia, write alongside a Star of David: 'And maybe, maybe . . . from the deepest pit of innocent pain will spring forth the strongest light of hope and love.' For one person 'The righteous have never been nor will they ever be forsaken. May God bless and keep every soul that passed through these walls. Amen.'[108] Others draw the lesson that we should be grateful for our freedom, and that we should be sure

[100] Book 544. [101] Book 563, 2 February 2001. [102] Book 563, 3 February 2001.
[103] Book 563, 4 February 2001, and book 556 (undated). [104] Book 556 (no date).
[105] Book 549 (no date). [106] Book 563, 8 February 2001.
[107] Book 563 (no date). [108] Book 563 (no date).

we 'don't forget what life means. Live every day good!' They are 'inspired to live . . . life with thoughts of the people who died here, and to treat others with benevolence and good will'.[109]

Some visitors express their disbelief or disorientation: 'One will almost not believe it really happened'; 'How could such a terrible tragedy have even taken place?' 'How brutal was Hitler? No one can believe it! But a day will come for everything!'[110] Others cannot express their feelings: Ferrara from Italy writes '*No abbiamo parole (Wir haben keine Worte)*', and Joanne Callahan from Galway, Ireland, 'No words!!'[111] Lynda Pezygoda wrote on 29 July 2000, 'It's been a crazy experience walking through all this. I had family here. Thank God he's still alive. I mourn for all those who have lost [their lives] here in Dachau'.[112] Many are prompted to think of the victims: 'I pray to those that have been here. You were brave'; or from Cheryl Barnes: 'May they rest in peace. My heart goes out to every last one!' Some have come specifically because of their work with victims: Tamara Tillman, from the USA, for example, writes: 'In loving memory of all the patients I have taken care of who bore the constant pain of the memory of the 'Tattoo' they wore. Today I make this journey for them.'[113] Of course, visitors extend their thoughts to the perpetrators as well: 'Let's pray for the torturers and killers as well as the victims and their families', and a Korean visitor: 'Forgive them, but never forget their behaviour.'[114] Others seem more impressed by their own suffering, and more concerned that they would never recover: 'I will never forget what I saw today and how awful I felt', wrote Lisa O'Donnell from Dublin, and Amy Hoey (also from Ireland) added 'What I saw here today distressed me greatly and I'll never forget it'. Yet another wrote 'I'm still crying'. For others their visit seemed like a rather frightening movie: A. Ariosa from the USA wrote 'This stuff is scary dude', and Sheridan Fields' verdict was 'Spooky but interesting'.[115]

A theme that runs throughout the comments in the visitors' books is the question of blame and responsibility. Germans (and others) express their shame: 'Germany, for which I am ashamed after these pictures', says Janina Knobel; 'In reaction to this you just have to be ashamed as a German citizen'; '*Hont, d'avoir un quelconque rapport avec les gens qui ont donné un nouveau sens aux mots: Horreur, torture, mort, agonie*', writes Sandrierre Fayard. In February 2000 we find a debate between young German visitors, all of them around fifteen or sixteen years old: 'it is terrifying what the German people have done!' writes the first,

[109] Book 563 (no date), Matt Webber, Virginia, USA.
[110] Books 563 and 556 (undated). [111] Book 563, 15 February 2001.
[112] Book 556, 29 July 2000. [113] Book 549 (no date).
[114] Book 563 and book 556, 28 July 2000. [115] Book 563, February 2001.

A. S. R. Heidenheim. 'It is indeed not just the Germans who did something like this! In Russia people were brutalised in the same way and tortured to death! Something like this must not happen again!' respond Maren Kling and Andrea Stadler. 'What the Germans did is horrible! What was done *to* the Germans *AS WELL*!' is the final contribution to this particular exchange. Other youngsters protest: 'Our generation should not be held responsible for something the one before committed.'[116] There are many who more specifically lay the blame on Hitler, and anti-Hitler or anti-Nazi diatribes are fairly frequently found. Here are a few examples of this type of comment: 'We gonna kill this fuckin Nazis'; and, in German, 'Hitler's mother was a Jew and the whole German people were blind he was not Aryan'; '*Hitler danke das du tot bist du Arsch.* Forever!' (Hitler thank you that you are dead you arsehole.)[117] Less frequent are pro-Hitler statements. Here is one: '*Hitler war ein guter Mann, brannte alle Juden an*', which roughly translates as: 'Hitler was a good man – he began burning all the Jews'. A subsequent writer has crossed out 'guter' (good) replacing it with 'scheiss' (shit) and 'Juden' (Jews) replacing it with 'Deutsche' (Germans). Later on 'guter' has been reinstated. On the same page we find two adjacent comments, first: 'We nearly escaped from all Jewish people but somebody stopped the genocide'; and then 'All Nazis were the black sheep of humanity. But we can never tell the reason why.'[118]

It is interesting that even in this context, many visitors sign themselves by noting their nationality or at least their country of origin. One resists this trend, noting 'From India, A human'.[119] A few others note that it is humanity that bears responsibility: Renata Isogo from Canada writes, 'Shame, shame, shame to humanity. Barbarism in the spirit of man has no place in this world'; and Len May from England notes, 'Under the right conditions *all* men are capable of this'.[120] Another blames civilisation: 'hard to believe another civilised human being could have done this to other civilised human beings . . . maybe civilisation is overrated'.[121]

What is most striking about this collection of comments is the huge range and diversity of responses people have when they visit Dachau. And the way people – not all, by any means, only a small proportion – take up the invitation to interact. They want to bring wreaths, memorial plaques and the like to Dachau, and they also want to contribute their thoughts to the ongoing debate about how we should deal with the events of 1933–45. Visitors interact with each other through the

[116] Book 549, 17 February 2000. [117] Books 563 and 556.
[118] Book 549, 16 February 2000. [119] Book 549.
[120] Book 549 (no date). [121] Book 556.

visitors' books. They read and respond to each other's comments. And they are happy to address their comments to the world in general as it passes through Dachau. In this way the memorial is more than just a static, official memory of the Nazi terror. The comments in the books remind us that things are by no means settled. We do not all agree with some comfortable version of 'Never again!' The museum engages the visitor, demanding their involvement. It does not have a strong storyline, and much of the text is in German, consisting as it does of photographs of the original Nazi documents. Translations are provided in the exhibition catalogue, but visitors on the whole do not consult this as they go round. They have to piece together the story themselves. The site too is not one that directs the visitor in a particular way. Guided tours are provided for school groups and once a day for general visitors, but on the whole people make their own sense of what they see. It is to be hoped that the reorganisation will increase the opportunities for thought, engagement and interaction, not stifle them under an expectation of conformity. At present there is a striking diversity of reasons for visiting and responses to the camp site.

Relics at Auschwitz

Auschwitz is also the site of contested memories and it has been co-opted for different purposes. James Young charts the difficulty of building a memorial at Birkenau, and tells us how the inscriptions on the tablets of the memorial unveiled in 1967 were erased with the fall of the communist régime.[122] Today, Auschwitz has become a site of what has been called atrocity tourism. Educational visits and even day trips from the UK take place to this site that is now central to the symbolism of the 'Holocaust'.[123]

The conflicts between authenticity and memory, and between mourning and tourism, are similar to those I have traced at Dachau. Tim Cole argues that Auschwitz is 'not simply a symbol contested by "Poles" and Jews, but a site contested by "pilgrims" and "tourists" '.[124] The tourism, he argues, includes an element of voyeurism. There are various concentration camp sites at Auschwitz: three main sites (Auschwitz I, Auschwitz II-Birkenau and Auschwitz-Monowitz) and a large number of other satellite sites. According to Cole the effect of the presentation of the sites for tourists is a merging of all three into a curious amalgamation of history and theme park. The site where the museum is situated – Auschwitz I –

[122] Young, *Texture of Memory*, 132–44.
[123] The Holocaust Educational Trust: Future Events, http://www.het.org.uk/FutureEvents.html, 28 January 2001.
[124] Cole, *Images of the Holocaust*, 115.

has come to stand in for all the others. At this site there is a mixture of original ruins and reconstruction. The building that houses the tourist shop, cafeteria, toilets and cinema, which visitors assume was built when the site became a museum, is in reality a building that between 1942 and 1944 was where prisoners were put through the humiliating rituals of shaving, tattooing and de-lousing. In contrast, the gas chamber and crematoria displayed at the museum site as authentic is a reconstruction of a building that began as an experimental gas chamber, was then used as an air raid shelter, was demolished by the Soviet army and only later reconstructed to resemble its original form. A chimney was reconstructed and furnaces re-built. Other reconstructions include the execution wall and the gallows in the roll-call square.[125] The mass killings of Jews took place not at Auschwitz I, which accommodated mainly political prisoners and Poles, but at Birkenau, a mile-and-a-half away. The relics now on show at Auschwitz I have been transported there from Birkenau.

It is these relics, the piles of eyeglasses, shoes, shorn hair and suitcases, that visitors to Auschwitz and Majdanek remember and find most directly affecting and moving. For some commentators it is difficult to understand what it is that makes this sight such an emotional one. James Young laments the fact that 'these artefacts . . . force us to remember the victims as the Germans have remembered them to us: in the collected debris of a destroyed civilisation. . . . Nowhere among this debris do we find traces of what bound these people together into a civilisation, a nation, a culture. Heaps of scattered artefacts belie the interconnectedness of lives that made these victims a people. The sum of these dismembered fragments can never approach the whole of what was lost.'[126] However, as Elaine Scarry points out, 'a made object is a projection of the human body'.[127] This applies not only to large objects like nations, civilisations or cultures, but to smaller objects such as suitcases, clothes, eyeglasses, shoes. Some sense of what Elaine Scarry means can best be grasped from her description of a woman making a coat:

> The woman making the coat . . . has no interest in making a coat per se but in making someone warm: her skilled attention to threads, materials, seams, linings are all objectifications of the fact that she is at work to remake human tissue to be free of the problem of being cold. She could do this by putting her arms around the shivering person (or by hugging her own body if it is her own warmth on

[125] The Municipal Office and the Silesian University in Katowice, 'National Museum in Oswiecim: Collection', http://www.man.katowice.pl/katowice/informator/tekst/english/m172.shtml, 30 December 1998, no longer at this address.

[126] Young, *Texture of Memory*, 132.

[127] Elaine Scarry, *The Body in Pain: the Making and Unmaking of the World* (New York: Oxford University Press, 1985), 281.

behalf of which she works), but she instead successfully accomplishes her goal by indirection – by making the freestanding object which then remakes the human site that is her actual object.[128]

To appreciate what is meant here we have to forget how under capitalist ways of making the world people are alienated from the purposes and the products of their labour. We are talking of objects that are designed and made for people, not profit. The objects displayed in the museum at Auschwitz are the type of objects that obviously embodied that sense of concern for the sentient beings to whom they belonged: shoes, prosthetic limbs, umbrellas, leg braces, spectacles or eyeglasses. They are all objects that protect the human body from the elements or extend the capacities of the body like a coat does, enabling it to walk further, withstand cold, rain, or see further when the eyes are no longer able to do so unaided. Personal possessions, 'armless sleeves, eyeless lenses, headless caps, footless shoes',[129] lying in great mounds in the museum testify poignantly to the absence of the sentient beings to whom they belonged. But they do much more. They draw our attention to the disregard of sentience, *its unmaking*, that was necessary for the persecution and killing to take place: 'Torture and war are not simply occurrences which incidentally deconstruct the made world but occurrences which deconstruct the structure of making itself; conversely . . . the ongoing work of civilisation is not simply making x or y but "making making" itself, "remaking making", rescuing, repairing, and restoring it to its proper path every time it threatens to collapse into, or become conflated with, its opposite.'[130] Scarry argues that those involved in acts of torture or brutality are 'stupid', a description she uses not 'as a term of rhetorical contempt for those who wilfully hurt others but as a descriptive term for the "nonsentience" or the "lack of sentient awareness", or most precisely, the "inability to sense the sentience of other persons" that is incontestably present in the act of hurting another person'.[131] The perpetrators of these acts employ false motives to prevent any awareness of the pain or injury to human sentience and feeling they are inflicting. They focus on their own hardship – the cost of the bullet, or having to watch concentration camp brutalities – instead of the experience of being shot or being the victim of massive brutality in the camps.[132] They become unable to sense the sentience of other people.

Visitors to Auschwitz have been confronted with the unfeeling brutality of the camp and the nonsentience of the guards. What the sight of the artefacts does is juxtapose to this unawareness in an unbearably moving

[128] Scarry, *Body in Pain*, 307. [129] Young, *Texture of Memory*, 132.
[130] Scarry, *Body in Pain*, 279. [131] *Ibid.*, 294. [132] *Ibid.*, 59.

way the sentience of their victims *preserved in these artefacts*. The shoes speak to us:

> We are the shoes, we are the last witnesses,
> We are shoes from grandchildren and grandfathers,
> From Prague, Paris and Amsterdam,
> And because we are only made from fabric and leather
> And not of blood and flesh, each one of us avoided the hellfire.[133]

As objects they escape temporality. As bodily extensions, like hair, they are intimately connected with the living body yet survive it. Not sentient or alive they are nevertheless the last witnesses. In a sense they are true witnesses, comparable to the Muselmanner, the no longer alive. I return to this point in Chapter 5.

We must, of course, be wary of taking the 'apparent-aliveness [of artefacts] as a basis for revering the object world' and making relics of the shoes or the hair, but rather use this 'apparent-aliveness as a basis for revering the actual-aliveness of the human source of that projected attribute'.[134] The projected sentience of objects here reminds us of the way soldiers' personal belongings from the First World War were kept by their descendants and referred to in discussions of memory. In a very real way, the objects preserve the sentience of their owners or their makers (when the object is such that the owner remakes it through its use). They are repositories of sentience that are timeless. Places of memory, in the sense of the actual sites where things took place, are the same. The place is remade by the human events that took place there. The built surroundings, like other objects, embody the human beings who produced them. The buildings at Dachau are much more problematic, embodying as they do the forced labour of inmates slaving to build the instruments of their own torture and destruction. The site at Dachau, as visitors are shown, included what purports to be a gas chamber, situated in a room immediately adjacent to the crematoria ovens. I return to the ambiguity of these remains at the end of the chapter.

Finding the small remnants of the concern and compassion of ordinary life multiplied thousand-fold in the museum at Auschwitz is an unexpected and jarring juxtaposition. It places side-by-side the thoughtfulness and consideration of daily existence, where people together make

[133] This poem, credited to Moses Schulstein, appears in the US Holocaust Memorial Museum above a display of shoes confiscated from prisoners in the Majdanek Concentration Camp, near Lublin, Poland (Jeshajahu Weinberg and Rina Elieli, *The Holocaust Museum in Washington* (New York: Rizzoli in collaboration with the United States Holocaust Memorial Museum, 1995)).

[134] Scarry, *Body in Pain*, 286.

and remake the social world, and the destruction of war and torture carried to its extreme, the unmaking of the world.

This discussion throws new light on the 'things' brought to the Vietnam Wall that were discussed in Chapter 3, and can be linked to the use of domestic objects in political protest such as the women's anti-nuclear protests of the 1980s in Britain. Protesters brought small domestic items – babygros, children's toys and the like – and attached them to the fence of the missile base at Greenham Common.

Narrative museums

Of course, the focus on 'authentic' inanimate objects as containers of time was in the past central to the concept of the museum. A museum grew up around a collection of some sort. Its primary function was the display of objects. In a sense it still is, although recent museums and exhibits have self-consciously adopted what they call a narrative approach. The famine museum in Ireland and the United States Holocaust Memorial Museum (USHMM) in Washington are examples of this new philosophy.[135] Despite this, the designers of the latter, for example, acknowledge how 'authentic three-dimensional artefacts constitute a direct link to the events, which are embedded in them, as it were. Having been there, they become silent witnesses.'[136] Not only is there a continuing focus on the authentic object, but this focus again brings into question the way in which these objects are treated as sacred relics. In some senses this can be seen as a way of bringing back the sanctity of the lives lost, giving them back their individuality and uniqueness. Museums become places of pilgrimage since they contain relics, and in the case of 'holocaust museums' even sometimes soil or ashes from the camps.[137] Like the Vietnam Wall, the USHMM has become a site to which survivors bring memorabilia of the events of 1933–45, 'objects which had witnessed and survived the Holocaust'.[138] The museum's collections department maintains two large storage facilities near Baltimore, and it holds some 26,000 authentic objects of which only around 1,000 are on display. But receiving and preserving the donated objects involves much more than the museum expected. Staff have 'to deal not only with artefacts but also . . . with [the] very sensitive human emotions' of the hundreds of survivor donors who

[135] Campbell, *The Great Irish Famine*; see also, for example, Sharon Macdonald and Gordon Fyfe, eds. *Theorizing Museums: Representing Identity and Diversity in a Changing World* (Oxford: Blackwell, 1996).

[136] Weinberg and Elieli, *The Holocaust Museum in Washington*, 67.

[137] Cole, *Images of the Holocaust*, 165–9.

[138] Weinberg and Elieli, *The Holocaust Museum in Washington*, 186.

maintain contact with the museum about their donations.[139] However, the authentic object is of significance to the curators of the USHMM for a different reason too. Authentic artefacts 'constitute a powerful argument against Holocaust denial'.[140] Although the museum focuses on telling a narrative, it still searches for objects because objects 'provide the strongest historical evidence, stronger even [than] that [of] documentary photographs'.[141]

The US Holocaust Memorial Museum is situated just off the Mall in Washington, DC, the centre of the administrative capital of the US empire and the area around which memorials to past rulers of the United States and their wars are to be found. In this location, any museum commemorating the destruction of the European Jews – to borrow from Raul Hilberg – is bound to be a specifically American museum.[142] As we have seen with other memorials, there were the usual struggles over who or what should be represented – specifically, was 'the Holocaust' the murder of six million Jews or the extermination of the eleven million victims of Nazism?[143] Although the museum has not given a definite answer to the question 'Are the "other millions" victims of *the Holocaust*, or *in addition* to the Holocaust?'[144] its response, in the narrative that it tells, has produced a particular but authoritative Americanised 'Holocaust'.

The museum was established with three distinct objectives in view: education, remembrance and moralising. These are expressed in two versions of the official statement:

> The United States Holocaust Memorial Museum is dedicated to presenting the history of the persecution and murder of six million Jews and millions of other victims of Nazi tyranny from 1933 to 1945. The museum's primary mission is to inform Americans about this unprecedented tragedy, to remember those who suffered, and to inspire visitors to contemplate the moral implications of their choices and responsibilities as citizens in an interdependent world.[145]

The second version, which appeared on the illustrated pamphlet handed out to visitors in 1999, reads:

> The United States Holocaust Memorial Museum is America's national institution for the documentation, study, and interpretation of Holocaust history and serves as this country's memorial to the millions of people murdered during the Holocaust. The museum's primary mission is to advance and disseminate knowledge about this unprecedented tragedy, to preserve the memory of those

[139] *Ibid.*, 187 [140] *Ibid.* [141] *Ibid.*, 67.
[142] Raul Hilberg, *The Destruction of the European Jews*, student edn (New York: Holmes & Meier, 1985).
[143] For a discussion of this debate see Novick, *The Holocaust and Collective Memory*, 217–20.
[144] Hyman Bookbinder quoted in Novick, *The Holocaust and Collective Memory*, 220.
[145] *The Holocaust: a Historical Summary* (Washington, DC: USHMM, n.d.), 32pp.

who suffered, and to encourage its visitors to reflect upon the moral and spiritual questions raised by the events of the Holocaust as well as their own responsibilities as citizens of a democracy.[146]

The difference between these two statements is an interesting reflection of how the museum evolved and shows not only how it gained in authority but also how the term 'Holocaust' became established. In the first statement it appears only in the name of the museum itself. By the time the second statement was composed, the term is used three times in the text itself. We can also see how the way the museum's statement figures its visitors has changed slightly. Although they remain unambiguously American, they are now citizens of 'a democracy', not 'an interdependent world'.

The building in which the museum is housed was seen by its architect James Ingo Freed as 'a resonator of memory'.[147] Visitors enter into the huge and echoing Hall of Witness. This is an evocative space, 'disturbing and fractured', where a number of the visual symbols of 'the Holocaust' and its death camps are used: brick arches that reflect the famous entrance to Auschwitz-Birkenau, watchtower-like structures, steel and brick walls and skylights, shadows cast by the skylights and steel beams.[148] The result is an 'ambience [that] although unfriendly, hard, and oppressive, grips visitors rather than [driving] them away'.[149] If the Hall of Witness, with its summons 'You are my witnesses', is what the visitor encounters when first entering the building, the last space is the Hall of Remembrance (Figure 25). Here the text links bearing witness with remembrance, and visitors are given space to reflect and compose themselves. It is on the way into this space that one finds for the first and only time images of recent genocides: Rwanda, Bosnia. This is where the moral message is driven home. It is also where its limitations become apparent: what we have here is a museum designed to confirm American values by showing their opposite. It can reduce complex webs of responsibility to a simple 'telling [of] the story of an un-American crime to Americans. . . . We reaffirm who we are in opposition to the historical "them". . . . It carries the danger of inducing in us a feeling of self-righteousness.'[150] This danger haunts such museums.

146 *United States Holocaust Memorial Museum Visitors Guide* (Washington, DC: USHMM, n.d.), folded pamphlet.
147 Weinberg and Elieli, *The Holocaust Museum in Washington*, 25.
148 Adrian Dannatt, *United States Holocaust Memorial Museum: James Ingo Freed* (London: Phaidon, 1995).
149 Weinberg and Elieli, *The Holocaust Museum in Washington*, 26.
150 Cole, *Images of the Holocaust*, 158.

Figure 25 Hall of Remembrance, US Holocaust Memorial Museum

In pursuit of their three objectives, of education, remembrance and conveying a moral message, the designers of the USHMM paid great attention to leading the visitor through the exhibit, telling the story, controlling the route and manipulating the emotions: things should be powerful enough to elicit the required response and avoid the criticism of 'sanitisation' and yet should not be such as to provoke the opposite criticism, that of 'voyeurism'. They saw what they were doing as producing a 'history museum, though not a history museum in the traditional sense'. Unlike the traditional museum, 'it takes as its point of departure a historical narrative'. It is a 'narrative museum', because 'its display is organised along a story line'. There is, of course, and it is quite trite to acknowledge this, no way in which 'even the most imaginative description of the Holocaust can truly reflect the horror of those days'. But, despite this, those who built the museum stress, 'even survivors who emphasise the inability of any narrative to fully portray their sufferings, even they wanted the story to be told'.[151] Survivors found their fellow Americans unwilling in the immediate post-war years to listen to what they had to say. The opening of this new museum, so the museum's founding narrative goes, is 'both the realisation of the survivors' dream and an admission of the bystanders' historic guilt'. With this, the story is 'presented and validated with the

[151] Weinberg and Elieli, *The Holocaust Museum in Washington*, 17.

authoritative voice of a federal museum by the American people'.[152] But it is not just the telling of the story for survivors that interests the museum planners. A narrative form as they understand it enables them to educate their visitors, their first aim. But a narrative is much more than just an educational tool, it 'affects visitors not only intellectually but also emotionally; it arouses processes of identification. Visitors project themselves into the story and thus experience it like insiders while at the same time remaining at a distance, with the intellectual perspective of outsiders.'[153] Visitors are 'drawn into the flow of the narrative' and 'not only register isolated facts, they also search for meaning'. A narrative has plot which triggers identification: 'we get emotionally involved [which] opens us to educational influence'. The term 'educational' here turns out to have a broad, and in some ways sinister, meaning. The USHMM designers 'consider it their task to affect and change the mental and moral attitudes of their visitors.... Thanks to the plot-based narrative embodied in its exhibits, it is endowed with an educational power likely to act on mental attitudes and behaviour patterns'.[154] This implies a large degree of control, and a view that does not seek to engage with visitors but to influence them in a predetermined way. Indeed, 'visitors are not free to choose their own way through the museum' but are forced 'to follow a preconceived circulation path'.[155] Like a film, the narrative museum has to be viewed in a particular sequence and at a particular speed. It was perhaps no accident that in this context the person chosen as first head of the Exhibition Department was a film director.

However, not only, as the museum's designers admit, does a narrative fail to fully convey what happened, a linear narrative was not to prove a suitable vehicle for telling the story the designers had in mind. Reality itself, it was discovered, was not linear. The solution in the end was a combination of a linear, chronological approach for the first part of the exhibition, covering from 1933 to 1939, and a structure for the second part based on the 'main stages' of the 'Final Solution': ghettos, deportations, concentration camps, death camps. In the final part a return to the chronological structure is seen alongside three thematic sections: rescue, resistance and the fate of children. The sections on rescue and resistance, minor parts of the historical record, were controversial within the planning team. But they obviously provided a good 'ending' for the narrative: a moral could be drawn and 'role models' provided.[156]

Despite the clear and somewhat disturbingly controlling intent of the exhibition designers, the story they had to tell didn't quite fit the linear narrative they wanted to impose. Neither did the process of identification

[152] *Ibid.*, 18. [153] *Ibid.*, 49. [154] *Ibid.*, 50. [155] *Ibid.*, 51. [156] *Ibid.*, 55.

work out quite as planned, and it is this that I want to explore a little further. A central part of the USHMM is its use of photographs: 'The narrative history museum is essentially an attempt at visual historiography. . . . Photographs are the primary carrier of its narrative.'[157] I want to look particularly at how the reliance on photographs and visuals disrupts the narrative to an extent. I will also examine the way that identity cards are used as an obvious and somewhat naive attempt to tie visitors in to a particular identification.

There is no doubt that the identity cards that visitors are offered at the start of their visit – cards detailing men and women who lived during the Nazi period – are intended to give the visitor a point from which to view the 'Holocaust': the point of view of the 'victim'. As part of the 'educational' intent, and 'to facilitate the emotional identification process, it was essential that visitors perceive the victims as human individuals'.[158] Once given the ID card, 'the visitor then goes through the exhibition of the Holocaust with a companion as it were'.[159] In a sense this is similar to the device of soliloquy in theatre or to what happens in film, where the shot/reverse shot enables us to take on the viewpoint of a particular character in the film. In a shot/reverse shot sequence, the second shot shows the point from which the first shot can be assumed to have been taken. Normally the camera is invisible, giving the illusion that what we see has an autonomous existence. However, the viewer demands to know whose gaze they are occupying. When the reverse shot shows them, they are then 'sutured' or sewn into that particular subject position. The illusion that there is no camera, nothing controlling the image, remains, and 'the gaze which directs our look seems to belong to a fictional character rather than to the camera'.[160] At first sight the initial shot represents an imaginary fullness or wholeness – an ideal image – but the pleasure in this fullness soon disappears as it becomes clear to the viewer that something is amiss. There are limitations in what is seen: something is missing – the camera is hiding things. The reverse shot functions to again conceal this limit and maintain the fiction, by substituting the fictional character's viewpoint for the camera. Identification with the character conceals the controlling gaze of the camera. This only works, of course, if the viewing subject is willing to be passive, 'to become absent to

[157] *Ibid.*, 66.

[158] *Ibid.*, 71. Despite the intention to project the human face of the victim, of course, this process also dehumanises them again. One wonders whether their permission has been sought before their details were included in this way.

[159] Weinberg and Elieli, *The Holocaust Museum in Washington*, 72.

[160] Kaja Silverman, 'Suture: the cinematic model', in *Identity: a Reader*, ed. Paul du Gay, Jessica Evans and Peter Redman (London: Sage, 2000), 76–86; 78.

itself by permitting a fictional character to "stand in" for it, or by allowing a particular point of view to define what it sees'.[161]

In film this identification can be disrupted in a number of ways. In the Hitchcock film *Psycho*, for example, these conventions are deliberately refused. Hitchcock 'unabashedly foregrounds the voyeuristic dimensions of the filmic experience' and forces the viewer 'to make abrupt shifts in identification... the viewing subject finds itself inscribed into the cinematic discourse at one juncture as victim, and at the next juncture as victimiser'.[162] The same thing happens in the Holocaust museum. An initial conflict takes place when we arrive and are introduced to the exhibit.[163] At the entrance on the ground floor, there are identity cards for visitors to collect – cards depicting real people from the Nazi era. We then file into the lift that will take us to the start of the exhibition on the top floor. The identity cards are those of victims, but the voices that we hear as we travel up in the lift are those of shocked American troops facing the encounter with the German concentration camps for the first time. As the doors of the lift open, we come face to face with a huge photograph of the charred corpses that greeted the liberators when they arrived at the camps. Not only this, though. We appear as liberators. We stand on one side of the charred corpses, the other American liberators on the other side. We reflect their postures even: hands in pockets, arms crossed, blank faces. The photo is entitled 'Americans encounter the camps'.

The problem of identification is one that resurfaces through the museum, and in part is what makes it such a disturbing experience. In some sense this parallels the dislocation and trauma of the events of persecution themselves. The narrative museum, as its designers say, 'works through the image, through the photograph'. Many of the images we see, certainly the more horrific, the images too violent and hidden behind screens like 'peepshow, snuff movies' are images taken by perpetrators, images of people being rushed to their deaths.[164] As Geoffrey Hartman puts it: 'Our Holocaust museums are full of photos drawn from the picturebook of the murderers.'[165] The screens behind which the video monitors sit give us the choice of whether to put ourselves in the camera's place or not: to look or to look away. Other images were taken in secret, by bystanders who saw what was going on and intervened only to the extent of taking

[161] Silverman, 'Suture', 80. [162] *Ibid.* [163] Cole, *Images of the Holocaust*, 152.

[164] As Barbie Zelizer points out, these days most images of this sort are no longer credited to the original photographer but to the archive which now owns them (Barbie Zelizer, *Remembering to Forget: Holocaust Memory through the Camera's Eye* (University of Chicago Press, 1998), 196–7).

[165] Hartman, *Longest Shadow*, 22.

photographs. We are positioned in the same ambiguous position ourselves. We see propaganda films, newsreels and films of speeches by prominent Nazis, filmed to persuade, to pass on the message of triumphant National Socialism. We recognise the same elements of rhetoric and oratory that are still used by our politicians in present-day democracies. Then finally, we see the images taken by Allied propaganda teams, images of liberation: pictures of camp inmates gathered together for the victory photographs, where in the past they had been gathered together to listen to Hitler's speeches. We are shown pictures of individuals (perhaps thankfully) in such distress that they cannot object to being photographed. Some of these pictures are taken by the Nazi camp guards, recording their treatment of their captives, some by the Allied liberators standing helplessly by as those who are now their prisoners continue to suffer. There is little difference.

Occasionally, just occasionally, the position of 'voyeur', the gaze of the all-powerful camera, is disrupted. The usual blank stare, the distress, the fear, disappears, to be replaced by a return of the gaze. These are the most disturbing pictures of all. The victim is not only looking directly at the camera: they are looking defiantly directly at us. Across the years and the continents, the accusation still holds: 'You see what is happening. What are you doing?'

One of the most powerful parts of the exhibition is said to be the tower of photographs.[166] The photographs here are posed portraits for the most part, often taken in a photographer's studio against a painted background, commissioned by the sitters. Some are groups – schools, workmates, sisters, families – and others are snapshots. The people are relaxed, poised, dignified. They smile out at us, or look serious and composed. These pictures contrast starkly with the photographs that appear under the display on Nazi 'race' science, where people are shown as racial types, and with the criminal mugshots, the record made of concentration camp inmates as prisoners: front view; profile; with a hat. The latter were almost certainly taken by fellow inmates, just as hair was shaved, personal possessions removed and sorted, and the new arrivals abused and brutalised by their fellow victims, in what Levi calls 'the grey zone'.

In our walk through the museum accompanied by our ghostly alter-ego whose identification card we hold, we are shown objects which, like the photographs, position us differently. We walk across a bridge in the

[166] For an interesting reading of the USHMM that sees the tower of photographs as counter-monumental, see Richard Crownshaw, 'Performing Memory in Holocaust Museums', *Performance Research*, 5, no. 3 (2000): 18–27. Crownshaw concludes that museums remain open to memory work, whether they are counter-monumental or prescriptive.

Warsaw ghetto, accompanied by life-size blow-ups of other people – real victims – on the walls alongside us. We are forced to walk into cattle cars like those in which people were transported to the camps, and out into an enlarged photograph of a selection process on the ramps at the camp. We walk under a replica of the sign that hangs at the entrance to Auschwitz, and into a reconstructed Auschwitz barracks. We are the victims. Yet, at the same time, we, like the Nazi camp guards and the inmates who helped with the unloading of the transports, *know* what fate awaits them. And this is made horribly explicit in the scale model of the killing process. We are shown a god's-eye view of the gassing process, where we see the victims undressing, being gassed, and their bodies being pushed into the crematoria ovens. We are shown the memorabilia from the voyage of the *St Louis* and hear the victims' stories. Yet, at the same time, we hear the debates around whether they should be allowed ashore, how the boat is to be turned around, what their ultimate fate is as they are returned to France, Belgium, Britain and Holland, just before the expansion of Hitler's empire. With hindsight we see the press cuttings that appeared in the US newspapers long before the end of the war detailing what was happening in Nazi Germany.

In fact, as several commentators have pointed out, the exhibition works to provide us with 'hindsight', with comforting closure, even before we begin the 'journey into darkness'. The first sight we meet when we get out of the elevator that brings us to the start of the exhibition is, as we have seen, a huge, life-size photograph of the arrival of American troops and the liberation of a concentration camp. We know, before we take on our persona as victim, that we will be liberated. We know that there is an end to the persecutions. For most victims, there wasn't. Most did not survive.

The generally upbeat tone of the exhibition has been widely noted, and was a topic of some contention even among the planning committee. Several writers have noted that more than half of the identity cards issued to visitors to the museum relate to people who did survive – a gross distortion of statistics. Despite the very small proportion of 'rescuers', this theme forms a very significant part of the final stage of the exhibition, as do the foundation of the Israeli state and the role of Jewish resistance. The lesson we are left to draw, as part of our moral education, would appear to be that what is important is the role that outsiders can play as liberators or rescuers, or as we phrase it today, as nations who take part in humanitarian intervention. Barbie Zelizer has argued that even this lesson may not be drawn: 'remembering earlier atrocities may not necessarily promote active responses to new instances of brutality. . . . The opposite may in fact be true: we may remember earlier atrocities so as to forget the contemporary ones.'[167] Even if the lesson is effective, it is limited. We are not given any pointers as to how we might have been implicated in what happened – our responsibility is solely that of an external bystander.[168]

For many of us, however, the most disturbing question is not what we would do if we were again in the position the USA or the UK were in during the Nazi era – outsiders who chose to ignore what was reported to be going on – but what we would do if we were called upon to participate in such atrocities ourselves or if those we knew were doing so. Would a conquered USA have deported its Jews or collaborated in their extermination? This is a question that the museum completely fails to come to grips with. In its attempts to re-humanise the victims, it totally forgets to examine the perpetrators in their (in)humanity. In its attempts to portray American values by presenting their opposite, it conveniently forgets that Americans have themselves been involved in the extermination or enslavement of different racialised groups in the past, and that these actions existed quite comfortably alongside liberal values of tolerance, individual liberty and democracy.

In the final section of the museum, we find ourselves positioned differently again. This section consists of an amphitheatre where a continuous video is playing. The film gives a series of survivor accounts. People talk directly to camera about their experiences. Here again, it is obvious that the upbeat aspects of resistance, hope and the survival of human dignity despite all the odds are given great, perhaps undue, emphasis. But despite this, there are searing accounts of parting and loss. In watching these accounts, we assume the place of those to whom the survivors are talking. We no longer pretend that we too were victims, nor that we were the rescuing American forces. We are just people, those to whom these people are telling their stories. It is a much more personal encounter than those we have experienced in the museum so far. We sit, passive, listening. But that listening is in many ways harder than all the attempts at empathy that we have encountered. We have to recognise that these events happened, not only to real people – people with a history and a culture as the tower of photographs attempts to show – but that they happened to people's mothers, sisters, children. We also have to recognise that there was no escape, no way out: there was no fairy-tale ending. Even, perhaps especially, for those who survived. In this section of the museum what we have learnt so far in our progress along the route charted out for us by the museum's designers, even disrupted as it has perhaps been by the images we have encountered along the way, is now thrown into question

[167] Zelizer, *Remembering to Forget*, 227.

[168] This term is discussed in Daniella Kroslak's work on French involvement in Rwanda (Ph.D. thesis in progress, University of Wales Aberystwyth).

again. What understanding we thought we had gained is challenged by these quiet voices speaking directly to each of us of incredible horrors. In this account, what is *not* said can weigh equally alongside what *is* said. We are made into witnesses; the responsibility for the unmasterable tale is handed over to us.

We are not just liberators, then. Nor are we just victims. We are also witnesses. Let us think back to the photograph with which the museum displays began. The photograph we confronted at the start shows not just the corpses of victims. It shows American servicemen bearing witness to those corpses. The soldiers, and the reporters and photographers that accompanied them, did not only liberate the camps, they bore witness to the atrocities that had been committed in them. When we are positioned so as to identify with the liberators, we are also called upon, as we were in the Hall of Witness as we entered the building, to become witnesses ourselves.

In an important sense the excesses of the story that is told breach the constraints of the narrative museum. The way in which the processes of identification are disrupted also takes away any pleasure we might have felt on being given a comforting story. But as Silverman emphasises in his analysis of Hitchcock's *Psycho* the abrupt shifts that seem to thwart the process of identification do not actually work like that. The more intense the apparent disruption, 'the more intense the viewing subject's desire for narrative closure'.[169] And hence, in the context of the US Holocaust Memorial Museum, the more receptive the visitor might be to the museum's moralising, and in particular to the various forms of closure – the importance of resistance and rescue, the founding of the state of Israel – that are offered at the end of the exhibition. If the essence of what the survivor wants to say is that all possibility of endings – or of stories that make sense or of meaning – has been removed, then the museum in succeeding in its 'educational' aim has failed the survivor. It uses the 'Holocaust' story to elicit a desire for answers. It then provides those answers – in the form of American values.

The format of the USHMM has been very influential indeed and other museums and memorial sites are rushing to emulate the format in the hope of reaping the same success. The Imperial War Museum in London opened a new exhibit in 2000 that draws its inspiration from Washington, and indeed sought advice from Washington's creator, Jeshajahu Weinberg.[170] It shares with the USHMM the same rather dictatorial approach to its visitors, and the same notion of its narrative as a

[169] Silverman, 'Suture', 81.

[170] Suzanne Bardgett, 'The Holocaust Exhibition at the Imperial War Museum', Imperial War Museum, http://www.iwm.org.uk/lambeth/pdf files/hol bardgett.pdf, 2 February 2003. (Article appeared in *News of Museums of History* (2000), 3.)

Figure 26 Museum of Jewish Heritage, New York

route through space. The search for and the use of artefacts was a key part of what the designers saw as their role, mainly because of what artefacts could contribute to bringing the reality of the subject home rather than as a contribution to the refutation of denial. The tension between voyeurism and sanitisation was a feature here too. A difference is the use made of sound – videotaped survivor testimonies – throughout, as 'a vital substrand' that humanises the narrative.[171] It is a smaller-scale reiteration of Washington, constructed of the same elements.

There are other approaches. The New York Museum of Jewish Heritage is quite distinct, with its emphasis on setting the Nazi persecution of the Jews within the framework of the traditions and history of worldwide Jewish culture (Figure 26). It is set out in three sections: 'Jewish Life a Century Ago', 'The War against the Jews' and 'Jewish Renewal'. It is unambiguously about the Jews as 'a people' and the legacy of a 'vibrant Jewish community'. Compared with the US Holocaust Museum in Washington and the Holocaust exhibit in London it is deserted. Each visitor gets individual attention from the staff. The Washington model is being followed in Germany as well as in London. As we saw, Dachau Concentration Camp Memorial is in the process of redesigning its museum, and it is taking inspiration from the USHMM.

[171] Bardgett, 'The Holocaust Exhibition at the Imperial War Museum', 3.

Sites of memory become museums and the debate comes full circle with authenticity requiring narrative and narrative the authentic object.

Commercialisation, denial and truth

The proliferation of museums and monuments in the USA and Europe at the end of the twentieth century led to the charge that 'the Holocaust' had been commercialised: it had become a 'Shoah business' or a 'Holocaust industry'.[172] In addition to the opening of museums in Washington and other locations, several new films appeared: *Schindler's List* was distributed in 1994, and *Life is Beautiful* in 1999. In Britain, Nazi Germany formed such a prominent part of the school syllabus that historians complained that it was the only period of history children were familiar with. The accusation made by writers such as Peter Novick, Tim Cole and Norman Finkelstein is not just that the scale and appeal of museums makes them a commercial enterprise, but that what they tell represents an appropriation of the story of the Nazi persecution and genocide for specific political purposes and financial gain. 'The Holocaust' has been packaged and sold as a commodity. A simplified collective memory has been manufactured by different groups in the pursuit of their various political objectives. In the USA the Nazi persecutions – marginalised immediately after the war – have been brought to the centre of cultural life. But all the attention paid to the subject is not necessarily to be welcomed. Peter Novick makes two points: first, that the presentation of the Jew-as-victim is undesirable as a basis for Jewish identity, and second, that the appropriation of 'the Holocaust' as an American memory allows an evasion of historical responsibility.[173] Discourses of 'the Holocaust' from the Anne Frank story onwards have been cast in terms of redemption and heroism.[174] In the Israeli museum and memorial at Yad Vashem the Nazi persecutions are seen in terms of the heroism of the rescuers and the rebirth of the Jewish nation; in the US Holocaust Memorial Museum, the liberation of the camps provides the source of consolation. Tim Cole argues that we should at least acknowledge that the various accounts are partial and historically situated. How we remember and use the narrative of the Nazi period depends on where and when we are.

The labelling of recent forms of memory and memorialising as a 'Holocaust industry' is hugely controversial, especially among Jewish groups. There are even those who suggest that such criticism comes close to supporting the case of those who wish to contend that 'the Holocaust'

[172] Cole, *Images of the Holocaust*; Finkelstein, *The Holocaust Industry*.
[173] Novick, *The Holocaust and Collective Memory*. [174] Cole, *Images of the Holocaust*.

never took place, the Holocaust deniers. Critics point out that the opening of museums to commemorate the Nazi genocides coincided with a feeling that some such initiative was needed to counter the growing claims of the deniers, and as we have seen such a concern is behind the USHMM's focus on absolute historical accuracy. Deborah Lipstadt certainly claims that deniers are dealt a blow by the opening of the US Holocaust Museum and the filming of *Schindler's List*.[175] In her book *Denying the Holocaust: the Growing Assault on Truth and Memory* – the book which led to David Irving's libel action in the UK – Lipstadt sets the denial movement in the context of a continuum between cold war revisionists[176] and those who contest the uniqueness of 'the Holocaust'.[177] Others, like Tim Cole for example, contend that it is precisely the insistence on the uniqueness of Jewish suffering that motivates the deniers.

In 2000, the publication of Norman Finkelstein's book *The Holocaust Industry* coincided with the end of the Irving-Lipstadt libel trial in the UK. David Cesarani argued that the 'backlash against the so-called Holocaust industry collides disturbingly with the events [in the Irving-Lipstadt case] in the high court and their background'.[178] Those who, like Novick and Cole, contest the view that 'the Holocaust' be seen as a unique phenomenon, particular to the Jews, were accused by Cesarani of pursuing 'an assimilationist agenda' and he argued that there was 'a danger of an inadvertent collision between the man who sees himself as the victim of "a hidden international conspiracy" [Irving] and the critics of the Holocaust industry who depict it as a manipulative ramp for the benefit of one ethnic interest group and the State of Israel.'[179]

The Irving-Lipstadt case in the UK led to a fairly widespread discussion and debate. A typical popular presentation of the issues saw the case as a question of 'freedom of speech'. In this view, what was at issue was allowing historians (of whom David Irving was one) the freedom to discuss and debate the question of 'historical truth' in any manner they saw fit. This intellectual quest for truth was seen as being more important than any respect for the feeling of survivors of the Nazi persecutions, or at least as essential to giving due respect to those who suffered. If historians saw fit to doubt the veracity of existing versions of history, they should be free to voice those doubts, however extreme, even if they amounted to a denial that 'the Holocaust' had ever happened. To try to outlaw such statements, as was the case in Germany, was an affront to basic

[175] Deborah Lipstadt, *Denying the Holocaust: the Growing Assault on Truth and Memory* (London: Penguin, 1994), xvii.
[176] Lipstadt, *Denying the Holocaust*, 20–1. [177] *Ibid.*, 212–13.
[178] David Cesarani, 'History on trial', *The Guardian*, G2, London, 18 January 2000, 3.
[179] *Ibid.*

human freedoms. Holocaust deniers were just historians who had come to a particular conclusion; they should be respected and accorded the right to publish their conclusions.

There are two points that are interesting in relation to the way this discussion unfolded. First, what are the politics of framing the debate in terms of 'Holocaust denial' versus 'historical truth'? Second, what tends to get left out or silenced when the debate is presented in this form? What form of speech can never be 'free'? I would argue that as the meanings of the Holocaust become ever more contested, what can easily be written out or silenced is survivor accounts. These contain a different form of 'truth'. As such they are resistant to incorporation in narratives as we have seen. They *take a long time.* Claude Lanzmann's film *Shoah,* which is based around such accounts, lasts for nine hours. And they are difficult to watch. Holocaust deniers in particular write out survivor accounts: for David Irving, for example, all survivors are liars and their testimony must be disregarded.

The Irving-Lipstadt case was fairly widely represented as a trial to establish whether 'the Holocaust' took place or not. This was not how the trial judge saw it. According to Mr Justice Gray 'What was at issue – it cannot be said too often – was Irving's methodology and historiography, not what happened back in the 40s'.[180] This did not stop others claiming that it had precisely been concerned with deciding what happened: both Israeli commentators, who saw it as a clear vindication of the Jewish account of the Holocaust,[181] and Irving supporters, who were pleased that what they saw as the Jewish lobby had been forced to produce evidence.[182] The case was also widely presented as the trial of David Irving but, it was not, of course. As a libel case it was in fact initiated by Irving: Lipstadt was the one who was at risk of being silenced, not Irving. He claimed that the publication of Lipstadt's book had destroyed his reputation as a serious historian. Lipstadt and her publisher Penguin Books' defence was that of justification. They set out to prove that their assertions that Irving had distorted historical evidence, and that he was a Hitler partisan, a neo-Nazi and a Holocaust denier were justified. They succeeded, winning a notably forthright judgement.

However, where victory in the end lay is not certain. One thing that is clear is that Irving, who began the case, had sought publicity throughout. He ran a website with daily transcripts alongside appeals for cash. Lipstadt on the other hand refused to enter into a debate with Irving. It was not

[180] Clare Dyer, 'Judging history', *The Guardian*, G2, London, 17 April 2000, 10.
[181] *Jewish Chronicle*, 14 April, quoted in *The Guardian*, London, The Editor, 14 April 2000, 4.
[182] http://www2.prestel.co.uk/littleton/irving-v-lipstadt.htm, 1 May 2000, no longer active.

necessary for her to give evidence in the case, and she chose not to. Like other writers on Holocaust denial before,[183] she had refused to appear with deniers on television on the basis that this would allow them to present themselves as a legitimate 'other side'. She would argue, like a previous French writer on Holocaust denial, 'one can and should enter into discussion *concerning* the [deniers]; one can analyse their texts as one might the anatomy of a lie; one can and should analyse their specific place in the configuration of ideologies.... But one should not enter into debate *with* [them]'.[184] This would be to give their challenge unwarranted legitimacy.

What happened in the Irving case? Was a debate engaged? Strictly speaking, no. What happened was that evidence from which Irving drew certain conclusions was examined in the light of those conclusions. In most of the critical cases his conclusions were shown to be distortions of the evidence. However, this led to the discussion of issues in a certain manner. For example, in a debate over the existence of gas chambers at Auschwitz, there was a lengthy exchange in court concerning how much fuel – how many kilograms of coke – were necessary to burn a human corpse, and how many tonnes millions of human corpses would weigh. This would depend, of course, on whether the prisoners had been held in Auschwitz for a time before they died or not. It turned out that the ovens were designed in such a way as to require a mixture of well-fed and emaciated corpses.

People like Irving win *not* by proving their case – in many senses that is not important to them – but by making it a question of evidence or factual 'truth'. They win by insisting that we fight *on this ground*. But the question is not one of this kind of simplistic truth but one of ethics, politics and historical analysis. By making it a question of truth, a dangerous polarisation of debate occurs: we seem to be witnessing a contest between supporters of the Israeli state and their neo-fascist opponents.[185] What gets lost is the possibility of nuanced scholarly discussion, where the ambiguity of evidence and the necessity of interpretation and re-interpretation is recognised. By making it a question of truth it is technologised. It becomes an issue of who has the most accurate reading of the documents, who looked at which document, how exactly the crematoria worked, and so forth. Questions of responsibility and trauma disappear. What is at stake is not whether we should accept or deny 'the truth' of

[183] Pierre Vidal-Naquet, *Assassins of Memory: Essays on the Denial of the Holocaust*, trans. Jeffrey Mehlman (New York: Columbia University Press, 1992).
[184] Vidal-Naquet, *Assassins of Memory*, xxiv.
[185] D. D. Guttenplan, 'Why history matters', *The Guardian Saturday Review*, London, 15 April 2000, 1–2.

'the Holocaust', as if 'truth' or 'the Holocaust' were monolithic, but how a contest over that truth can betray what we owe to different ways of remembering.

The reduction of suffering and trauma to a question of truth silences the voices of survivors, as does the appropriation of their truth to a discursive contest in the service of power relations. They have something important to say, something that is almost impossible to communicate, and we should listen. In the camps, there was no room for anything other than indifference towards the violence and suffering of fellow inmates; we risk demonstrating exactly that same technologised indifference again in our refusal to listen. As Geoffrey Hartman reminds us, 'questions arise... about the limits of representation: questions less about whether the extreme event can be represented than whether truth is served by our refusal to set limits to representation'.[186] Here, of course, he is referring to truth of a different order.

This different truth is reflected in the conclusion of the film *Martin*, directed by Ra'anan Alexandrowicz.[187] This film is an astute examination of what happens when our need to know, our desire for certainty, collides with the impossibility of knowing. Martin Zaidenstadt, the subject of the film, is a mysterious figure. A self-styled survivor of the Dachau concentration camp, he still lives in the town nearby. He spends each day as an unpaid and unofficial guide, accosting visitors outside the crematoria buildings with his own account of what happened in the camp. He has his photograph taken with those he meets, and asks them to send him copies. He gives them copies of his business card, and asks for a contribution to the printing costs. Many visitors are clearly very moved by this encounter with a real survivor; others don't know what to make of it. The film traces two visitors who decide to pursue Martin, to find out more about him and his story. The two are so intrigued by their first meeting that they return the following day determined to track him down again and to try to get more information from him.

Martin's main concern seems to be to set right what he claims are certain misrepresentations at the memorial site, particularly the area around the old crematorium. First and foremost, he insists that the gas chamber at Dachau was in fact used, although the notices in the chamber itself say 'Gas chamber disguised as a "shower room" – never used as a gas chamber'. He also claims that a tree in the grounds against which people were tortured has been removed. He points out the firing range where prisoners were shot, now concealed by a screen of trees. He takes visitors

[186] Hartman, *Longest Shadow*, 151.
[187] *Martin*, directed by Ra'anan Alexandrowicz, Israel, 1999.

behind the trees to show them the bullet holes in the wall. In the film the two visitors, intrigued but not convinced, are determined to track down the truth. They follow Martin home. Eventually, he warms to their interest. He shows them photographs that back up his claim to be a survivor and he tells them tales of his previous life. But the two never get a satisfactory answer to their main question: was the gas chamber used? Did Martin hear the screams of those being gassed, as he claims? Or was the chamber constructed but never functional as the camp authorities claim? Their searches extend to the archives in Jerusalem, where they are told that survivor testimony is notoriously unreliable. At Dachau they question the camp staff, who say they know Martin well but then cannot find his name in the list of camp inmates. The film ends with the whole story surrounded by doubt and uncertainty. If Martin the survivor is not to be believed, whom can we trust to be telling 'the truth'? Perhaps we have to be content with something less. Perhaps it is not possible to be certain, even about such a basic piece of information as whether the gas chamber at Dachau was ever used or not.

Timothy Ryback's book *The Last Survivor: in Search of Martin Zaidenstadt*[188] does not solve the question, although it adds another layer of possibility. Ryback, like the two characters in the film, is fascinated by Martin Zaidenstadt. He spends two years and several trips to Dachau trying to get to know Martin and to establish the veracity of what he is saying and his status as a survivor. In the end, his search too is inconclusive. He does, however, elicit from Martin the story of what happened immediately after the liberation of Dachau. Martin travelled back to Poland in search of his family. He discovered that they, along with the rest of the Jewish population of the village of Jedwabne, had been herded into a barn that was then set on fire. He visits the site, and the graveyard where some of the victims' remains were buried. This is the story Martin doesn't want to tell, the account that it takes two years to get out of him. Everyday he tells the tale of how he heard the screams of those gassed in Dachau to anyone and everyone who will listen. The story of what happened to his own family is never recounted. It is what is absent: the silence, the void. The story he does tell functions perhaps in some way to conceal the tale he cannot tell. The screams he maybe didn't hear at Dachau stand in for the screams he didn't hear at Jedwabne: the screams of his wife and child.

[188] Timothy W. Ryback, *The Last Survivor: in Search of Martin Zaidenstadt* (New York: Pantheon, 1999).

Conclusion

In no sense is this story a picture of resolution. The difficulties that beset the practices of memory in all the cases that we have examined indicate not only the difficulty of representing the horrors involved in genocides and famines, but the ease through which processes of memory become recipes for forgetting. Practices of memory also indicate the extent to which we are still embroiled in the very questions and dilemmas that led to the atrocities we commemorate. Narratives seem unable to get away from rhetorics of state or nation, and they fail to escape the racialisation upon which the genocides, enslavements and famines were themselves based.

An important question to consider is why remembering 'the Holocaust' became so important towards the end of the twentieth century and the beginning of the twenty-first. Why did the British government inaugurate a Holocaust Memorial Day some fifty-six years after the event it was to commemorate? Why the intense debates in Germany over the question of memorials? It is not just that a period of time has elapsed and that we are now able to come to terms with what happened. As in the case of the Irish famine, the role of memory can be directly linked with what else is going on in the political arena. In the Irish case, as we saw, the beginning of the peace process coincided with the first major commemorations of the famine, on its 150th anniversary. In the period with which we are concerned, alongside the increased concern with 'Holocaust commemoration', a new form of sovereign power, one that operates alongside the globalisation of finance, emerged: globalised humanitarian power. I shall argue in the next chapter that remembering 'the Holocaust' is not a way of ensuring that genocides do not happen, but of ensuring that, as in Kosovo, they do. In the 1990s we find governments promoting narratives of memory. Not just narratives glorifying heroism in war (though the Israeli narrative of the Holocaust is very similar to these). In the earlier commemorations, memorials at concentration camp sites, as we have seen, reflected nationalistic narratives too. In the new museums and on the new anniversaries, the narrative is different: it is one of rescue. It is perhaps no accident that the day chosen as Holocaust Memorial Day in Britain was a day of liberation – the liberation of Auschwitz by Russian troops. After September 11, as we have seen, there was yet another twist: governments using narratives of memory not after a war, to glorify the losses that sovereign power had produced, but before a war, to claim lives lost as a justification for a militarised response. The prevalence of memorialisation and the awareness of past horrors at the turn of the last century made it easy perhaps for humanitarian war to become the war against terror. Practices of memorialisation insisting on bearing witness to past traumas were co-opted and used as a legitimation for more trauma.

The focus on authenticity, like the focus on truth, is a search for a chimera that distracts from the need to face the horror. Like the word 'frightful', the search for certainty in the form of authenticity or truth can be a shield against uncomfortable questions. As Santayana reminds us, in a quotation that forms the motto of the Imperial War Museum Holocaust Exhibition in London, 'those who cannot remember the past are condemned to repeat it'.[189] However, we need to pay attention to the sort of remembering he is calling for. It is not a remembering of *history*, the narrative that we tell ourselves about the past, but a remembering of the *past*. To explore what the difference might be, consider the example of Leonard in the film *Memento*.[190] Leonard has what he calls 'a condition'. Since he and his wife were attacked in their home, he can no longer make new memories. He forgets what he is doing after about ten minutes. He is not suffering from amnesia – he can still remember exactly who he is and how to do even complex tasks, but he can't remember someone he met a few minutes earlier. In order to cope, to track down his wife's killer and exact his revenge, Leonard perfects a system of habit and note taking. He photographs his car, his motel, and important people in his life with a Polaroid camera. He writes their name and phone number on the front of the photos. On the back, he writes his decisions. He writes facts about the killer he is looking for on index cards and then later tattoos the facts on his body. His friend Teddy urges caution, saying 'You can't trust a man's life to your little notes and pictures... your notes could be unreliable'. Leonard responds: 'Memory's unreliable. Memory's not perfect. It's not even that good. Ask the police. Eyewitness testimony is unreliable.... [The police] collect facts, they make notes and they draw conclusions. Facts, not memories. That's how you investigate.'

The film begins at the end and moves step-wise backwards through time. We see a few minutes of action, and then the previous few minutes up to where we started before, and so on. As the film progresses backwards in this way we slowly realise that Leonard is caught in a trap. He is compelled to repeat the killing of his wife's murderer, each time with a new victim. He cannot remember the last act of revenge. We think he is being manipulated, and try to work out who is behind it, who is controlling him. However, it turns out that he is manipulating himself. Leonard's

[189] G. Santayana, *Life of Reason* (New York, 1922).
[190] *Memento*, produced by Suzanne Todd and Jennifer Todd, directed by Christopher Nolan, Newmarket, 2000.

past is much more tragic than the story he tells. He and his wife were not simply victims of an attack, and he is implicated in his wife's suffering. He chooses to lie to himself – by writing false notes on photographs, for example – to maintain the story of heroism and revenge that has enabled him to go on living. In other words, *he* is the one who is driving himself around in endless cycles of violence. It gives him a sense of purpose and a reason for living, and it is the only way to avoid facing the traumatic reality of what happened.

This is a parable for the importance of traumatic memory in political life. At present we use the image of 'the Holocaust' to justify our treatment of Iraq or Serbia. We see ourselves as heroic figures, saving strangers, fighting terror.[191] An alternative would be to try to remember the Nazi mass murders, not as history, not as part of some neatly scripted 'Holocaust' narrative, but in all the ambiguity and difficulty of the accounts of those survivors brave enough to give us their stories. We should not seek for 'the truth' or 'the facts' since so often these are given to us as heroic narratives or written as convenient lies. In what happened, there are no neat distinctions between victims and perpetrators, between Jews and Germans, between survivors and their tormentors. If we were to remember this, however, we might not be able to go on with life as it is: a life and a politics which rely on distinctions that echo those of the past – between economic migrants and refugees, between Hutu and Tutsi, between humanitarian intervention and war, between us and them. As Slavoj Žižek argues, we cannot forget the 'Holocaust' because we are still implicated in it. The reason for

> This impossibility of representing the Holocaust is not simply that it is 'too traumatic', but rather, that we, observing subjects, are still involved in it, are still part of the process which generated it (we need only recall a scene from Shoah in which Polish peasants from a village near the concentration camp, interviewed now, in our present time, continue to find Jews 'strange', that is, repeat the very logic that brought the Holocaust about . . .)[192]

Remembering what happened, in all its traumatic reality, is the only way to escape the cycle of violence that our present reliance on neat and heroic stories of the past traps us in. It is not enough to arm ourselves with the word 'frightful' and create a narrative of 'the Holocaust' that conceals its traumatic nature. We have to attend to the details, however much we would rather put them to one side: 'The point is not simply to "tell the entire truth about it", but, above all, to confront the way we ourselves, by means of our subjective position of enunciation, are always-already

[191] Nicholas Wheeler, *Saving Strangers* (Oxford University Press, 2000).
[192] Slavoj Žižek, *The Plague of Fantasies* (London: Verso, 1997), 215.

involved, engaged in it.'[193] We cannot assume a neutral view, because we are not in a neutral position, we are within, not outside, the trauma.

This is what leads to the difficulty witnesses face, as we saw at the start of the chapter. We saw how those recently liberated in Dachau discovered a gulf opening up between what they had to say and the words at their disposal. But this is not just a question of the inexpressibility of trauma. It has to be seen alongside the imperative that survivors feel to speak. They have something to say, and it is the thought of bearing witness that has kept them alive. They face a redoubled trauma when it becomes clear that the trauma cannot be shared, because it cannot be expressed in the symbolic structures of language – not because it is outside language, 'but precisely because it is inherent to it, its internal limit'. The trauma cannot be expressed, 'it can only be *shown*, in a negative gesture, as the inherent failure of symbolisation'.[194] Such a showing, if it succeeds where expression failed, can itself produce something approaching trauma in those who in their turn witness the showing. In Claude Lanzmann's *Shoah*, testimony itself forms the exclusive content of the film.[195] According to Shoshana Felman, 'this film revives the holocaust with such a power... that it radically displaces and shakes up not only any common notion we might have entertained about it, but our very vision of reality as such, our very sense of what the world, culture, history and our life within it are all about'. We need to pay attention to the accounts of survivors of Levi's grey zone if we are to do justice to the lessons of the Nazi period.

In the next chapter I explore more fully the question of what we call testimony and what it means to bear witness.

[193] Žižek, *Plague of Fantasies*, 215.
[194] *Ibid.*, 217.
[195] Shoshana Felman, 'The return of the voice: Claude Lanzmann's *Shoah*', in *Testimony: Crises of Witnessing in Literature, Psychoanalysis and History*, ed. Shoshana Felman and Dori Laub (London: Routledge, 1992), 204–83; 205.

5 Testimony and sovereign power after Auschwitz: Holocaust witness and Kosovo refugees

> Since Auschwitz all men, Jews (and) non-Jews, die differently: they do not really die; they survive death, because what took place – back there – without taking place, death in Auschwitz, was worse than death.[1]
>
> – Sarah Kofman

In the face of the horror of the Nazi concentration camps, there is a temptation to retreat into the comfort of easy solutions to the question of memory. There are several ways of doing this, as we saw in the last chapter. One is to represent what happened in a linear narrative – the historical account of the Holocaust. Museums like the US Holocaust Memorial Museum in Washington or exhibits like that at the Imperial War Museum in London attempt to present such a narrative: a coherent story that promotes a clear moral message. They focus on historical accuracy, displaying authentic artefacts to back up their claims to irrefutability. Historical research in its search for the truth about the events of the National Socialist persecutions can appear obsessed with factual detail, evidence and proof, particularly in the face of those who would deny that anything called 'the Holocaust' ever took place. There is a reassuring assumption that a historical narrative based on firm evidence can lead to a form of closure, a final solution to outstanding questions.

Such approaches seek to understand and explain what happened. Claude Lanzmann argues that 'there is an absolute obscenity in the very project of understanding', which is revealed if we formulate the historians' question 'in simplistic terms – Why have the Jews been killed?'[2] It is

[1] Sarah Kofman, *Smothered Words*, trans. Madeleine Dobie (Evanston, Illinois: Northwestern University Press, 1998), 9. Kofman quotes Theodor Adorno: 'the administrative murder of millions made of death a thing one had never yet to fear in just this fashion.... The last, the poorest possession left to the individual is expropriated. That in the concentration camps it was no longer the individual who died but a specimen – this is a fact bound to affect the dying of those who escaped the administrative measure' (*Negative Dialectics*, 371, quoted in Kofman, *Smothered Words*, 76).

[2] Quoted in Claude Lanzmann, 'The obscenity of understanding: an evening with Claude Lanzmann', in *Trauma: Explorations in Memory*, ed. Cathy Caruth (Baltimore: The Johns Hopkins University Press, 1995), 200–20; 204.

necessary to cultivate a certain 'refusal of understanding' if we are to be able to look at what happened without yielding to the temptation to produce an abstraction in its place. In the making of the film *Shoah*, Lanzmann used 'this blindness' as 'the vital condition of creation'. He refused to accept that the testimony he elicited in the film could lead to an understanding of why the events concerned happened. There is he argues 'a gap, an abyss' between the background – the previous events – and the killings, such that to seek to understand, to generate 'harmoniously... the destruction of six million people', is an obscenity.[3] He refused the response 'I understand'. But he is by no means recommending that this refusal of understanding, this blindness, should stand in the way of an attempt to see. On the contrary, in a totally different way he argues that 'blindness has to be understood here as the purest mode of looking, of the gaze, the only way to not turn away from a reality which is literally blinding'.[4]

Museums and memorial sites combine their quest for truth with a duty of remembrance, which can be seen as a second attempt to bring a form of closure. What is remembered is a story of humanity unbowed in the face of untold suffering, a story of redemption, heroism and rescue. These elements are present in an exaggerated form in museum exhibits devoted to 'rescuers', 'resistance', and the continuation of the Jewish community after persecution or the foundation of the state of Israel. In memorial halls we are enjoined to bear witness and to remember, but in the imaginary safety of a world where what happened is in the past and where our actions can guarantee the 'never again'. We have a label for what happened: we call it 'the Holocaust'. We can talk about it as if we knew what it was. In these ways we are shielded from the horror.

A third approach, and one which still involves shielding ourselves from the reality of what happened, is when we acknowledge the event as unimaginable and unsayable. The result of this is that we are excused from further enquiry. As we have seen, Robert Antelme noted that 'most consciences are satisfied quickly enough, and need only a few words in order to reach a definitive opinion of the unknowable.... *Unimaginable*: a word that doesn't divide, doesn't restrict. The most convenient word. When you walk around with this word as your shield, this word for emptiness, your step becomes better assured, more resolute, your conscience pulls itself together.'[5] The soldiers who entered Dachau to liberate the concentration camp were content with the verdict 'frightful'. But it was

[3] Lanzmann, 'The obscenity of understanding', 206. [4] *Ibid.*, 204.

[5] Robert Antelme, *The Human Race*, trans. Jeffrey Haight and Annie Mahler (Evanston, Illinois: The Marlboro Press/Northwestern, 1992), 289–90.

not only they who had problems. Even the survivors, who 'wanted to speak, to be heard' and to describe their experience, even they saw that there was 'a gap opening up between the words' at their disposal and that experience. As Antelme describes it, 'even to us, what we had to tell would start to seem *unimaginable*'.[6] However, significantly, he stresses that his conclusion is not to be taken as an excuse for silence, but as a call for a resumption of the effort.

For Sarah Kofman 'about Auschwitz and after Auschwitz no story is possible, if by a story one means: to tell a story of events which makes sense'.[7] On the other hand she insists with Antelme that 'there remains, nonetheless, a duty to speak, to speak endlessly for those who could not speak... To speak in order to bear witness. But how? How can testimony escape the idyllic law of the story?'[8] Again there is a chasm between the duty to speak and the impossibility of speech:

> How can one speak of that before which all possibility of speech ceases?... To speak: it is necessary – *without (the) power*: without allowing language, too powerful, sovereign, to master the most aporetic situation, absolute powerlessness and very distress, to enclose it in the clarity and happiness of daylight. And how can one not speak of it, when the wish of all those who returned... has been to tell, to tell endlessly, as if only an 'infinite conversation' could match the infinite privation?[9]

This aporia between speaking and not speaking, between the compulsion to bear witness and the impossibility of doing so, is for Giorgio Agamben the very structure of testimony. Survivors of the camps bore witness to something it was impossible to bear witness to.[10] We should listen to this gap. For survivors, what happened in the camps was the only true thing. The facts of their persecution are so real, nothing is truer. But at the same time, what happened in the camps is unimaginable. It is a reality that exceeds facts. This aporia of historical knowledge, between facts and verification, on the one hand, and truth and comprehension, on the other, is the lacuna that forms the very structure of testimony.[11]

In this chapter I examine Agamben's analysis of Auschwitz. His work draws on Primo Levi to argue that testimony arises in the gap between the human and the inhuman produced in the camp. It also examines more broadly the role of the camp in the biopolitics of the west. This sets out the politics at stake, and reveals testimony to be one of a number

[6] Antelme, *The Human Race*, 3. [7] Kofman, *Smothered Words*, 14.
[8] *Ibid.*, 36. [9] *Ibid.*, 9–10.
[10] Giorgio Agamben, *Remnants of Auschwitz: the Witness and the Archive*, trans. Daniel Heller-Roazen (New York: Zone Books, 1999), 13.
[11] Agamben, *Remnants of Auschwitz*, 12.

of forms of resistance that involve 'traversing the fantasy' or assuming 'bare life'.[12] However, the potential of testimony to resist is not often realised in contemporary practices. Survivor testimony is appropriated and co-opted in projects of state-building or money-making. Moreover, it is possible to argue that in contemporary practices of sovereign power we find the subversive power of testimony dissolved from the start. In the second part of the chapter, I discuss the Nato intervention in Kosovo in 1999. In this case, we can see the camp as central to the production of sovereignty – here the sovereignty not of the state but of an international body. The establishment of the camp as a site of emergency helps Nato to present itself as a sovereign power. Importantly, we find testimony incorporated in sovereign power, and resistance defused, by the way in which the gathering of testimony for future war crimes tribunals was central to the action from the beginning.

Biopolitics of the camp

Although some may seek an easy answer to the memory of horrific events, many survivors have a compulsion to bear witness. They have to offer atonement for their survival. To their audience they are both frightful and compelling. Like Coleridge's ancient mariner who fixes us with his glittering eye and forces us to hear his tale of horror,[13] survivors seize the attention of their unwilling listeners.[14] Levi, for instance, summons those who live safe in their warm houses to consider his words or face his curse.[15] And the listeners in their turn become witnesses to anguish. They cannot choose but hear – and yet, of course, they cannot fully understand. The misery that passes down the generations in this way is an uncomprehending, visceral grief.[16]

For survivors of the camps the obligation to bear witness is just one of the ways in which there is no return to past worlds. For Levi there

[12] 'Traversing the fantasy' is used here in Slavoj Žižek's sense (see for example Slavoj Žižek, *Tarrying with the Negative: Kant, Hegel and the Critique of Ideology* (Durham, North Carolina: Duke University Press, 1993); and Slavoj Žižek, *The Sublime Object of Ideology* (London: Verso, 1989)) and 'bare life' or naked life is a term used by Agamben which will be discussed below.

[13] Samuel Taylor Coleridge, *The Rime of the Ancient Mariner*, II, 582–5.

[14] The parallel is suggested by Primo Levi's use of this verse from Coleridge as an epigraph to *The Drowned and the Saved*, trans. Raymond Rosenthal (London: Abacus, 1989), v.

[15] Primo Levi, *If This is a Man and The Truce*, trans. Stuart Woolf (London: Abacus, 1987), 17.

[16] This is captured in Anne Michaels' *Fugitive Pieces* (New York: Vintage, 1998), where Ben is an example of the response of the second generation. It is not until the end of the novel that Ben is able to tell us: 'I know the elation of ordinary sorrow. At last my unhappiness is my own.' (*Fugitive Pieces*, 292.)

were others too. Liberation did not bring rejoicing but rather a 'vague discomfort... not precisely shame'.[17] In part there was the humiliation of having lived an inhuman existence: in the camp overwhelming hunger, fatigue, cold and fear supplanted any possibility of reflection or a more specifically human emotion. Further, there was remorse at having survived arbitrarily, in someone else's place. More than this though, and perhaps more unexpected, was the shame of survivors at the misdeeds of others and at the way those actions and the survivors' own involvement in them represented a permanent change in the conditions of possibility of human interaction. The survivors 'sensed that what had happened around them in their presence, and in them, was irrevocable. It would never again be able to be cleansed.'[18]

For Agamben too the camps are emblematic of a point of no return. For him, they symbolise the moment after which it is no longer possible to sustain the separation between the biological body and politically qualified life, a separation seemingly in place since Aristotle:

> There is no return from the camps to classical politics. In the camps, city and house became indistinguishable, and the possibility of differentiating between our biological body and our political body – between what is incommunicable and mute and what is communicable and sayable – was taken from us forever.[19]

According to Agamben's account in *Homo Sacer*, the first move of classical western politics was the separation of the biological and the political. The natural life of *zoe*, understood as the simple fact of living common to all living beings, was excluded from the *polis* and confined to the *oikos* or domestic sphere. The life of the *polis*, for the Greeks, was *bios*, a form of living particular to an individual or group. The simple natural life of *zoe* was separated from the politically qualified life that was part of the *polis*. Of course, in the process the female figure becomes invisible.[20] As feminist political theorists have long argued, from the Greeks onwards the political has operated through the inclusion by exclusion of the female.[21] Women are invisible in international politics too.[22] Crucial to both exclusions is the way the domestic is excluded from the political or the international. There is disagreement on the implications. Jean Elshtain

[17] Levi, *The Drowned and the Saved*, 54. [18] *Ibid.*, 66.

[19] Giorgio Agamben, *Homo Sacer: Sovereign Power and Bare Life*, trans. Daniel Heller-Roazen (Stanford University Press, 1998), 188.

[20] In Agamben's account this invisibility remains. The figure of bare life is continually referenced as male. I return to this point in the conclusion.

[21] Jean Bethke Elshtain, *Public Man, Private Woman: Women in Social and Political Thought*, 2nd edn (Princeton University Press, 1993).

[22] Cynthia Enloe, *Bananas, Beaches and Bases: Making Feminist Sense of International Politics* (Berkeley: University of California Press, 1990).

wants us to resist the extension of the political to the domestic or family realm since she regards that realm as emblematic of values more conducive to the feminine. Cynthia Enloe argues that we should regard the personal as international. Indeed Enloe stresses the impossibility of making the distinction. However, both agree on the importance to western sovereign order of the dichotomies of female and male, the *oikos* and the *polis*, domestic politics and the international, inside and outside.[23]

Like the feminists, Agamben argues that the separation of *zoe* and *bios* is a practice of inclusion by exclusion that is constitutive of sovereignty in the modern western sense from the beginning.[24] In other words, the exclusion of *zoe* from the *polis* is at the same time an inclusion. It is not just with the rise of the modern state, as Michel Foucault would have us believe, that *zoe* is included in state power. Foucault argues that at the beginning of the modern era natural life comes to be included more and more in the mechanisms and calculations of state power. At this point politics becomes biopolitics and whereas for Aristotle man was a living animal with a capacity for political existence, modern man becomes 'an animal whose politics calls his existence as a living being into question'.[25] Modernity for Foucault is the point at which the species and the individual as a simple living body become what are at stake in a society's political strategies. At one and the same time it becomes possible both to protect life and to organise a holocaust. However, as we have seen, according to Agamben this picture needs to be corrected and Foucault's analysis of power in modernity completed. Sovereign power in the west *from the start* is constituted by the exclusion of natural life. However, the way in which natural life is excluded from political life ensures its inclusion in it. Natural life or *zoe* is there as that which is excluded, the outlaw that haunts the sovereign order: it is thus included by the very process of exclusion.

More than this inclusion by exclusion, sovereign power in the west is constituted by its ability to suspend itself in a state of exception or ban: 'the originary relation of law to life is not application but abandonment'.[26] The paradox of sovereignty is that the sovereign is at the same time inside and outside the sovereign order: the sovereign can suspend the law. What defines the rule of law is the state of exception when law is suspended.

[23] For a discussion of these separations see R. B. J. Walker, *Inside/Outside: International Relations as Political Theory* (Cambridge University Press, 1993).

[24] As defined by Carl Schmitt, *Political Theology: Four Chapters on the Concept of Sovereignty*, trans. George Schwab (Cambridge, Massachusetts: MIT Press, 1985).

[25] Michel Foucault, *History of Sexuality. Volume 1: an Introduction*, trans. Robert Hurley (Harmondsworth: Penguin, 1978), 3.

[26] Agamben, *Homo Sacer*, 29.

The very space in which juridical order can have validity is created and defined through the sovereign exception. However, the exception that defines the structure of sovereignty is more complex than the inclusion of what is outside by the very fact that it is placed outside or forbidden.[27] It is not just a question of creating a distinction between inside and outside. It is the tracing of a threshold between the two, a location where inside and outside enter into a *zone of indistinction. It is this state of exception or zone of indistinction between inside and outside that makes the modern juridical order of the west possible.*

The camp is exemplary as a location of a zone of indistinction. Although, in general, the camp is set up precisely as part of a state of emergency or martial law, under Nazi rule this becomes not so much a state of exception, in the sense of an external and provisional state of danger, as a means of establishing the Nazi state itself. The camp is 'the space opened up when the state of exception begins to become the rule'.[28] In the camp, the distinction between the rule of law and chaos disappears: decisions about life and death are entirely arbitrary and everything is possible. A zone of indistinction appears between outside and inside, exception and rule, licit and illicit. What happened in the twentieth century in the west, and paradigmatically since the advent of the camp, was that the space of the state of exception transgressed its boundaries and started to coincide with the normal order. The zone of indistinction expanded from a space of exclusion within the normal order to take over that order entirely.

In the concentration camp, inhabitants are stripped of every political status and the arbitrary power of the camp attendants confronts nothing but what Agamben calls bare life, or *homo sacer* (sacred man), the *Muselmann*: a creature who can be killed but not sacrificed.[29] This figure, according to Agamben's account an essential figure in modern politics, is constituted by and constitutive of sovereign power. *Homo sacer* is produced by the sovereign ban and is subject to two exceptions: he is excluded from human law (killing him does not count as homicide) and he is excluded from divine law (killing him is not a ritual killing and does not count as sacrilege). He is set outside human jurisdiction without being brought into the realm of divine law. This double exclusion, of course, also counts as a double inclusion: '*homo sacer* belongs to God in the form of unsacrificability and is included in the community in the form of being able to be killed'.[30] This exposes *homo sacer* to a new kind of human

[27] Which would correspond in a general way to the Derridean constitutive outside. (Henry Staten, *Wittgenstein and Derrida* (Oxford: Basil Blackwell, 1984).)
[28] Agamben, *Homo Sacer*, 168–9.
[29] This creature appears throughout Agamben's writing as male.
[30] Agamben, *Homo Sacer*, 82.

violence such as is found in the camp and constitutes the political as the double exception: the exclusion of both the sacred and the profane.

At the threshold of the modern era then, the realm of bare life begins to coincide with the political, and inclusion and exclusion, outside and inside, *bios* and *zoe*, right and left, enter into a zone of indistinction. In these zones of indistinction, bare life or *homo sacer* becomes both the subject and the object of the political order: it is both the place for the organisation of state power, in the forms of discipline and objectification described by Foucault, and the place for emancipation from it, through the birth of modern democracy and the demand for human rights.

This move of biological life to the centre of the political scene in the west leads to a transformation of the political realm itself, one that effectively constitutes its depoliticisation. That depoliticisation takes place side by side with the politicisation of bare life. Bare life is politicised and political life disappears. This irony is explained by the way the link forged in modernity between politics and bare life, a link that underpins ideologies from the right and the left, has been ignored. As Agamben says, 'if politics today seems to be passing through a lasting eclipse, this is because politics has failed to reckon with this foundational event of modernity.... Only a reflection that...interrogates the link between bare life and politics...will be able to bring the political out of its concealment.'[31] Any attempt to rethink the political space of the west must begin with an awareness of the impossibility of the classical distinction between private life and political existence, and examine the zones of indistinction into which the oppositions that produced modern politics in the west – inside/outside, right/left, public/private – have dissolved. Agamben proposes that 'it is on the basis of these uncertain and nameless terrains, these difficult zones of indistinction, that the ways and forms of a new politics must be thought'.[32] In the zone of indistinction, a claim to a politically qualified life can no longer be effective as such.

If the state of exception or ban that formed the original political relation has transgressed its boundaries in space and time and extended beyond the camp or the emergency as Agamben argues, a new way of thinking the political is called for. In global politics at the end of the twentieth century this appearance of an infinite extension of a zone of indistinction was symptomatic too of the production of a new order of sovereign power, one in which the west as a whole claimed sovereignty. This is what was happening in the politics of emergency in areas and events such as Kosovo. The appearance of the camp as a zone of indistinction was a crucial signal of the operation of sovereign power in these instances.

[31] *Ibid.*, 4. [32] *Ibid.*, 187.

The camp and the witness

In the Nazi concentration camp we find the features that Agamben identifies as part of the juridico-political structure of the camp exemplified. First, the camp is part not of criminal law but of a state of emergency or martial law. In Nazi Germany, normal law – and rights – are suspended. The camp is the location where the state of emergency gains a more permanent spatial setting, though still one that remains outside normal rule. Second, the space of exception began to become the rule. The camps in Germany became part of a permanent state of affairs. Finally, in the camps law is suspended and everything is possible: 'Fact and law are completely confused'.[33] The camps' inhabitants are transformed into *Muselmänner* – bare life. This is how the arbitrariness of the decisions made by camp guards and officials between life and death is to be understood:

> The camp is the space of this absolute impossibility of deciding between fact and law, rule and application, exception and rule, which nevertheless incessantly decides between them. [It] consists in the materialisation of the state of exception and the creation of a space in which bare life and the juridical rule enter into a threshold of indistinction . . . a space in which normal order is de facto suspended and in which whether or not atrocities are committed depends not on law but on the civility and ethical sense of the police who temporarily act as sovereign.[34]

In Levi's accounts of the concentration camp we find a vivid picture of bare life, arbitrary decision and the knowledge that everything is possible. Stripped of citizenship beforehand if they were categorised as Jewish, inmates arriving in the camp encountered a grey zone, where not only were they subject to cold, hunger and fear, but much more:

> The world into which one was precipitated was indecipherable: it did not conform to any model, the enemy was all around but also inside, the 'we' lost its limits, the contenders were not two, one could not discern a single frontier but rather many confused, perhaps innumerable frontiers, which stretched between each of us. One entered hoping at least for the solidarity of one's companions in misfortune, but the hoped-for allies, except in special cases, were not there; there were instead a thousand sealed-off monads, and in between them a desperate hidden and continuous struggle. This brusque revelation . . . was so harsh as to cause the immediate collapse of one's capacity to resist.[35]

The ritual of entry was part of this collapse: 'kicks and punches right away, often in the face; an orgy of orders screamed with true or simulated rage; complete nakedness after being stripped; the shaving off of all one's

[33] *Ibid.*, 170. [34] *Ibid.*, 173–4. [35] Levi, *The Drowned and the Saved*, 23–4.

hair; the fitting out in rags'.[36] But much more important in Levi's account is the grey zone inhabited by the prisoner-collaborators, and the way in which any distinction between victim and perpetrator is blurred: 'It is naïve, absurd and historically false to believe that an infernal system such as National Socialism was, sanctifies its victims: on the contrary, it degrades them, it makes them similar to itself, and this all the more when they are available, blank, and lack a political or moral armature.'[37] In the concentration camp the functionaries, from the lowest *Kapos* upwards, had unlimited power. There was no upper limit to the punishment they could impose for any perceived offence or for none: they were 'free to commit the worst atrocities on their subjects [without] having to fear any sanctions'.[38]

There was a sharp division between two types of prisoners, which Levi calls the saved and the drowned.[39] The drowned were those who had been disorientated from the beginning, had not made the rapid adjustment to camp life that the exigencies of the régime demanded, and had not found any way of circumventing the hardships and privations. Such prisoners were the majority. Their life expectancy in the camp was short. They soon succumbed to starvation and disease, exhaustion or the regular selections for the gas chamber. They were shunned by the other prisoners, who gave them the name '*Muselmänner*' – Muslims. Levi gives us this description:

> Their life is short, but their number is endless; they, the *Muselmänner*, the drowned, form the backbone of the camp, an anonymous mass, continually renewed and always identical, of non-men who march and labour in silence, the divine spark dead within them, already too empty to really suffer. One hesitates to call them living: one hesitates to call their death death, in the face of which they have no fear, as they are too tired to understand. They crowd my memory with their faceless presences, and if I could enclose all the evil of our time in one image, I would choose this image which is familiar to me: an emaciated man, with head dropped and shoulders curved, on whose face and in whose eyes not a trace of thought is to be seen.[40]

In ordinary life it rarely happens that a man loses himself and becomes totally destitute but in the harsh struggle of the Lager there was no one to help. The *Muselmänner* were not worth speaking to – their fellow prisoners knew that 'in a few weeks nothing [would] remain of them but a handful of ashes in some nearby field and a crossed out number on a register'.[41] By contrast, the saved were those who had a profession they were permitted to follow, those who became *Kapos* or Block captains, or those who in

[36] *Ibid.*, 24. Levi noted the similarity between the camp entry rituals and those of military barracks, 90.

[37] Levi, *The Drowned and the Saved*, 25. [38] *Ibid.*, 31.

[39] Levi, *If This is a Man and The Truce*, 93. [40] *Ibid.*, 96. [41] *Ibid.*, 95.

some other way managed to find a role and place in the camp that would gain them privileges.

Of course, those who survived the camps were drawn disproportionately from the ranks of the privileged: 'The saved of the Lager were not the best . . . the worst survived, the selfish, the violent, the insensitive, the collaborators of the "grey zones", the spies. The worst survived – that is, the fittest; the best all died.'[42] It is these survivors whose accounts have produced the description of the camps that we have. Levi acknowledges the extent to which this is incomplete:

> We, the survivors, are not the true witnesses. . . . We are those who by their prevarications or good luck did not touch bottom. Those who did so, those who saw the Gorgon, have not returned to tell about it or have returned mute, but they are the 'Muslims', the submerged, the complete witnesses.[43]

The survivors felt an obligation to attempt to tell of those who did not return, but this was 'a discourse "on behalf of third parties", the story of things seen from close by, not experienced personally'.[44] The drowned would not have been able to speak for themselves, even if they had paper and pen, because long before their death they 'had already lost the ability to observe, to remember, compare and express themselves'. The survivors spoke 'in their stead, by proxy'.[45] This impossibility of bearing witness is central to Agamben's discussion of testimony.

The distinction that Levi points to between the drowned and the saved arises because the purpose or outcome of the concentration camp is much more than 'mere' extermination. Specifically, the camp transforms the Jew into the *Muselmann*. This is the final stage of the operation of ontological categories as 'devastating' biopolitical weapons[46] that in the Nazi state transmutes the citizen into the non-Aryan, the non-Aryan into the Jew, the Jew into the deportee, the deported Jew into the prisoner or *Häfling*, and the *Häfling* into the *Muselmann*.[47] The *Muselmann* is a limit figure beyond which no further division is possible, the figure that makes it impossible to distinguish life from death, the human from the non-human.

The existence of the *Muselmann*, so vividly described for us by Levi and signalled in the title of his memoir *If This is a Man*, raises important questions about the meaning of human being. Is there any sense, for example, in which there is some 'essence' of humanity that can be identified that is any more than just the biological membership of a particular species? In the camp, the answer has to be 'no'. Human

[42] *Ibid.*, 62–3. [43] *Ibid.*, 63–4. [44] *Ibid.*, 64. [45] *Ibid.*
[46] Agamben, *Remnants of Auschwitz*, 146–7. [47] *Ibid.*, 84–5.

being becomes nothing more than a question of biological belonging. In the camp, 'the calling into question of our quality as men provokes an almost biological claim of belonging to the human race'.[48] What of those who did not become *Muselmänner*, those who strove to retain what they saw as emblematic of their 'human dignity' in the face of the indignities of the camp? Were they more human, or less so? For Levi, the survivors, those who resisted 'following the slope down to the bottom',[49] were the worst. In Auschwitz, it was not decent to remain decent: the inhuman were those who retained their humanity. To remain decent was shameful.[50] Agamben argues that in the face of Auschwitz we have to 'withdraw the meaning of the term "man" to the point at which the very sense of the question is transformed'.[51] In other words 'if one establishes a limit beyond which one ceases to be human and if all or most of humankind passes beyond it, this proves not the inhumanity of human beings but the insufficiency and abstraction of the limit'.[52]

What happens then is that we have to rethink our notions of human being. To do otherwise, to deny the humanity of the *Muselmänner*, for example, would be to repeat the gesture of the persecutors. We are driven to a point where the very humanity of human being is called into question and where we can no longer make a distinction between the human and the inhuman. In Antelme's words, 'it brings us to a clear vision of its indivisible oneness'.[53] The notion of survival is key here. In Auschwitz, survival had two meanings. Either it was the survival of the *Muselmann* as bare life when his more human life had already been extinguished. Or it was the survival of the prisoner who succeeded in his struggle not to succumb to the degradation of the inhuman existence of the *Muselmann*. In the first, the inhuman, vegetative life has survived the conscious, human life. In the second, the case of the survivor, human life has survived the threat of the inhuman. What the testimony of Auschwitz tells us is that these two senses converge. In Levi's formulation 'they are "the Muslims," the submerged, the complete witnesses'.[54] Agamben re-articulates this as follows: '*the human being is the inhuman; the one whose humanity is completely destroyed is the one who is truly human*'.[55] This paradox, significantly, is what leaves open a space for testimony:

> Testimony takes place where the speechless one makes the speaking one speak and where the one who speaks bears the impossibility of speaking in his own

[48] Antelme, *The Human Race*, 5–6. [49] Levi, *If This is a Man and The Truce*, 96.
[50] Agamben, *Remnants of Auschwitz*, 60. [51] *Ibid.*, 58. [52] *Ibid.*, 63.
[53] Antelme, *The Human Race*, 6. [54] Levi, *The Drowned and the Saved*, 64.
[55] Agamben, *Remnants of Auschwitz*, 133.

speech, such that the silent and the speaking, the human and the inhuman enter into a zone of indistinction in which it is impossible to establish . . . the true witness.[56]

Testimony is to be read as 'the impossible dialectic between the survivor and the *Muselmann*, the pseudo-witness and the "complete witness", the human and the inhuman'.[57] This is not a comfortable position for either: 'For the one who knows, it is felt as an impossibility of speaking; for the one who speaks, it is experienced as an equally bitter impossibility to know.'[58]

The human and the inhuman, animal life and vegetative life, are both *separate* and *inseparable*. This is the paradox. Or, as Agamben puts it, '*Muselmann* and witness, the inhuman and the human are coextensive and at the same time, non-coincident; they are divided and nevertheless inseparable'.[59] He means this somewhat in the sense that, for example, buyer and seller or teacher and pupil are interdependent – together they 'authorise' each other. It is also meant in another sense, one that takes us back to the notion of trauma and the discussion of the psychoanalytic view of subjectivity that we encountered in Chapter 1. In that discussion we saw that the subject is formed around a lack, and in the face of trauma. The problem is that subjecthood involves taking a place in the symbolic or social order into which we are born. In a sense that is what enables us to become what can be called human. However, the places that the social order provides are not ones that 'fit' exactly who we are. We are more than that. There is a non-coincidence between the subject we are, or the subject we think we are, and the subject we would like to be. We are striving for an imaginary wholeness, when these things would be reconciled, but that is impossible. There is always something more, a surplus or an excess – what Agamben calls the remnant, what remains, perhaps – and this in the psychoanalytic account is called the real. In order to take our place within the social order, we are obliged to forget the real and hide the trauma at the root of subjectivity. This, as we noted in Chapter 1, is one part of what is called 'the real', the real that arises with the entry of the subject into the symbolic or social order. We noted the non-linear temporality inherent in this process: the way in which, like our view of the distant stars, we only know what we were, not what we are. The other part of the real is the real *before* the symbolic order. This, Agamben notes, is like the way 'the stars shine surrounded by a

[56] *Ibid.*, 120. [57] *Ibid.*
[58] *Ibid.*, 123. The symmetry here is an exact reflection of Heisenberg's uncertainty principle in modern physics where it is impossible to know the speed and position of a particle simultaneously: one or the other can be known, not both.
[59] Agamben, *Remnants of Auschwitz*, 151.

total darkness that, according to cosmologists, is nothing other than a testimony of a time in which the stars did not yet shine'. It is the real before the advent of the symbolic order, before language, before speech: 'so the speech of the witness bears witness to a time in which human beings did not yet speak; and so the testimony of human beings attests to a time in which they were not yet human'.[60] In other words, *it bears witness to the real*. The temporality involved here is what Agamben calls 'remaining time'. In a sense, since subjectivity involves the traumatic encounter with the real, the ability to bear witness is inherent in all subjects. Agamben extends this further, noting that 'to be a subject and to bear witness are in the final analysis one and the same'.[61] The implication of this is that one's own subjectivity depends on and demands one's bearing witness.

The act of biopower is to try and separate the human from the inhuman, producing 'in the human body the absolute separation of the living being and the speaking being, *zoe* and *bios*, the inhuman and the human – survival'.[62] Testimony (and remembrance more broadly), by accepting and bearing witness to the trauma at the basis of human subjectivity, asserts the inseparability of the human and the inhuman and contests biopower. 'With its every word, testimony refutes precisely [the] isolation of survival from life.'[63] The difficulty that testimony experiences – that there are no words to express what the witness needs to say – is an extreme and exemplary form of the difficulty with language more broadly. To speak is to put oneself in a position in language, to take on the 'I' as the subject. But language is not one's own: it in a sense 'speaks us', we do not speak language. We cannot control it, and this means that what provides the very possibility of speaking, language, also makes speaking, in the sense of saying what we want to say, impossible.

The concentration camp marks a threshold in western biopolitics. The camp is the point at which the inhumanity of biopolitics becomes apparent and takes on its most horrific form. Biopolitics has moved beyond the transformation Foucault traced from the old sovereign power (*to make die and let live*) to the new biopower (*to make live and let die*). According to Agamben, contemporary biopolitics, the act of contemporary sovereign power, can be encapsulated in the phrase *to make survive*:

> The decisive activity of biopower in our time consists in the production not of life or death, but rather of a mutable and virtually infinite survival. In every case, it is a matter of dividing animal life from organic life, the human from the inhuman, the witness from the *Muselmann*, conscious life from vegetative life maintained

[60] *Ibid.*, 162. [61] *Ibid.*, 158. [62] *Ibid.*, 156. [63] *Ibid.*, 157.

functionally through resuscitation techniques, until a threshold is reached: an essentially mobile threshold that, like the borders of geopolitics, moves according to the progress of scientific and political technologies.[64]

The production of survival, in other words, would be accomplished by the absolute separation of *zoe* and *bios*, the inhuman and the human. The *Muselmänner* would be the end point of this ambition, *were it not for their intimate connection with the witness*. The Nazis sought to produce survival separated from every possibility of testimony. The *Muselmänner* were intended to be invisible, empty, unseen: 'Bare, unassignable, unwitnessable life.'[65] The Nazis saw covering their tracks as essential to their enterprise. Survivors remember their warning to inhabitants of the camp:

However this war may end, we have won the war against you; none of you will be left to bear witness, but even if someone were to survive, the world would not believe him. There will perhaps be suspicions, discussions, research by historians, but there will be no certainties, because we will destroy the evidence together with you. And even if some proof should remain and some of you survive, people will say that the events you describe are too monstrous to be believed: they will say that they are the exaggerations of Allied propaganda and will believe us, who will deny everything, and not you. We will be the ones to dictate the history of the Lagers.[66]

They almost succeed. And those who today assert the 'unsayability' of the horrors of Auschwitz risk repeating the Nazis' gesture. Testimony, on the contrary, refutes it. Testimony demonstrates the impossibility of the separation between the human and the inhuman. It is because *human being* resides 'in the fracture between the living being and the speaking being, the inhuman and the human', and bears witness to their inseparability, that testimony is possible.[67] The distinction between *zoe* and *bios* underlies sovereign power – is fundamental to it. Hence in its very form, testimony contests sovereign power.

Practices of testimony

However, although the very structure of testimony makes it a challenge to sovereign power, to what extent can that potential be realised? As we have seen, testimony would appear to challenge biopower at its roots, by exposing the way it produces violent distinctions and exclusions. But in practice how has testimony functioned politically after Auschwitz?

[64] *Ibid.*, 155–6. [65] *Ibid.*, 157.
[66] Simon Wiesenthal, *The Murderers Are Among Us*, quoted in Levi, *The Drowned and the Saved*, 1.
[67] Agamben, *Remnants of Auschwitz*, 134.

The accounts trauma survivors tell are emotionally charged and difficult to listen to. Clearly the content is shocking, but there is more to it than that. Often they involve a reliving of the events described, producing an account that is not selective, incoherent in many ways, and not designed for any particular audience. Sessions take a long time, and once begun cannot be abbreviated or condensed. Lanzmann's *Shoah*, based on testimonies given direct to camera, runs for nine hours whereas even *Schindler's List*, which is longer than average for a film, tells the whole story in three-and-a-half hours. Witness accounts have to be told in a particular way, and survivors themselves are in some sense not in control of the telling. Perhaps inevitably the tendency is for testimony to become routinised or codified. Kalí Tal identifies three distinct strategies of coping with testimony: mythologisation, medicalisation and disappearance. These combine to produce what she calls the 'cultural codification' and appropriation of the trauma.[68] Mythologisation works by reducing the traumatic event to a set of contained and controlled narratives. These are no longer disturbing or frightening. This is the strategy we see on the whole in museums and documentaries. The standard narrative ploys are used, and notions of rescue, redemption and overcoming figure large. Medicalisation takes place when survivors are treated as victims of an illness – post-traumatic stress syndrome. They are treated by various forms of psychiatric and medical practice, the aim being rehabilitation and the resumption of normal life. The testimony is seen as a product of the illness, a symptom, and its political value destroyed. We have seen this most notably with Vietnam veterans in the USA, but survivors of the Nazi camps have also been treated in this way. The third strategy, disappearance, means 'a refusal to admit to the existence of a particular kind of trauma' and is 'accomplished by undermining the credibility of the survivor'.[69]

Once codified in one or several of these ways, the traumatic experience becomes something that can be appropriated. Witnesses lose control over the interpretation of their testimony. Because testimony is highly political, and if as such 'it threatens the status quo, powerful political, economic and social forces will pressure survivors either to keep their silence or to revise their stories'.[70] Survivors who are marginal or isolated will be most at risk of the appropriation; if there is a powerful community a measure of control can be retained. The pressures for conformity will be strong, precisely in reflection of the strength of the testimony itself:

[68] Kalí Tal, *Worlds of Hurt: Reading the Literature of Trauma* (Cambridge University Press, 1996), 6.

[69] Tal, *Worlds of Hurt*, 6. [70] *Ibid.*, 7.

Bearing witness is an aggressive act. It is born out of refusal to bow to outside pressure to revise or repress experience, a decision to embrace conflict rather than conformity, to endure a lifetime of anger and pain rather than to submit to the seductive pull of revision and repression. Its goal is change. If survivors retain control over the interpretation of their trauma, they can sometimes force a shift in the social and political structure.[71]

Tal argues that the case of the concentration camps demonstrates clearly the appropriation and codification of a traumatic event. The label 'Holocaust' symbolises that appropriation. There are many examples as we have already noted of the retreat into easy solutions. For example, museums and exhibits tell an accepted story.[72] In the exhibit at the Imperial War Museum, testimony is even used as aural wallpaper. Eighteen survivor witnesses speak of their experiences on video monitors placed at intervals along the exhibit. As the project director describes it, 'their voices are almost constantly within earshot throughout the display'. This is 'an additional layer' which humanises the narrative providing 'a substrand... which enriches the story of Nazi oppression by giving back the voice to those who suffered'.[73] Their testimony is, of course, carefully selected and framed. All their stories tell of 'innocent pleasures and frustrations' later irrevocably 'overturned' by the Nazi occupation and 'the progressive breaking up of each survivor's family'. The dangers of testimony are thoroughly contained, no doubt to avoid any risk that the exhibit would 'lose [its] public through upset or exhaustion'.[74]

The Yale archive is one of the best known and longest standing attempts to gather survivor testimony. The Fortunoff Video Archive for Holocaust Testimonies at Yale University was founded in 1981. This was the most recent of three periods when survivors 'recovered their voice and an audience materialised for them' – after the showing of the television series *Holocaust* in 1978.[75] The first period was immediately after the war, the second the occasion of the Eichmann trial in Jerusalem in 1960. The archive project grew out of a grassroots project that later found support from Yale. The work of the interviewing relies on a non-directive format designed to give the survivor a chance to be spontaneous. The emphasis is on a collection of depositions. Only later are these excerpted and put

[71] *Ibid.*
[72] Despite the best intentions of the museum designers, there is room for ruptures to appear in the narrative structure. I discussed this in Chapter 4.
[73] Suzanne Bardgett, 'The Holocaust Exhibition at the Imperial War Museum', *News of Museums of History* (2000), 3.
[74] Bardgett, 'The Holocaust Exhibition at the Imperial War Museum', 3.
[75] Geoffrey H. Hartman, *The Longest Shadow: in the Aftermath of the Holocaust* (Bloomington and Indianapolis: Indiana University Press, 1996), 143.

together into compilations for pedagogic purposes.[76] The role of the interviewers can be intrusive at times; despite their best intentions there is a tendency to acknowledge privation but stress a heroic meaning found in survival.[77] On the whole though, the archive seems to succeed in 'giving survivors their voice'.[78] Here at least there is some evidence that testimony escapes codification and appropriation. Geoffrey Hartman remarks that 'face to face with that world, it is our search for meaning which is disclosed, as if we had to be comforted for what they suffered. For us, who were not there, the classical axiom holds that "Nothing human is alien"; for them, "Nothing human is entirely familiar." The sense of the human has always to be restored.'[79]

Lawrence Langer's *Holocaust Testimonies* draws on material from the Yale archive. In this text the testimonies are very much mediated once more, despite the fact that viewing the witnesses on video Langer himself felt 'naked before their nakedness, defenceless in the presence of their vulnerability'.[80] In preparing the book, he 'dons such clothing' as he could. Whilst he does not intrude a narrative on the testimonies as such, the book does impose a structure, as books must. The accounts are framed by a study of forms of memory and corresponding forms of selfhood.[81] Claude Lanzmann's *Shoah* is another example of the use of direct survivor testimony in such a way that it is framed by the director's specific conception of the finished product. Lanzmann perfects certain devices to prompt the testimony he requires, and as we have seen he has a clear vision of what the aim of his film is.

Very much at the other end of the spectrum, the *Voices of the Shoah* CD collection is an 'audio documentary' produced specifically because the initiator of the project identified a gap in the market. Looking round the gift shop after a visit to the US Holocaust Memorial Museum he was 'disappointed that there was no oral history of the Holocaust available' and decided 'a collection of first-person accounts was desperately needed now, while survivors can share their stories with us in their own words'.[82]

[76] Hartman, *The Longest Shadow*, 144.

[77] Lawrence L. Langer, *Holocaust Testimonies: the Ruins of Memory* (New Haven: Yale University Press, 1991), contains examples of intrusions of this sort by interviewers.

[78] Hartman, *The Longest Shadow*, 144. [79] *Ibid.*, 133.

[80] Langer, *Holocaust Testimonies*, xiii.

[81] It is instructive to compare the raw accounts collected in the immediate aftermath of the war and recently published in Eugene Aroneanu, *Inside the Concentration Camps: Eyewitness Accounts of Life in Hitler's Death Camps*, trans. Thomas Whissen (Westport, Connecticut: Praeger, 1996). Although they are collected into a rough narrative sequence, this is the only editorial intervention.

[82] Richard Foos, President, Rhino Records, quoted in David Notowitz, *Voices of the Shoah: Remembrances of the Holocaust*, with 4 CDs, narrated by Elliot Gould (Los Angeles: Rhino Entertainment Company, 2000), 3.

This collection, 'featuring a 100-page hardbound book with complete transcripts of the audio selections, historic photos, comprehensive time-line, explanatory essays, glossary and more', is, of course, commercially available.

As well as the danger of appropriation and commercialisation of survivor testimony, there is the vexed issue of the claim to 'survivorship'. Tal points to the way in which certain 'survivors'' voices have been selected over others.[83] Elie Wiesel, now accorded the status of 'the' voice of the survivor in the USA, was not always 'Elie Wiesel'. At one time he was just one of a number of anonymous voices. And how do people get to become 'survivors'? Is someone who left Germany before the war began considered a survivor? Where is the line drawn? How about second-generation survivors? There is a developing literature on the second generation, and increasingly the children of survivors are taking up the torch from their parents. An example of the issues at stake here is the heated public debate that took place in London on 19 July 2000, the day of the British publication of Norman Finkelstein's book *The Holocaust Industry: Reflections on the Exploitation of Jewish Suffering*, between Finkelstein and Steve Paulsson, Senior Historian of the Holocaust Exhibition Project at the Imperial War Museum.[84]

The discussion was highly charged, the protagonists trading accusation and counter-accusation about scholarship, accuracy and method. The question of authority to speak is raised. Finkelstein sets out his position as a child of survivors: his parents were Warsaw Jews who survived the concentration camps. Paulsson points out that Finkelstein – a political theorist – has no specific qualifications as a 'Holocaust scholar'. A questioner from the floor asks about the tension between Finkelstein's argument for rationality rather than passion, distortion or kitsch, on the one hand, and his own use of his personal history, on the other. Finkelstein responds with a passionate defence. He tells of how his mother was 'a Holocaust bore' – she turned every conversation whether about a rose bush or whatever into a reflection on her experiences in the Second World War. He cursed his parents in their last years, but now he feels himself to be the carrier of responsibility for their memory. This outburst elicits a response in an unexpected manner from Paulsson. Not only does it produce a moderating of his own tone, but the admission, in his closing speech, that he too is the child of survivors. His parents, like Finkelstein's, were in the Warsaw ghetto and survived the camps. He acknowledges that his own

[83] Tal, *Worlds of Hurt*, 1–3.

[84] Organised by the Institute of Contemporary Arts as part of its film season *Out of that Darkness*, 16–23 July 2000, in conjunction with the conference *Remembering for the Future 2000*.

activity as a 'Holocaust scholar' is more recent – and more precarious – than he has so far revealed. He spent twenty-odd years in computing, as far away as he could get, and it was only after his own mother's death that he felt able or free to become a historian of the Nazi period. Strangely, in the emotionally charged atmosphere of this debate, the contest over authority was suddenly muted. The two second-generation survivors – in complete disagreement over tactics – were united by their ambiguous status.

Witnessing and responses to trauma are not limited to survivors, but extend to those to whom survivors speak, as Shoshana Felman's account of a class on literature and testimony that she taught and the class reaction to a viewing of videotaped survivor accounts shows. These accounts included those of a husband and wife who, separated during the war, had come together and remained together afterwards because, as the wife said in her testimony: 'He knew who I was':

> The man I married and the man he was after the war were not the same person. And I'm sure I was not the same person either... but somehow we had a need for each other because, he knew who I was, he was the only person who knew... He knew who I was, and I knew who he was... And we're here, we're here to tell you the story.[85]

The class reacted in a way that Felman, as teacher, had not anticipated. She describes what happened. The students felt that instead of studying and talking about testimony, 'the testimony of an accident', what had happened in the penultimate session with the screening of survivor testimony of the Holocaust was that 'all of a sudden, *the accident happened* in the class, happened *to* the class. The accident *passed through* the class.'[86] The class, which had been silent at the close of the showing of the testimony, felt obliged, after the session, in the days that followed, to tell anyone they could coerce into listening, about what they had 'witnessed'. In the end Felman gave them a class task of writing an account of their testimony, and she reports that 'the written work the class had finally submitted turned out to be an amazingly articulate, reflective and profound statement of the trauma they had gone through and of the significance of their assuming the position of witness'.[87]

[85] Fortunoff Video Archive for Holocaust Testimonies, Yale University, T58. Quoted in Shoshana Felman, 'Education and crisis, or the vicissitudes of teaching', in *Trauma: Explorations in Memory*, ed. Cathy Caruth (Baltimore: Johns Hopkins University Press, 1995), 47.

[86] Felman, 'Education and crisis', 52. Also printed in Shoshana Felman and Dori Laub, *Testimony: Crises of Witnessing in Literature, Psychoanalysis and History* (London: Routledge, 1992), 1–56.

[87] Felman, 'Education and crisis', 13–60.

Dori Laub also recognises distinct 'levels' of witnessing: being a witness to the experience oneself; being a witness to the testimonies of others, and 'being a witness to the process of witnessing itself'.[88] After the First World War, there were 'two nations': those who had fought, and the rest: 'there was no way for those at the front to explain to those at home what the war was like'.[89] But there were two communities of suffering: 'those at the front, who saw and purveyed *death*, and those at home, who saw no death, no carnage and no corpses, but who experienced *bereavement*.'[90] The war changed attitudes to death; in Freud's words: 'Death will no longer be denied; we are forced to believe in it. People really die.'[91]

During the First World War another form of witnessing was important, and that was the testimony of soldiers concerning what had happened to their fellow soldiers killed in action. The families of the bereaved needed to know more than the bare details, partly to confirm their loss, and partly to provide more information. Red Cross workers during the First World War spent time going beyond the 'official', sanitised account and seeking out the reports of survivors, comrades and fellow soldiers, of incidents they had witnessed. These witness accounts were important for relatives and the Red Cross passed them on verbatim, however graphic or horrific they might appear. This need for information, where possible, about how and where people had died continues today, and is part of the role of the Red Cross in cases of disaster.

Kosovo and the camp

The discussions so far have demonstrated how sovereign power is implicated in abominations such as the Nazi camps. The form of the camp can be traced through a series of locations – not only the Nazi concentration camps, but also refugee and famine relief camps in Africa, and camps for refugees in Kosovo. In doing this, I am not intending to equate the experience of the inhabitants of these different camps in general terms. There is, of course, no way in which the horrors of the Nazi concentration and death camps are encompassed by an analysis of the production

[88] Dori Laub, 'Truth and testimony: the process and the struggle', in *Trauma: Explorations in Memory*, ed. Cathy Caruth (Baltimore: Johns Hopkins University Press, 1995), 61–75; 61.

[89] David Cannadine, 'War and death, grief and mourning in modern Britain', in *Mirrors of Mortality. Studies in the Social History of Death*, ed. Joachim Whaley (London: Europa, 1981), 187–242; 212.

[90] Cannadine, 'War and death', 213.

[91] Sigmund Freud, 'Thoughts for the times on war and death, II: Our attitude towards death (1915)', in *The Standard Edition of the Complete Psychological Works of Sigmund Freud*, ed. J. Strachey (London, 1957), 289–91; quoted in Cannadine, 'War and death', 218.

of sovereignty in which the camp is embroiled. According to one set of figures in this period 5,100,000 people were killed: over 800,000 starved to death in ghettos and elsewhere; over 1,300,000 were shot in the open-air or gassed in mobile vans; and up to 3,000,000 died in death camps, concentration camps and transit camps.[92] I wish only to draw a parallel in one sense: in all these locations we find people who are produced as *bare life*, a form of life that can be killed but not sacrificed, a form of life with no political voice. I want to focus, in this second part of the chapter, on the refugee camps in Kosovo. In the first part of this chapter we saw how testimony had the potential to contest the sovereign politics of the concentration camp, and how the Nazis tried to ensure that none would survive to bear witness. In the last section we traced how this possibility is controlled by strategies of mythologisation, medicalisation and disappearance that contain the traumatic impact. In this section, we look at the way in which the collection of testimony accompanied the unfolding of violence and the setting up of the camp. In Kosovo it appeared that the politics of testimony became central to the production of sovereignty.

Agamben chooses the camp as the paradigmatic form of the political space of modernity in the west. Foucault examined the asylum and the prison, but not the concentration camp. Hannah Arendt, in contrast, studied the totalitarian state and argued that the concentration camp was necessary in such states as an instrument of total domination. Agamben argues, however, that the process is the inverse of this: it was 'the radical transformation of politics into the realm of bare life (that is, into a camp) [that] legitimated and necessitated total domination'.[93] Only when politics has become biopolitics is totalitarian politics then both possible and, in some sense, necessary. Hence 'the camp – as the pure, absolute, and impassable biopolitical space (insofar as it is founded only on the state of exception) – will appear as the hidden paradigm of the political space of modernity, whose metamorphoses and disguises we will have to learn to recognise'.[94] He notes that the movement of populations typical of modernity leads to locations similar to the camp, such as the holding zones at airports for asylum seekers, and considers the figure of the refugee. He does not analyse the politics of emergency or exception that produces this movement or the global liberal governance that arguably represents the contemporary form of biopolitics.[95]

[92] Raul Hilberg, *The Destruction of the European Jews*, student edn (New York: Holmes & Meier, 1985), 338.

[93] Agamben, *Homo Sacer*, 120. [94] *Ibid.*, 123.

[95] As discussed in Michael Dillon and Julian Reid, 'Global Governance, Liberal Peace and Complex Emergency', *Alternatives*, 25, no. 1 (2000): 117–43.

Like the concentration camp, the famine or refugee camp set up during a state of emergency after a disaster or drought also rapidly becomes a permanent space of exception.[96] Camps are in place for generations: the returnees to Eritrea from the famine camps of the mid-1980s in the Sudan were not the people that had originally been displaced but their descendants. Many people did not wish to return when they were given the chance. The places to which they *would* return had in any case long since disappeared or been settled by others. Like the concentration camp, the famine relief camp is the site of arbitrary decisions between life and death, where aid workers are forced to choose which of the starving they are able to help. Unlike the distribution of relief through local government or community councils, where account can be taken of the personal situation and social circumstances of the individuals involved, in famine relief camps, victims appear only as a form of life that can be saved (as bare life) not as people whose communities and livelihoods have been destroyed but who still have political views. The camp administrators assume total control of recipients' actions and responsibility for their well-being. In an account of the camps in the Sudan, Barbara Hendrie recounts an episode where an entire group of refugees decided they wished to return home.[97] The people who had crossed from Ethiopia to Sudan between October 1984 and June 1985 were a highly politicised group. Most were supporters of the Tigray People's Liberation Front (TPLF) and had been living in areas controlled by the Front and taking part in their political reform programmes. The agencies involved in the relief operation that was mounted in the camps were largely unaware of this background: the refugees were seen as usual as victims of drought and war. Families, households and communities were split up on arrival, priority being given to the ordering of camp spaces into a series of zones and grids, with new arrivals simply allocated the next available space on the grid. Later, the refugees began to reorganise themselves according to their district of origin. This caused so much anger from camp administrators concerned at the disruption to their systems that eventually it was carried out secretly and at night. The physical condition of the refugees was by contrast a focus of attention, with data being collected on births and deaths, disease and nutritional

[96] The political process that produces and involves famine itself remains largely invisible; see Amrita Rangasami's argument that famine is the final stage of a process of oppression. Amrita Rangasami, 'Failure of Exchange Entitlements Theory of Famine 1', *Economic and Political Weekly*, 20, no. 41 (1985): 1747–52; Amrita Rangasami, 'Failure of Exchange Entitlements Theory of Famine 2', *Economic and Political Weekly*, 20, no. 42 (1985): 1797–801.

[97] Barbara Hendrie, 'Knowledge and Power: a Critique of an International Relief Operation', *Disasters*, 21, no. 1 (1997): 57–76.

status. As far as assistance to refugees was concerned, the main objective of the camp officials was 'to get the death rates down'.[98] Restoring productivity and economic livelihoods was a secondary concern, relegated to 'phase two' of the relief operation.

The Tigrayans themselves did not share this view. Matters came to a head when large numbers of refugees began returning home to begin cultivation in time for the new agricultural season. The camp personnel were alarmed: 'Here we were trying to save lives, trying to provide food and services, and the refugees wanted to leave!'[99] The operation of power in the relief effort, and particularly the role of the camp, meant that the refugees had been produced as bare life, life that could be saved but not life that had a political voice. The sovereign power, the power that produced and was produced by the state of exception that was the relief camp, was the international community with its humanitarian agencies. Victims of famines are expected to be passive recipients of aid and the camp is the location where that passivity is expected to be played out.[100] In this case, this sovereignty was contested. Hendrie reports a telling exchange that took place between the UN High Commissioner for Refugees (UNHCR) and the relief organisation of the TPLF over who had the more legitimate claim to speak for the refugees, 'Geneva' or 'Tigray'. To the UNHCR representative's statement: 'You must tell these refugees to turn back. We are waiting for orders from Geneva'; the response was 'We are waiting for orders from Tigray not Geneva. Get out of the way – we will take our people home.'[101] The exchange makes very clear the issues of sovereign power over bare life at play here.[102]

It is interesting how the image of the camp in the international media prevails despite the preponderance of local relief efforts, for example, those by the TPLF in the case I have been discussing.[103] Although these days 'trauma is displacing hunger in the West's conceptualisation of the

[98] NGO staff member quoted in Hendrie, 'Knowledge and Power', 66.

[99] UNHCR staff member, quoted in Hendrie, 'Knowledge and Power', 69.

[100] These expectations blind the agencies to the political activities that take place in the camps (and render them unable to respond when that blindness lifts) as was the case in the Rwandan refugee camps in Zaire.

[101] Hendrie, 'Knowledge and Power', 71.

[102] Another aspect that I have not discussed here is, of course, the use by the Ethiopian authorities of relief camps run by international agencies in Ethiopia itself as collecting grounds for resettlement programmes, where political opponents of the then government were forcibly relocated to areas in the south of the country, away from the disputed territories and the influence of the TPLF.

[103] Jennifer Hyndman argues that while camps continue to house refugees, a new set of 'safe spaces' has arisen, under the names of UN protected areas, preventive zones or most notably 'safe havens'. Jennifer Hyndman, 'A Post-Cold War Geography of Forced Migration in Kenya and Somalia', *Professional Geographer*, 51, no. 1 (1999): 104–14.

impact of wars and disasters',[104] the location of our concern and the predominant media image is still the camp, and what is ultimately at stake is not nutrition or post-traumatic stress, but sovereign power, governance and the production of life as bare life. In the case of the Nato campaign in Kosovo in 1999, although accommodation of refugees with host families was widespread it was the setting up of large camps that made the headlines.[105] I want to explore the question of why and how the refugee and the camp figured so prominently in this case. Kosovo raises many issues, but two are of particular interest in the context of our discussions here: the camp and testimony. In order to address the question of the camp, I will examine the relationship of the Nato campaign to the humanitarian crisis and the way in which the trope of 'the Holocaust' and Nazism were used. What Kosovo represented was by no means the beginning of a new form of governance where humanitarianism overrides state sovereignty, as liberal humanitarians might argue. What happened was, in contrast, a repetition of a very old form of sovereign politics, a politics of exclusion or a politics of the sovereign ban. The sovereign power produced this time was Nato.[106] In this campaign the collection of testimony proceeded in tandem with, not in opposition to, the military action.

In discussions of Kosovo a key point of contention is to what extent the Nato action produced the refugee, on the one hand, or to what extent it was a response to the refugee, on the other. This lack of clarity would be expected were the subject (the refugee) being produced *at the same time as* the order of power/knowledge by which the subject is to be

[104] Vanessa Pupavac, 'Therapeutic Governance: Psycho-social Intervention and Trauma Risk Management', *Disasters*, 25, no. 4 (2001): 358–72; 358.

[105] By May 1999, there were 173,000 refugees in Macedonia, 74,300 confined to camps and 91,300 with host families. Steve Boggan, 'From the war rooms of Whitehall to the squalor of Stankovic No 1', *The Independent*, London, 4 May 1999, 3.

[106] Martin Shaw makes what is in some ways a similar argument based on a neo-Weberian approach. He sees the Kosovo war as part of the evolution of a historically unique 'Western state conglomerate', a pooling of monopolies of violence and a concentration of state power that means that the west can be regarded as a single state (centred around though not exclusively based on Nato). He argues that this state is being produced as part of a global-democratic revolution. I argue with Agamben that far from being a revolutionary or emancipatory movement, the spread of democracy is just an integral part of sovereign biopolitics. The apparent genocidal dynamics of contemporary warfare can better be understood in terms of accounts of biopolitics found in Foucault and Agamben than in terms of a counter-revolutionary movement by authoritarian states outside the western state conglomerate. The distinction is crucial since Shaw's analysis leads him to call for a further expansion of western state power, though admittedly through global state institutions rather than war. Martin Shaw, 'The Kosovan War, 1998–99: the historical sociology of state, war and genocide in global revolution', paper presented at *Bringing Historical Sociologies into International Relations* (University of Wales Aberystwyth, 2–4 July 1999).

governed (Nato).[107] Extending that analysis using Agamben enables us to trace the involvement of sovereignty in the production of the refugee as subject. In this process not only an order of governmentality but also an order of sovereign power is born, together with the monopoly of legitimate violence as the means peculiar to that sovereign power. What we encounter is not just disciplinary power (though disciplinary power in the form of documentation and surveillance is fundamental to the pattern of life in concentration, refugee or famine camps) but also a power that involves the ban or exception. In producing the refugee as outside but at the same time inside its power, sovereignty is produced, in this case Nato's sovereignty.

There was some movement of people within Kosovo before the beginning of the Nato bombing campaign on 24 March 1999. Evacuations of civilians from the war zone were organised by soldiers of the Kosovo Liberation Army (KLA). In other cases people fled the approaching Serbian offensive while police officers went from house to house demanding money and looking for KLA sympathisers.[108] After that date the movement escalated rapidly. In reports it was unclear whether people were fleeing the Nato bombing or the Serbian police and militia. Nato was criticised for having not reduced the civilian distress in Kosovo: the ostensible humanitarian aim. Although it emerged later that Nato officials had warned that an air campaign would worsen the humanitarian situation, at the time the suggestion that the violence had increased as a result of the Nato action was denied by western ministers.[109] A British official disingenuously admitted 'a failure of imagination'.[110] Other reports spoke of Serbian revenge for Nato strikes.[111] Stories emerged of people being told by Serbian soldiers: 'Now Nato is going to help you. Go to America – Clinton will help you too. Tell them this place is Serbia',[112]

[107] See, for example, Michel Foucault, 'Truth and power', in *Power/Knowledge: Selected Interviews and Other Writings 1972–1977 by Michel Foucault*, ed. Colin Gordon (Brighton: Harvester, 1980) and Michel Foucault, *Discipline and Punish: the Birth of the Prison*, trans. Alan Sheridan (Harmondsworth: Penguin Books, 1991).

[108] Emma Daly, 'Serbs drive thousands from homes', *The Independent Monday Review*, London, 22 March 1999, 11.

[109] John Davison, Rachel Sylvester, Steve Crawshaw and David Usbourne, 'Nato urged to hit Serb death squads as massacres spread', *The Independent on Sunday*, London, 28 March 1999, 1; Sarah Schaefer, 'Blair rejects criticism of Nato bombing', *The Independent*, London, 30 March 1999, 8.

[110] Peter Beaumont, Patrick Wintour, Stephen Bates and Burhan Wazir, 'Nato's tragic errors', *The Observer*, London, 4 April 1999, 15.

[111] Emma Daly and Rachel Sylvester, 'Serbs wreak revenge after raids', *The Independent on Sunday*, London, 28 March 1999, 3.

[112] Emma Daly, 'Numbed by fatigue and fear the refugees flee Serb death squads', *The Independent*, London, 30 March 1999, 1.

or 'You wanted Nato, now go and ask them for help'.[113] Yet further reports show Nato escalating its campaign supposedly 'to stop the organised and systematic campaign by Serbian police'.[114] It was ineffectual in this – unsurprisingly given the nature of the air campaign – and the movement of refugees became overwhelming.

The distress that media commentators claimed to see from the start on the faces of those crossing borders became clear enough by the time the flow of refugees had increased to a torrent. Wildly improbable figures were quoted at the time, but the movement was clearly huge by any account. Refugees had been stripped of their vehicles, their money and their documents before they crossed the border, leaving them in possession only of their lives: 'At a stroke they had been turned into invisible human beings, stateless, landless and derelict. . . . Now they really were all equal. But they were alive.'[115] By 3 April, the scale of what was happening was visible: refugees were spending the night in their thousands in fields on the Macedonian border.[116] The scene was reported as 'biblical' in proportions and the capital of Kosovo, Pristina, was transformed into 'a vision not seen in Europe since the Nazis cleared the ghettos of the Jews'.[117] The aid agencies struggled to keep up, shipping in water, food and tents.

Refugee camps were eventually set up in Macedonia not by the UNHCR but by Nato. The camps were sanctuaries, 'specially designated safe areas, policed by Nato troops and funded by the international community'.[118] British, Dutch, French and German troops from the Nato forces erected tents and installed water facilities supplied by Oxfam.[119] They also erected wire fencing: 3.5 km of fencing at Brazda camp.[120] US Marines distributed food from UNHCR trucks at Nato's

[113] James Dalrymple and Emma Daly, 'In just a week, Kosovo is swept clean', *The Independent on Sunday*, London, 4 April 1999, 13.

[114] Nato spokesman Jamie Shea, quoted in Patrick Wintour and Justin Brown, 'Nato bombers open attack on Serbian murder squads', *The Observer*, London, 28 March 1999, 1.

[115] James Dalrymple, 'Stateless, landless and derelict: the forlorn lost tribe of Kosovo', *The Independent*, London, 1 April 1999, 1.

[116] James Dalrymple, 'Like an oil painting of hell and still the dispossessed flood in', *The Independent*, London, 3 April 1999, 1.

[117] Beaumont, Wintour, Bates and Wazir, 'Nato's tragic errors', 15.

[118] Rachel Sylvester and John Davison, 'Nato to set up sanctuaries', *The Independent on Sunday*, London, 4 April 1999, 1; proposals for 'safe havens' inside Kosovo were also mooted at that time: 'Operation Safe Haven', *The Sunday Times*, London, 4 April 1999, 13.

[119] Tim Butcher, 'British troops given new orders to help Kosovars', *The Daily Telegraph*, London, 5 April 1999, 3.

[120] 'Conflict briefing: day 14', *The Independent*, London, 7 April 1999, 2.

Stenkovic camp.[121] When Nato established a Refugee Co-ordination Centre at its headquarters in Mons, the Russians lodged a complaint in the UN that the UNHCR was coming under Nato control. In the camps Nato was everything, 'the provider of food, water and shelter; the guarantor of peace and security'.[122] The Nato military were the camp guards. The inaction of the UNHCR was said to have arisen from Nato's unwillingness to antagonise the Macedonian government, expressed through Nato members on the Security Council. But it left the refugee camps without legal status under international refugee law.[123] According to Daniel Puillet-Breton of Action Against Hunger, 'the government [of Macedonia] has given a humanitarian status to these people, rather than a refugee status.... They have no civil rights, no human rights, no access to health services or legal advice'.[124] For refugees airlifted out of Macedonia, with no say over their destination, army camps and prisons were considered suitable accommodation.[125] Twenty thousand refugees were to be housed in a prison camp at the US naval base at Guantanamo Bay in Cuba, later the location of the holding camp for suspects after the war in Afghanistan. The camp did have shops and a McDonald's, but was 'surrounded by high metal fences festooned in barbed wire'.[126] The refugees had nothing but bare life: they were *homines sacri*.

During the war over Kosovo, leaders on both sides were equated with Adolf Hitler, the Nato/Nazi slogan was chanted in Belgrade and accusations of genocide were levelled at Milosevic.[127] While, as has been argued by many, comparisons with the Nazi genocide were dreadfully overstated, I would argue that they were accurate in one precise and limited sense.[128] The parallel that can be drawn is with the camp and not with the atrocities

[121] *The Independent*, London, 8 April 1999, AP photograph, 4.

[122] Richard Lloyd Parry, 'Nato acquits itself with honour', *The Independent on Sunday*, London, 18 April 1999, 16.

[123] Later the UNHCR did register people as refugees and the International Committee of the Red Cross (ICRC) set up tracing centres (Richard Lloyd Parry, 'Database of hope helps the missing', *The Independent*, London, 14 April 1999, 4), although the handing over from Nato was continually delayed as more refugees crossed into Macedonia (Richard Lloyd Parry, 'Thousands more head for Macedonia', *The Independent*, London, 15 April 1999, 4).

[124] John Hooper, 'Powerless UN looks on as refugee crisis grows', *The Observer*, London, 11 April 1999, 16.

[125] Paul Waugh and Jason Bennetto, 'UK opens old prisons to refugees', *The Independent*, London, 7 April 1999, 2.

[126] Mary Dejevsky, 'Cuban prison camp has McDonald's and golf course', *The Independent*, London, 8 April 1999, 4.

[127] Fergal Keane, 'What Milosevic is doing is evil but it is no Final Solution', *The Independent Weekend Review*, London, 17 April 1999, 3.

[128] Felipe Fernández-Armesto, 'Crimes against truth', *The Independent on Sunday*, London, 4 April 1999, 25. R. Ruth Linden, 'Deportations and Discursive Displacements', *Sociological Research Online*, 4, no. 2 (1999): http://www.socresonline.org.uk/4/2/linden.html

inside Kosovo. In this sense the Nato/Nazi equation is the one that holds good. The bombing campaign that accompanied the constitution of the Kosovan refugee as bare life or *homo sacer* inaugurates Nato as sovereign power and at the same time legitimates its assumption of the monopoly of legitimate violence. It is only with the refugee crisis that the bombing becomes justifiable and Nato emerges as a new 'state' with a claim to sovereign force and the sovereign ban.

Another characteristic of the action, which was much remarked, was the avoidance of Nato casualties. This seems more typical of the enforcement and production of an area of jurisdiction rather than a conflict between sovereign powers. It does not arise because of squeamishness and a fear of body bags but because what is happening is a police action not a contest of sovereigns.[129] The soldiers are not expendable: they are not conscripts who can be killed.[130] Rather they are the law enforcement officers of the new régime.[131] They expect to wield overwhelming force and to face little or no opposition. The situation in Kosovo was criminalised from the start and reports of atrocities solicited. People arriving in the camps on the border were questioned in order to compile dossiers that could be used to bring criminal prosecutions. The emphasis on punishment was so great that prevention seemed largely sidelined.

As we have seen, Agamben argues that 'humanitarian organisations ... can only grasp human life in the figure of bare or sacred life, and therefore, despite themselves, maintain a secret solidarity with the very powers they ought to fight'.[132] More broadly, humanitarianism, generally seen by liberal commentators as the challenge to sovereign authority on behalf of common humanity, turns out to be the very manner in which a sovereign order is achieved. Humanitarian intervention is nothing more than another example of the way the biopolitical principle and the production of bare life are two-faced. The rise of human rights discourse and democracy paralleled the rise of the modern sovereign state, and the trope of humanitarianism itself has been emblematic of international orders from colonial empires through the international society of sovereign states to the so-called 'new humanitarianism' of the late twentieth century. The

[129] Anne McElvoy, 'Milosevic has caught Nato still living by its cold war creed', *The Independent Wednesday Review*, London, 7 April 1999, 3.

[130] Conscripts are compelled to surrender their rights as citizens when they enter military service. This is symbolised by the shaving of hair, the parade ground discipline and humiliation of the military training camp. It is a rendering *bare*: forming the soldier into *homo sacer*: life that can be killed but not sacrificed.

[131] John Davison and Kim Sengupta, 'Cook pledges "we'll hunt down all war criminals" ', *The Independent*, London, 30 March 1999, 5.

[132] Agamben, *Homo Sacer*, 133.

only new thing about this later humanitarianism is the new sovereign order of violence that it institutes. The relation between humanitarianism and either violent militarism or politics is not an oxymoron. Humanitarianism is essential to both: it is deeply implicated in the production of a sovereign political power that claims the monopoly of the legitimate use of violence.

In the new order, humanitarianism plays as significant a role as it did in the original colonial empires which were established through a sovereign ban where the figure of *homo sacer* was a figure of the slave or the native, a figure seen as outside either because of its child-like inability to govern itself, or because of its dark, outlaw capacity for atrocity and inhuman violence. In the colonial order, the nation-state order and the new humanitarianism of the Nato world order we can trace a parallel drive for the instatement of sovereignty through the ban. The new humanitarianism of the emergency is simply a new form of sovereign politics.

After the negotiated settlement and the end of the war, the zone of indistinction produced in the camps extended and deepened to embrace the whole of the territory of Kosovo. Alongside the destruction was confusion: how people were treated and whether and which atrocities were condoned depended on how each different group of armed forces used their authority. The refugees were returned to their homes, but there was no restoration of law and order, nor, most importantly, did the refugees cease to be *homines sacri*. In their victimhood they had no political voice.[133] In the so-called post-conflict period the biopolitics of ethnicity predominated and violence escalated. Moderate, multi-ethnic parties, whose political aims were not based on the exclusion of one racial group or another, were marginalised. In this zone of indistinction the reduction to bare life goes alongside both the assumption of victim status in relation to liberal humanitarianism and the resurgence of racist or separatist parties. Both rely on the inclusion of life in politics only by its exclusion from it. The refugee or victim can be included in the calculations of liberal humanitarians only through a surrender of political status. Membership of an ethnic group or race is a form of belonging that claims to be biologically or culturally determined. Ethnic purity takes priority over and displaces political allegiance in the totalitarian state by itself becoming political. We enter a zone of indistinction where the possibility of the political disappears.

[133] Jasmina Husanovic, 'Promises and incompetencies in the "post-conflict" Kosovo: a view from below', paper presented at the Carr Workshop held in Aberystwyth, University of Wales, 20 November 1999. A later version of this paper is published as Jasmina Husanovic, '"Post-conflict Kosovo": an Anatomy Lesson in Ethics/Politics of Human Rights', *International Journal of Human Rights*, 4, Nos. 3–4 (2000): 263–80.

Kosovo and testimony

In the case of Kosovo and the Nato intervention there is another important issue, alongside the camp and the references to 'the Holocaust'. From the beginning of the crisis the possibility of testimony was taken account of. The planning of the Nato action incorporated from the start the assembling of witness statements and the collecting of evidence – forensic and other – of atrocity. It was almost as if this gathering of material was more important than the prevention of the crimes in the first place. It certainly seemed during the crisis that the need to get witness statements from victims of rape, for example, was seen as of overriding importance. Since Nato and the international community assumed authority in Kosovo, forensic teams have been brought in to unearth mass graves and the painstaking process of the identification of bodies through DNA profiling is taking place.

Agamben points out the difference between two notions of witness. The first is the witness in a court of law, a third party who can produce neutral facts for a trial. The second is the survivor, someone who has lived through something and can therefore bear witness to it. The function of a court of law is to produce something that will stand in for truth, in other words, something that will henceforth be taken as true. The juridical process produces something that *counts as true*. Survivors, in total contrast, are not concerned solely with judgement or allocation of responsibility. They are interested in 'what makes judgement impossible: the grey zone in which victims become executioners and executioners become victims'.[134] They do no want to duck the question of judgement: they would have no hesitation in condemning those who committed crimes. It is just that the law does not exhaust the question. Juridical categories and ethical categories should not be confused: the survivor is concerned with what is beyond the law. The Nuremberg trials 'helped spread the idea that the problem of Auschwitz had been overcome'.[135] The guilty had been brought to justice, judgements had been passed. But this was not the case, and 'it has taken almost half a century to understand that law did not exhaust the problem, but rather that the very problem was so enormous as to call into question law itself'.[136]

In contemporary politics we find several arenas for testimony of the first sort: the practice of apology, and the institutions of the tribunal and the truth commission. When a government apologises for wrong doing in the past, as, for example, the Blair government (almost) did in the celebrations of the 150th anniversary of the Irish famine, this is an invocation of

[134] Agamben, *Remnants of Auschwitz*, 17. [135] *Ibid.*, 19. [136] *Ibid.*, 20.

moral responsibility as an exemption from the responsibilities demanded under the law. Such apologies are made to deflect legal consequences: the Japanese government apologised for its mistreatment of British prisoners of war in the 1940s without being prepared to pay any form of compensation, monetary or otherwise, to its victims. Acceptance of moral responsibility is meant to be the end of the matter. In the case of the tribunal, whether a truth commission or a war crimes tribunal, what is sought is closure, either in the form of reconciliation between perpetrator and victim, or the conviction of those responsible for the crime. In the case of the Truth and Reconciliation Commission (TRC) in South Africa, an alternative outcome was the granting of amnesty. Both conviction and amnesty are judgements that establish what is to count as truth. Despite general support for the TRC, there was considerable unhappiness with the details of its procedures and outcomes. The even-handedness with which the commission treated victims and perpetrators was criticised, as was the way in which those who testified before the commission were treated afterwards. It was noted that while perpetrators received individual amnesty from prosecution, reparations were to communities.[137] Mario Di Paolantonio, in his analysis of the Argentine National Commission on the Disappeared (CONADEP), points to the ethical limits of using truth commissions as a means for coming to terms with the past.[138] He argues that this ultimately relies on a way of understanding that fails to get to grips with how the traumatic event exceeds the 'we' within which reconciliation is sought. In the case of Argentina, mass disappearances exceeded the legal term 'murder': in the phrase of the Mothers of the Plaza de Mayo: 'Our children are not dead. They are disappeared.' The process of the commission, with its assumptions of equality before the law, produces a disconnected and individualised version of the events: the collective dimension disappears. The Mothers contest reconciliation. For them wounds should remain open, and their impossible cry is 'they took them away alive; we want them back alive!'

In the case of Kosovo, it seems to have been decided before the Nato intervention that the collection of testimony for future criminal prosecutions would form a part of the strategy from the very beginning. Diana Johnstone describes the order of events. The punishment – the bombing

[137] See, for example, the various essays in Charles Villa-Vicencio and Wilhelm Verwoerd, eds., *Looking Back, Reaching Forward: Reflections on the Truth and Reconciliation Commission of South Africa* (Cape Town and London: University of Cape Town Press and Zed Books, 2000).

[138] Mario Di Paolantonio, 'Pedagogical Law and Abject Rage in Post-trauma Society', *Cultural Values*, 5, no. 4 (2001): 445–76.

campaign – began in March; the indictment of Milosevic by the International Criminal Tribunal for former Yugoslavia (ICTY) was issued in May; 'then, in late June, the Clinton administration dispatched 56 forensic experts from the Federal Bureau of Investigation to Kosovo to gather material evidence of the crimes. . . . The only crimes of interest were those for which Milosevic had previously been accused.'[139] During the bombing campaign, anti-Serb testimony was collected from the Kosovan refugees, the work being funded by 'a special $27 million appropriation' from Clinton.[140] Less than six days after the bombing began, the UK Foreign Secretary Robin Cook said that those responsible for the 'régime of terror' in Kosovo would be 'hunted down, arrested and brought before the International War Crimes Tribunal'. The Ministry of Defence published a list of high-ranking officers it held responsible for war crimes, and Defence Secretary George Robinson was quoted as saying 'We are saying to them, "we are watching, we know what you are doing, we know who is doing it, and that information is going to The Hague" '.[141] Video footage hailed as 'hard evidence', 'the first pictures of the slaughter inside Kosovo . . . graphic footage of young men executed in the village of Male Krushe, apparently taken by a survivor' was shown by the BBC a few days later.[142] A report compiled by David Scheffer, ambassador-at-large for war crimes, from interviews with refugees was presented to the US Secretary of State at the beginning of April. A state department spokesperson said, 'We believe these reports, coupled with what we are learning from other sources, clearly demonstrate that ethnic cleansing, war crimes, crimes against humanity, are occurring in Kosovo.'[143] Spy planes and satellite photographs were providing evidence of possible mass grave sites and Pentagon officials had reports of rape camps. Scheffer had put monitors in place to interview eyewitnesses and pass their reports directly to the war crimes tribunal in the Hague, where the material was unclassified.[144] Other reports stressed the need for hard evidence to back up eyewitness reports and the necessity of a ground invasion to provide

[139] Diana Johnstone, 'Humanitarian war: making the crime fit the punishment', in *Masters of the Universe? Nato's Balkan Crusade*, ed. Tariq Ali (London: Verso, 2000), 147–70; 147.
[140] Johnstone, 'Humanitarian war', 165.
[141] Davison and Sengupta, 'Cook pledges', 5.
[142] John Sweeney, Patrick Wintour, Stephen Bates and Burhan Wazir, 'Finally, the brutal truth of Serb massacres in Kosovo', *The Observer*, London, 4 April 1999, 1; John Sweeney, 'The cleansing of Krushe', *The Observer*, London, 4 April 1999, 17.
[143] Ben Fenton, 'Expert gathers war crimes evidence', *The Daily Telegraph*, London, 6 April 1999, 5.
[144] Ed Vullamy, 'Allies seek missing hordes', *The Observer*, London, 11 April 1999, 2.

such material since the Serbs were reportedly expert at covering their tracks.[145]

There is little discussion of the willingness of survivors to speak of their distress. One article reported the 'harrowing stories stored in a shiny red dossier' by Silvia Miria, a psychologist and director of the Counselling Centre for Women and Girls in Tirana who was gathering evidence for war crimes tribunals. She and another fourteen workers were visiting camps to collect testimonies, though women's reluctance to testify due both to the stigma of rape and the trauma of war was recognised – and then largely ignored.[146] Aid agencies were also involved in collecting testimony, aware of the need to collect evidence in tandem with the provision of aid. The prosecution service in Albania, where the camps were located, was involved too, with eighty staff working full time on the programme. The UN-funded International Criminal Tribunal itself had some seventy investigators and a budget of $100 million.[147] Their concern according to Judge Louise Arbour, chief prosecutor of the tribunal, was to 'find a way of obtaining credible, usable courtroom product', and specifically, to enable them 'to point [their] efforts all the way up the chain of command [and] ascertain where the highest level of responsibility is among the political and military structures'.[148] It was unusual that the investigators this time, when they went in with the peacekeeping force, would have access to an uncontaminated crime scene where 'each atrocity can be collated, corroborated and cross-checked. The graves have already been identified. The bodies, and the bullets inside them, are still fresh'.[149]

An indictment was issued against Milosevic, three of his ministers and his army chief on 27 May, as a peace deal was being brokered. There were contradictory allegations in the press, on the one hand that the indictment was politically motivated and, on the other, that it was politically inconvenient.[150] The indictment accused the five of expulsions and mass killings, and individual victims of a series of separate incidents, one on 15 January, before the bombing began, and others on 25, 26, 27 March

[145] Henry Porter, 'Ruthless Serbs may yet dodge justice: proving war crimes will be extremely difficult', *The Observer*, London, 11 April 1999, 18.

[146] Steve Boggan, 'Victims tell harrowing tales of rape', *The Independent*, London, 13 April 1999, 1.

[147] Steve Boggan, '15 mass grave sites found in Kosovo: War crimes', *The Independent*, London, 16 April 1999, 4.

[148] James Dalrymple, 'One tiny woman against the war criminals', *The Independent*, London, 12 May 1999, 5.

[149] Dalrymple, 'One tiny woman', 5.

[150] Marcus Tanner, 'Milosevic charge splits Allies', *The Independent*, London, 28 May 1999, 1; Ed Vullamy and Patrick Wintour, 'Hawks smell a tyrant's blood', *The Observer*, London, 30 May 1999, 15–18.

and 2 April were named.[151] Later it was announced that the charges might be revised to include genocide.[152] Intelligence reports supplied by the US, British and German governments made it possible to connect those indicted with the incidents and the deaths of named victims by tracing the chain of command.[153]

When the peacekeeping force entered Kosovo it was accompanied by senior detectives from the British anti-terrorist squad, forensic pathologists, anthropologists and ballistic and explosives experts in an effort co-ordinated by the Foreign Office.[154] These formed part of a contingent of 350 to 400 investigators seconded from a number of countries and they focused first on sites mentioned in the Milosevic indictment.[155] At the same time the Serbs responsible fled, after attempting to conceal evidence.[156] Immediately stories began to surface in the press of how the atrocities had been even worse than feared, based at this stage on very little.[157] Phillip Knightley argues that such stories are a common means throughout history of justifying violence, and most melt away when subjected to investigation.[158]

John Laughland pointed out that the International Criminal Tribunal for the former Yugoslavia had been set up and funded by those who had supported the attacks on Yugoslavia. Although its establishment was claimed to be an extension of human rights and a curbing of the power of states to abuse their own citizens, in fact it could be seen as merely handing that power to Nato and the 'international community'. When asked whether Nato leaders could ever be indicted by the tribunal, spokesman Jamie Shea recalled that without Nato countries there would

[151] Extracts from the indictment were published ('Milosevic: crimes against humanity', *The Independent*, London, 28 May 1999, 16) and the text was available on the web: http://www.un.org/icty/indictment/English/miL-ii 990524ehtm, no longer active. Information about the case was later summarised on http://www.un.org/icty/glance/milosevic.htm, 18 January 2003.

[152] Stephen Castle, 'Milosevic may be charged with genocide', *The Independent*, London, 19 June 1999, 4.

[153] Vullamy and Wintour, 'Hawks smell a tyrant's blood', 15–18.

[154] Andrew Gilligan, 'Expert warns of "massive" war crimes', *The Sunday Telegraph*, London, 13 June 1999, 5; Stephen Farrell and Andrew Campbell, 'Massacre victims "run to thousands",' *The Times*, London, 17 June 1999, 13.

[155] Kim Sengupta, 'The long trail to justice', *The Independent on Sunday*, London, 20 June 1999, 25; Rupert Cornwell, 'Cook says Serbs will pay for atrocities', *The Independent*, London, 24 June 1999, 13.

[156] Fiona Fleck, 'Serb war criminals escaping justice', *The Times*, London, 17 June 1999, 13; Julian Borger and Owen Bowcott, 'Troops covered up massacres', *The Guardian*, London, 17 June 1999, 2.

[157] See, for example, '100 massacres, 10,000 dead – a catalogue of killing reveals the horror of Kosovo', *The Independent*, London, 18 June 1999, 3.

[158] Phillip Knightley, 'Propaganda wars', *The Independent on Sunday*, London, 27 June 1999, 29; see also Henry Porter's analysis of the differing view in the media, 'For the media, war goes on', *The Observer*, London, 4 July 1999, 16.

be no tribunal, and no International Court of Justice: 'Nato countries are at the forefront of those who have established these two tribunals, who fund these tribunals and who support on a daily basis their activities.'[159]

If the ICTY or any other court is in the hands of a particular sovereign power – whether it be an individual state or some form of imperial power – the possibility of testimony as a resistance to power will have been annulled from the start. The framework within which witnesses can recount their stories in any case may be limited to the one that leads to prosecutions; their testimony is a less valuable form of evidence in that context than forensic evidence or intelligence reports. What they can say is limited to what will be relevant to the accusations in the indictment. Once their words have been transcribed and correlated with other forms of data, they can be filed away and forgotten. There may be little respect for the needs of witnesses – who may not be ready to tell their stories, or may not wish to do so publicly. The whole focus is on linking the testimony to the chain of command so that those at the top of the political ladder can be convicted and debarred from office.

However, if the court is independent, and if the prosecutor and judges are well chosen, there is some possibility that an international legal system to prosecute war crimes and genocide will have a political impact. The setting up of the International Criminal Court (ICC) in 2002 builds on lessons learned by the tribunals in Rwanda and Yugoslavia. Its remit is vastly enlarged, and its influence may expand to match.[160] Certainly some states, notably the United States, seem to fear the impact on their sovereignty.[161] The USA, originally a proponent of the ICC, voted against the Rome treaty because by majority decision of the states that were party to the treaty, the court it created was to have an independent prosecutor. The USA preferred to retain its veto by having cases referred to the Security Council.[162]

Support for victims and witnesses was set up very late in the case of the International Criminal Tribunal for the former Yugoslavia. With the International Criminal Court, both a victims and witnesses unit and a

[159] John Laughland, ' "The anomalies of the International Criminal Tribunal are legion. This is not victors' justice in the former Yugoslavia – in fact, it is no justice at all," ' *The Times*, London, 17 June 1999, 24.

[160] Vesselin Popovski, 'The International Criminal Court: a Synthesis of Retributive and Restorative Justice', *International Relations*, 15, no. 3 (2000): 1–10.

[161] Guy Roberts. 'Assault on Sovereignty: the Clear and Present Danger of the New International Criminal Court', *American University International Law Review*, 17, no. 1 (2001): 35–77.

[162] Barrie Paskins and James Gow, 'The Creation of the International Tribunals for the Perspectives of Pragmatism, Realism and Liberalism', *International Relations*, 15, no. 3 (2000): 11–15.

trust fund for victims have been provided for in the statute. The victims and witnesses unit will be responsible for the care and protection of witnesses as they travel from their home countries to give evidence, and during the period of their court appearances. The unit will be involved in activities such as procuring travel documents, finding accommodation, transport to and from court and counselling, particularly in the case of traumatised children and rape victims. There may well be a need for permanent protection to be provided afterwards, possibly including resettlement in another country for the witness and their family. Witnesses will be compensated for loss of earnings, though there is a need to refrain from anything that might be construed as a payment for testimony.[163]

A crucial point about the ICC – as distinct from the ICTY at the time of Kosovo – is that it does not stand in the same relation to the state or sovereign power as domestic courts do. Normally, the state is on the side of the prosecution: the weight is on that side. In domestic courts, elaborate systems have to be set up to ensure that the defendant is adequately protected. In the case of the ICC, the position will be reversed. Although defence witnesses (and the defendant) will not be neglected, providing adequate protection for prosecution witnesses will be a vital element in the process.

Conclusion

One reason why the tale of the concentration camp survivor is so compelling is that although it is presented as a space of exception, the camp is nothing more than the coming to fruition of the horror contained in everyday existence under the sway of sovereign politics in the west. Thus our response to the camps is in part a recognition of our own predicament as participants in the reduction of life to bare life and politics to biopolitics. As Foucault reminds us 'we are all governed and, to that extent, in solidarity'.[164] But this is of no use if our invocation of the trope of humanitarian crisis repeats the metaphor that reinforces the very power that produces the humanitarian emergency in the first place. As Agamben puts it:

[163] Thordis Ingadottir, Françoise Ngendahayo and Patricia Viseur Sellers, 'The International Criminal Court: the Victims and Witnesses Unit (Article 43.6 of the Rome Statute): a Discussion Paper', *ICC Discussion Paper*, no. 1 (March 2000), Project on International Courts and Tribunals, New York University/School of Oriental and African Studies, University of London.

[164] Michel Foucault, quoted by David Campbell, 'Why Fight: Humanitarianism, Principles and Post-structuralism', *Millennium: Journal of International Studies*, vol. 27, no. 3 (1998): 497–521.

> It is almost as if, starting from a certain point, every decisive political event were double-sided: the spaces, the liberties, and the rights won by individuals in their conflicts with central powers always simultaneously prepared a tacit but increasing inscription of individuals' lives within the state order, thus offering a new and more dreadful foundation for the very sovereign power from which they wanted to liberate themselves.[165]

This double-sidedness, of course, recalls Jacques Derrida's double contradictory imperative where the question, for example, of whether and in what way to intervene in a humanitarian emergency is a dilemma that has to be resolved in any particular instance by a decision.[166] Aid cannot be both offered and withheld: only one course of action can take place. But to seek general rules, applicable overall to aid organisations and their operations, is to duck the very question of the political that is inherently involved.[167] Agamben's work enables us to analyse what is at stake in the politics of the decision. He elaborates how sovereign power operates through the state of emergency and how the very posing of the question through the trope of emergency is always already on the side of sovereignty. The implication of the argument in the final part of the chapter is that although the power of the sovereign state over the lives of its populations has been successfully challenged in the post-cold war period and the notion of humanitarian concern as overriding sovereignty widely accepted, this is not a liberation or an emancipation but merely the beginning of another and more authoritarian form of sovereign control over life. Just as the role of the revolution in the transition to modern state rule can be seen as an ironic strengthening of central authority,[168] so the role of humanitarian intervention can be seen as a tightening of a global structure of authority and control.

There is a 'fundamental biopolitical fracture' in the structure of the west.[169] From time to time the attempt is made to produce a unified political community by exterminating those that occupy the place of

[165] Agamben, *Homo Sacer*, 121.

[166] See, for example, Jacques Derrida, *The Other Heading: Reflections on Today's Europe*, trans. Pascale-Anne Brault and Michael B. Naas (Bloomington, Indiana: Indiana University Press, 1992); and 'Force of law: the "mystical foundation of authority",' in *Deconstruction and the Possibility of Justice*, ed. David Gray Carlson, Drucilla Cornell and Michel Rosenfeld (New York: Routledge, 1992), 3–67.

[167] These issues are explored in relation to famine relief in complex emergencies in Jenny Edkins, 'Legality with a Vengeance: Famines and Humanitarian Intervention in "Complex Emergencies",' *Millennium: Journal of International Studies*, 25, no. 3 (1996): 547–75; reprinted in *Poverty in World Politics: Whose Global Era?*, ed. Sarah Owen Vandersluis and Paris Yeros (Basingstoke: Macmillan, 1999), 59–90.

[168] Theda Skocpol, *States and Social Revolutions: a Comparative Analysis of France, Russia and China* (Cambridge University Press), 1979.

[169] Agamben, *Homo Sacer*, 180.

homines sacri or bare life, whether they be slaves, Jews, gypsies, people of the Third World or the underclass. Such attempts inevitably give rise to another *homo sacer*, in an endless cycle of exclusion, obliteration and reincarnation. In this way, every society decides who its 'sacred men' will be. However, this limit has been extended further and further and 'in the new biopolitical horizon of states with national sovereignty... bare life is no longer confined to a particular place or a definite category. It now dwells in the biological body of every living being.'[170]

As I have already noted Agamben's emblem of modern sovereign power, the *homo sacer*, is a male figure. In contrast, if we examine crises involving human rights violations, zones of indistinction or emergency, the figure that we come across there is female. The reason is not necessarily that those in famine or refugee camps are predominantly women.[171] The person of the female seems to occupy a fundamental place in the imagery of the humanitarian international. In Kosovo, women and women's distress were central to the television imagery.[172] When western commentators hovered at the edges of atrocity waiting for crimes to report, evidence was collected not only of murder but also of rape.[173] It is surely not accidental that the figure that appears as the victim, the bare life Nato is there to save, is the female Muslim, the figure that on two counts is included in western power by virtue of its exclusion from it.

Unfortunately the obstacle that survivors experience in finding words that bridge the chasm between language and the experience of inhumanity, between speaking and the unspeakable, is not the only difficulty they face. In the examples we considered we saw the survivor's hard won 'voice' being situated and used by others. Generally, bearing witness is normalised, categorised and appropriated. Only occasionally do we find testimony surviving the telling.

The gulf between the need to speak and the impossibility of doing so is discussed in psychoanalytic accounts of traumatic experiences and attempts to talk about them. There the traumatic experience is seen as something that takes place outside language. In that sense it is not experience at all, in that it cannot be made sense of or recounted in language. In Lacanian terms, it is an encounter with the real. The Lacanian real is that which is outside the linguistic realm, outside the symbolic or social

[170] *Ibid.*, 139–40.

[171] Margaret Kelleher, *The Feminisation of Famine: Expressions of the Inexpressible?* (Cork University Press, 1997).

[172] The overwhelming predominance of women and children in the camps, some 80 to 90 per cent rather than the 65 per cent usual in refugee camps, was attributed, of course, to Serb genocide rather than KLA recruitment: the figure of the refugee cannot be a political figure.

[173] Boggan, 'Victims tell harrowing tales of rape', 1.

order. Putting this in terms of the separation between the human and the inhuman, or as Agamben also expresses it, the speaking being and the living being, trauma becomes facing the inhumanity, the bare life, that lies at the heart of humanity – the social, symbolic or linguistic being. Trauma cannot for this reason be spoken. It is outside the realm of language, and to bring it back within that realm by speaking of it, by setting it within a linear narrative form, is to destroy its truth.

There is a gap or abyss at the heart of subjectivity, according to this account, because every formation of a subject in relation to language is flawed. It produces an excess or surplus: the real. Trauma is what happens when this abyss, normally hidden by the social reality in which we live our daily lives, is suddenly revealed – as it was in the camps. When Agamben speaks of a humanity without limits, unbounded, he is calling for us to set aside the social fantasy and accept the ungroundedness and indistinguishability of being. The ultimate protest against sovereign power's production of its subjects as 'bare life' is the unconditional acceptance of that designation. Protests *as bare life* are the effective contestation of sovereign power. In such actions, a solidarity of the shaken as Foucault calls it, protesters would accept or rather *inhabit* or *take on* their vulnerability. Certain forms of non-violence might work in this way, as indeed, as we have seen, might testimony. In the final chapter, I look at the way in which protests, and often explicitly non-violent protests, bring resistance back to the sites of memory and sovereign power.

6 Conclusion: the return of the political – the memory of politics

> Humans bear within themselves the mark of the inhuman . . . their spirit contains at its very centre the wound of the non-spirit.
>
> – Giorgio Agamben[1]

Before 11 September 2001 it seemed for many people living in North America and Europe that trauma was something distant in time and place. It was either something they knew about through their parents' or grandparents' war memories, or more distant folk memories of famines, wars or other upheavals, or something they might have come across through friends or relatives who had experienced private trauma of one sort or another – sexual or physical abuse within the family being perhaps the most common. Many people themselves would not have come closer to the sense of vulnerability and the fracturing of self that what we call trauma brings, than a war movie or a road traffic accident. In other parts of the world, of course, this was not the case. Wars, genocides, torture and persecutions formed part of the map of the second half of the twentieth century, as of the first, but they were exported for much of it to what was then called the Third World. And, of course, at the beginning of the twenty-first century not only were there older generations in Europe and North America with memories of when Europe was a far from peaceful continent. There were also many people living in those parts of the world, often much younger, who had more recent experiences of violent conflict and mass killings: people from Bosnia, from parts of Africa, from Chile and Argentina, from Pakistan, from Vietnam, from the Middle East and from China, for example. For the most part, however, trauma was a matter that was dealt with by memorial ceremonies and practices of remembrance, as we have seen in the chapters of this book so far.

On 11 September it seemed that this changed. All of a sudden, catastrophe was not something remote. Trauma was brought home – right to the centre of Manhattan Island in New York, and right to the heart

[1] Giorgio Agamben, *Remnants of Auschwitz: the Witness and the Archive*, trans. Daniel Heller-Roazen (New York: Zone Books, 1999), 77.

of Washington DC. The landscapes of our cities are hugely symbolic, composed as they are of the memorials through which we at once come to terms with past traumas and reinstate them as part of our national psyche. In this final chapter of the book I explore how such landscapes have been chosen as the site of protests by movements challenging the sovereign power of the contemporary state. Cityscapes such as the Mall in Washington and Tiananmen Square in Beijing are sites of memory and landscapes of political power. It is at these spots that, in a return of the repressed, we find political protest brought directly to the sites of state memory.

This concluding chapter argues that these sites and the protests that take place there are symptomatic of the centrality of memory and trauma to the production of political space. At the point at which changes in the political ordering of the state are demanded, protests move to the sites that are central to the current structure. The protests reclaim memory and rewrite it as a form of resistance. The story is never finished: the scripting of memory by those in power can always be challenged, and such challenges are found at moments and in places where the very foundations of the imagined community have been laid out. They play on, and demand a recognition of, the contingency of political community and its structure as social fantasy.

For the most part, these protests are insistently non-violent. As such they have a particular effectiveness in their appeal against the structures of sovereign power put into place by the treatment of life as bare life that was discussed in the previous chapter. In a sense that I shall explore in this chapter, they *assume*, or take on, bare life. The protesters, in refusing violent means, expose the violence of the state. This exposure is particularly poignant and powerful when it takes place in the face of the memorials to state violence.

It is in this context that I shall explore what was so shocking about the events of September 11, 2001 in New York and Washington. The so-called 'attacks' of that date can be seen as an instance in which resistance is brought into the cityscapes of imperial power, but as precisely the obscene reverse of non-violent resistance – a protest rather of the most grotesquely and gratuitously violent kind. What this chapter will explore is how this analysis of the symbolic power of the events can be combined with an analysis of the production of a particular form of life – life that can be treated as bare life. I shall argue that on September 11 the sovereign power of the state was usurped. Life was treated in an instrumental way – as life that could be killed but not sacrificed. We can see by the way in which the state authorities leapt in with memory practices almost before the events had taken place a desperate attempt to repossess power. It was as if only by rapidly assuming responsibility for their 'failure' to protect their citizens could the sovereignty of states be reinstated.

Landscapes of memory – sites of resistance

The Mall in Washington DC in its open, uncluttered greenness is testament to the relative newness of the USA as an imperial power. In contrast to London, where the lineaments of empire are covered and in parts concealed by the buildings which have over the generations grown up alongside and around them, and by the remnants of the monarchical power that preceded it, in Washington the layout is stark and plain, as if it had been staked out yesterday from unclaimed land. However, despite the newness the layout is assertive and grandiose in its scale and pretension. The central spine is the Mall, a grassy expanse running from Capitol Hill in the east to the Lincoln Memorial in the west. Like a vast cathedral in its east-west alignment, its raised altar is the democratic institutions represented by the Capitol building and its transepts encompass the White House and the Jefferson Memorial. The vestries – in the form of office buildings for senators and congressmen – surround the altar, and in the Lady Chapel at the far eastern end, behind the altar, are the Supreme Court and the Library of Congress. The aisle runs the full length of the Mall. Along the choir section are a series of side-chapels: museums dedicated to the various forms of knowledge and achievement represented by the arts, the sciences, natural history, botany, the conquest of air and space. And on the inner walls and floors of the nave of this cathedral are memorial tablets to the great and the good – chiefly, of course, previous presidents: Jefferson, Lincoln, FDR – and those who sacrificed themselves for the nation in the Vietnam or Korean wars. And in the centre of the crossing of nave and transept, where the spire of a cathedral would rise, is the Washington Monument. Just outside the cathedral building, across the Potomac River in Arlington, lies the graveyard where lesser or more recent members of the congregation are buried and remembered. And at the lych-gate, standing guard over the entrance through the south porch, is the Pentagon.

When demonstrations come to Washington the focus is often the west end of the Mall, furthest from the Capitol. These demonstrations often explicitly draw on the monumental architecture of Washington to make their rhetoric plain. In 1963 the Lincoln Memorial was the site of Martin Luther King Jr.'s famous 'I have a dream' speech. The Lincoln Memorial does not mention slavery or emancipation. It is, Kirk Savage claims, very much in the mould of other monuments to emancipation that still show the black as beholden to his white masters for liberation, as we saw in Chapter 4. Savage suggests remembering King's speech by another monument: a life-sized statue of King on the very steps of the Lincoln monument from which he gave his famous speech.[2] This would be a renegotiation of the monumental landscape, a veritable 'return of the repressed' in the figure of Martin Luther King.

The idea of the Aids quilt is credited to San Francisco activist Cleve Jones, who saw it as a message that would call upon the conscience of the nation, and a message specifically designed for exhibition on the Washington Mall.[3] It brought to the nation's attention those who had been rejected, and was both a commemorative and a political tool. However, it was according to its founder 'a political tool that does not threaten or exclude through its politics'; the political message was 'that human life is sacred'.[4] It expresses this through the way the panels are each crafted by people for specific friends, lovers or relations. The emphasis is not on sombre rituals of mourning, but on the celebration of individual lives lived. The quilt was first displayed in Washington DC in 1987, when it consisted of 1,920 panels. Each panel measures six feet by three feet and commemorates an individual who has died of Aids. Displays of the quilt, which take place in other locations as well, involve a ritual of unfolding and laying out the panels, which cover a vast area. Despite its location on the Mall, it is not subsumed into the Mall's nationalist discourse. There is an alternative. As Marita Sturken argues, 'the tradition of nationalism in which Jones wanted to situate the quilt is not the nationalist context of stone monuments on the Mall but rather the context of the Mall as a site of protest'.[5] It represents again the return of the repressed. Those who were outcasts are returning to claim their lives as lives worth living and their voice as a political voice.

If the Mall in Washington reveals the newness of the imperial power of the United States of America, Tiananmen Square is testament to the long pedigree of the imperialism still based in Beijing. The original Tiananmen, the Gate of Heavenly Peace from which the square takes its name, was built in 1417 as the entrance to what is now called the Forbidden City, the palace residence of the Chinese imperial family.[6] At that time the residence was the innermost of a series of three walled spaces: the inner palace complex or Forbidden City, a second palace and temple complex

[2] Kirk Savage, *Standing Soldiers, Kneeling Slaves: Race, War and Monument in Nineteenth-Century America* (Princeton University Press, 1997), 212.

[3] Marita Sturken, *Tangled Memories: the Vietnam War, the AIDS Epidemic, and the Politics of Remembering* (Berkeley: University of California Press, 1997), 194.

[4] Sturken, *Tangled Memories*, 195. [5] *Ibid.*, 216.

[6] A Sketch Map of the Imperial Palace, a folded map (Beijing: China Esperanto Press, 1998).

surrounding it – the imperial city – and the outer city of Beijing, itself twelve square miles protected by a third set of colossal walls sixty-two feet thick at the base and forty-one feet high.[7] The whole was laid out according to geomantic and cosmological principles, a series of enclosures around a central north-south axis. In this schema, Tiananmen was the symbolic platform at the southern end of the imperial city from which imperial edicts were read aloud to government officials below.

Tiananmen Square was the focus for a series of demonstrations in the years between the fall of the Qing dynasty in 1912 and the victory of the Communists in 1949. At that point the area around the square housed numerous universities and colleges, and Tiananmen was an obvious focus for student protests. The first of these was on 4 May 1919, when 3,000 students gathered in the square to voice their objections to China's treatment in the Treaty of Versailles. This protest 'marked Tiananmen Square's inauguration as a fully public and anti-governmental space'.[8] It led to the formation of what came to be known as the May 4 Movement, a movement that had a direct influence on the establishment of the Chinese Communist Party in 1921. In 1925, in the continuing public discontent with China's political and economic exploitation and their government's acceptance of Japanese demands, and in protest at the killing of Chinese demonstrators in Shanghai by British police, a series of major demonstrations began in Tiananmen Square. The demonstrations were tolerated for a while, but on 26 March 1926 regular troops opened fire on the crowd, killing at least 50 and injuring 200 or more.[9]

With the victory of the Communist Party in 1949, the square's role as an official public space and place of protest were fused in a new and different way. On 1 October 1949 Mao Zedong declared the founding of the People's Republic of China from Tiananmen itself, proclaiming that the Chinese people had now stood up. The day before, 30 September 1949, Mao had led a ceremony 'to take the first symbolic step in constructing a new nation' laying a cornerstone at the site of the Monument to the People's Heroes on the crucial central axis of Tiananmen Square.[10] With this move, interesting in the precedence it takes over the founding moment of the Republic, those who had fought and died as enemies of the government over the years of political and armed struggle were reinscribed as heroes of 'the people'. The following day, those same 'people' became the rulers of China. Today just as Dachau has its disturbing

[7] Jonathan Spence, 'The gate and the square', from *Children of the Dragon* (New York: Collier Macmillan, 1990), excerpted on http://www.tsquare.tv/links/spence.html, 18 January 2003.

[8] Spence, 'The gate and the square', 5. [9] *Ibid.*

[10] Hikotara Ando, *Peking* (Tokyo: Kodansha, 1968), 15–16.

persistence in the use of the SS barracks as the training centre for Germany's riot police, so the Imperial Palace Museum – now sponsored by American Express and visibly disintegrating – has its uncanny double in the Zhongmenai compound to the east, living and working quarters of present-day Chinese governing elites.

It was not until 1958 that the space was enlarged and Tiananmen Square took on its present form, with the Monument to the People's Heroes as its central marker. This change was largely to accommodate the Communist government's May Day rallies and 1 October anniversary parades. The two buildings flanking the present-day square were built at that time: as the Museums of Chinese History and of the Revolution, on one side, and the Great Hall of the People, on the other. At the same time the universities were re-located to a site on the outskirts of Beijing, four hours on foot from Tiananmen.[11] The square had been reclaimed for memory and for the state.

However, it was by calling specifically on the processes of remembrance and mourning that protesters found their way back into Tiananmen in April 1976. In what became known as the 'Tiananmen Incident', a large crowd gathered to mourn Premier Zhou Enlai, who had died the previous January. They chose the traditional festival for cleaning graves, 5 April. The gathering centred around the Monument to the People's Heroes, which carries on its south side an inscription by Zhou Enlai. People wrote poems, which were later collected and published, much to the consternation of the party hierarchy who had pronounced the incident counter-revolutionary.[12] The demonstration was not so much an act of mourning, however, as a protest against the power of Jiang Jing and her associates of the so-called Gang of Four. Demonstrators were beaten and arrested when they refused to leave the square at the end of the day.[13]

On the night of 3 June 1989 it was not clubs that were used in Tiananmen, but tanks and machine guns. The aim was not, as it had been in 1976, to clear the square, but rather to bring an end to all challenges to the authority of the ruling régime.[14] The democracy movement had begun, like the 1976 incident, as a response to a death – this time the death of Hu Yaobang, a leader who advocated reform and a supporter of the student movement. Again it began with poems extolling his virtues, poems that turned into criticisms of the party leadership. Memorial services

[11] Spence, 'The gate and the square', 7.

[12] Xiao Lan, ed., *The Tiananmen Poems* (Beijing: Foreign Languages Press, 1979).

[13] Richard Curt Kraus, *Brushes with Power: Modern Politics and the Chinese Art of Calligraphy* (Berkeley: University of California Press, 1991), 132–5.

[14] Perry Link, 'Commentary: June Fourth: Massacre and the Morality of Memory', *China Rights Forum*, Summer 1999: Special June Fourth 10-year Anniversary Issue, 1.

were a site for protests to begin.[15] On 13 May a hunger strike began in Tiananmen Square. For a brief period the square – and the whole of Beijing – was filled with hundreds of thousands of demonstrators supporting the hunger strikers. A temporary monument made of fibreglass representing the Goddess of Democracy was installed facing Mao's portrait on the Gate of Heavenly Peace itself.[16] For some days there was a stand-off between people and the People's Army. But on the night of 3 June, the party leadership was finally persuaded by hardliners to insist that the tanks move in to clear the students from the 'sacred ground' of Tiananmen.[17] Several hundreds died. Others fled abroad or were imprisoned and any remnant of the democracy movement was suppressed.

In Beijing that night, the violence was in the end disproportionate to the presumed objective of clearing the square and suppressing the movement. Student leaders were ready to surrender or negotiate as the violence began.[18] The extent of the violence is documented in a suit filed by relatives ten years after the events.[19] Tanks and exploding bullets were used against unarmed protesters, many of whom were shot in the back. Whoever was in the way of the tanks and armoured vehicles was crushed. Giorgio Agamben suggests that the Tiananmen protest of 1989 was put down with such violence because it was not a struggle to take over the state, but a struggle of a different sort, one more threatening to the state as such. In presenting themselves as bare life, with no identity or political grouping for which they claimed rights but just 'their being in common', the demonstrators were the state's 'principal enemy'. In such a case, 'sooner or later, the tanks will appear'.[20]

On the square today a flagpole has been erected on the central axis where the Goddess of Democracy once stood. Soldiers seemingly on ceremonial duty stand guard at the base. Every morning and evening traffic is halted and flag-raising and lowering ceremonies take place, watched by crowds of tourists: there is a regular changing of the guard. But the officers do not have the fixed gaze of those on formal duty. On the contrary, they continually scan the crowds, observing and noting, watching for the slightest sign of trouble. The Monument to the People's Heroes in the

[15] Li Lu, *Moving the Mountain: My Life in China from the Cultural Revolution to Tiananmen Square* (London: Pan, 1990), 115–25.
[16] Lu, *Moving the Mountain*, 207.
[17] John Gittings, 'Deng's Tiananmen paranoia revealed', *The Observer*, 7 January 2001, 20.
[18] Lu, *Moving the Mountain*.
[19] David Usbourne, 'Tiananmen anniversary: Chinese leaders are sued over the massacre', *The Independent*, London, 1 June 1999, 14.
[20] Giorgio Agamben, *The Coming Community*, trans. Michael Hardt (Minneapolis: University of Minnesota Press, 1993), 86.

centre of the square (Figure 27) is now as much forbidden territory as the Imperial Palace once was. Visitors are not allowed to approach the obelisk. An area of lawn has been planted with 'Care of the Green. No Entrance' notices and barriers to keep people at a distance. Any wreath-laying or other ceremonies require permission. A notice reads:

1. The Monument to the People's Heroes is a national historical relic of the Chinese revolution. Please be conscious to maintain its solemnity, grandeur and neatness.
2. Visitors may pay their respects to the Monument to the People's Heroes outside the bed platform. No entrance is allowed without approval.
3. It is strictly forbidden to scribble, score and put other articles on the Monument to the People's Heroes.
4. It is strictly forbidden to spit, scatter chewing gum, cigarette ends, wastepaper, skins or seeds of melons and fruits and other castoff, and to dump sewage and dirt.
5. Approval must be obtained from the management committee before holding any commemorative activity at the Monument.
6. Approval must be obtained from the management committee before laying wreath and basket of flowers at the Monument.
7. Approval must be obtained from the management committee before making video recording or taking photograph.
8. All visitors must observe the provisions mentioned above and obey the direction and management of the personnel on duty and working staff conscientiously.

Tian An Men Place Management Committee, Beijing People's Government, August 10, 1999.

Soldiers guard the monument too. There are four, one at each corner: two at ground level and two on the first level of the podium itself. The square is patrolled by officers, and at regular intervals 'public security' vans are parked.[21] The 1950s street lanterns have been supplemented with powerful floodlights on massive poles, and fire extinguishers stand ready at the foot of the monument. The authorities are clearly concerned to be able to retain control of this sacred space and the memories it invokes. At one time the immediate threat was from members of Falun Gong, who regularly attempted to perform their meditative poses or unfurl banners in the square.[22] This movement was banned in 1999 but not eradicated: analysts have likened it to the democracy movement of 1989 except that

[21] It is perhaps ironic that these vans carry the label 'Gong An': public security, or, literally, 'Public Peace'. The Chinese character for peace used here – 'An' – is the same character as in Tian 'An' Men, literally the Heavenly Peace Gate.

[22] Falun Dafa Information Centre, 'Tiananmen: Court of Last Resort: A Special Report Examining the Role of Tiananmen in the 2-year persecution of Falun Gong', at http://www.faluninfo.net/devstories/tiananmen/index.asp, 4pp, 20 October 2001.

Figure 27 Monument to the People's Heroes, Tiananmen Square, Beijing

it is more dispersed and more difficult to defeat. It chose Tiananmen as the site of its brief protests.

September 11, New York and Washington

In Tiananmen Square on 3 and 4 June 1989 we saw, not for the first time, the violent suppression of an explicitly non-violent protest. What happened was made all the more terrible by the fact that in different places later in the same year – 1989 – similar protests would have very different outcomes. Régimes were toppled as a result of protest movements demanding democratisation, as the movement in Beijing had done. In Beijing on 3 and 4 June, in contrast, what took place was the deliberate use of disproportionate violence to suppress political dissent.

On September 11, 2001 we saw what seemed to be the use of overwhelming and quite deliberate violence in the course of a terrorist action. This violence was played out, as the protest movements we have been discussing so far had been, in the centre of landscapes of power – downtown New York City and Washington DC. It made use, to devastating effect, of the symbolic capital invested in the layout and architecture of those cities. In one sense it was a return of the repressed: a return of the unbounded violence that it is the prerogative of the state alone to use on its citizens and others.

The events of that day were certainly an instance where life was treated with utter contempt. The people on the planes were used instrumentally, as what Agamben calls 'bare life', nothing more. Aircraft fully loaded with fuel were taken and flung into buildings like weapons, disregarding the passengers and crew on board entirely. We do not know whether the demolition of the towers was part of the plan, but even if not, the office workers, and the firefighters who rushed to help them, were treated as pawns in the game too. The fact that the planes were not full is not read as an attempt to involve as few people as possible, nor is the timing of the attacks at the start of the working day, before many of those with offices in the twin towers had arrived for work. The aim of the attackers is interpreted as being the combination of a spectacular televised event – the destruction of the symbolic heart of American secular capitalism – with the maximum civilian casualties.

The trauma of that day was very public. It could not be concealed or hidden. On the contrary, it was broadcast worldwide, by a media so thrown by events that it had little control of what it was transmitting. Rumour and counter-rumour prevailed, and there was confusion and chaos as people who could comment authoritatively on what was taking place were sought but not found. Without words, let alone explanations for what was happening, television channels were reduced to playing over and over again the images of the aircraft hitting the buildings, the scenes of people fleeing, others falling from the windows, and the final unbelievable collapse. As in traumatic nightmares or flashbacks, the scenes were endlessly repeated, the incredible, unbelievable events were relived time and time again as if in an attempt to overcome the shock and surprise of what had happened. All the while, in the background, there was a nightmare scenario unfolding where military forces were put on high alert, fighter jets were scrambled over New York and Washington, air space was cleared, flights were grounded indefinitely, the president and vice-president were spirited away to secure and secret locations. The panic reactions and the chaos that don't normally get revealed except to those intimately involved were shown to anyone watching, and, of course, by then everyone was.

In the succeeding days, the raw coverage continued. The experiences of survivors were recounted 'live'. The searches of relatives for the missing were covered in heart-rending close-ups. Reporters accosted in the street those trailing from hospital to mortuary to information point in the increasingly hopeless quest. The last words of many of those killed were relayed to the waiting public as answering machine tapes were replayed. And the vigils and commemorations – and later the funerals and memorial services – were covered too. The one thing that was absent from the coverage seemed to be death. In part this was inevitable given the manner of the majority of the deaths. Most of the bodies of the victims in New York were never recovered. In part it was censorship: pictures of people falling to their deaths from the burning towers were not shown after the first day, and such remains as were found at Ground Zero were removed discreetly, well away from the gaze of the cameras. This form of concealment does not reduce the traumatic impact of the event but increases it. As we have seen before, relatives need details, however horrific, of what happened. The imagination can always supply unimaginable horror.

The other absence from the coverage in the immediate aftermath was the protests. From the first hours there were debates and discussions between those opposed to any revenge and those who wanted to see immediate retaliation. There were controversial anti-war protests, and candlelit vigils. And there were anti-war performances, as we saw in Chapter 4. The process of reclaiming the streets and spaces of New York began with these gatherings, in Union Square and Washington Square initially, and later in the vicinity of Ground Zero. People came together to discuss and debate, to mourn and to comfort each other. Shrines were set up in neighbourhoods, and posters and flowers left on railings and barricades, marking the cityscape once more. It was significant that although the events in New York were taken by the federal authorities as an attack on

America, for those more closely involved it seemed more like an attack on New York. It was the city that had been violated. The figure of the Mayor of New York was more significant and more in tune with popular feeling in the immediate aftermath than that of the President. Although New Yorkers resorted to displays of the stars and stripes, like others elsewhere in the country, some claimed that this was because there was no other symbol available to them.

Six months or so later, the trauma could be re-lived through video coverage. Some was very raw. At an exhibition at the New York Historical Society two videotapes were showing on a rotating basis from the day following the six-month anniversary. The first, a twenty-minute film by freelance Evan Fairbanks, captured the horror, filming events at the World Trade Centre from the beginning of the attack to the collapse of the south tower. This intensely moving and gripping tape is almost unedited and without commentary. The second tape, Etienne Sauret's *WTC: the First 24 Hours*, shows the monochromatic silence in the immediate aftermath of the collapse, with strange figures wandering through the lunar landscape and the ruined buildings.[23] Two films were broadcast on US television, one at the six-month anniversary, another a few weeks later. The first, a film that began as an account of the life of New York firefighters, provides a bleak reminder of the trauma and the horror witnessed by those involved in the rescue and by New Yorkers in the streets surrounding the doomed buildings. It captures the unreality of the events from conversations between onlookers. 'You saw *a plane* go into the building?' asked one passer-by of another. 'A plane!' was the reply, 'Went straight into the building. Right there into the side of the building.' 'Two planes', someone else explained. 'There were *two* planes?' said the first man, incredulous, 'One in each building!' 'Yes, two planes: one like that', said the second man, gesticulating with his hands, 'then another...' 'What are those people going to do?' asked the first man again, 'All the elevators are blocked out!' Unable to accept the logic of what he was seeing, he answers his own question: 'Well, the staircases must still be... Right?'[24] In the second broadcast, made with the co-operation of the Mayor's Office, Rudolf Giuliani says 'I think we're going to have to remember September 11 in its *reality*, much the same way as we have to remember other horrific events in our history, because somehow I think it pushes the human consciousness toward finding ways of avoiding this

[23] *WTC: the First 24 Hours*, Camera and direction: Etienne Sauret, produced by Etienne Sauret and David Carrara, VHS 40 minutes, Isis, 2001.

[24] *9/11*, directors Jules Naudet, Gedeon Naudet and James Hanlon, Goldfish Pictures/ Silverstar Productions, 2002. Broadcast on CBS 10 March 2002.

in future. But if you censor it too much, if you try to find too many euphemisms for what happened, then I think you rob people of the ability to actually re-live it and therefore motivate them to prevent it from happening in the future'.[25] The broadcast opens with horrific scenes of people falling from the Trade Centre Towers, and those watching in the streets around beside themselves with anguish at what they are witnessing.

The events of 9/11 exposed the contingency of everyday life and the fragility of the taken-for-granted safety of the city. The intrusion of the real of death and devastation into New York on a sunny September morning was a brutal reminder that all security is a fantasy. New Yorkers were reminded of realities that they, like the rest of us, prefer to forget: the vulnerability and uncertainty of human existence and the horror that lies not so far beneath the surface of social life. But there was more than that – the destruction had a specific character. The attacks were not a protest against state violence. They did not bring it into question like the non-violent protests we discussed earlier. The latter draw their power from the contrast they point to with the state's monopoly of violence, and by their insistence on a different form of action. Nor were they an attack on the state as such. The events of 9/11 were rather an instance of state-like violence, a reflection of the state. Like the state they produced life as nothing more than bare life – life that could be taken with impunity. The lives of those that were killed were regarded as worthless, expendable. And their deaths too were taken from them. They did not die as individuals; they were obliterated, rubbed out, disappeared. They didn't die, they vanished. They became the missing. Their grieving families had no bodies to bury, and no certainty as to what had happened to them. Relatives obtained death certificates without a death. The trauma lay not so much in the fact of loss but in its manner: it was not an accident, it was deliberate. But the victims could have been anyone.

To the state, this action was a direct challenge to its monopoly. It was a throwing down of the gauntlet to sovereign authority. The terrorists had shown that they too could exercise what they would claim as justifiable violence. They could treat people the way the state does: as bare life. The state succumbed to the need to reinstate its authority, but it did so in an unfortunate way: by declaring a war on terrorism. By treating the attacks of 9/11 as an act of war, and responding in kind, the US government effectively treated the terrorist networks as a contending sovereign authority. It was tantamount to a recognition of terrorists' authority. To the victims, the attacks were very much an example of totally unjustifiable

[25] *In Memoriam. New York City 9/11/01*, Home Box Office, Brad Grey Pictures, 2002. Broadcast on HBO 26 May 2002.

violence, and many of them refused to countenance more such violence, in the form of attacks on innocent civilian populations, in response.

State-organised acts of remembrance and the rhetoric of war return sovereignty to the domain of the government and the state. The world is remade as a world of sovereign power. Practices of remembrance play a crucial role in this. The bodies of those killed, and their deaths, are reclaimed. But they are not reclaimed as people, as family members, as individuals with relationships and plans for the future. They are reclaimed in the rhetoric of the state only as bare life, as numbers of missing, as 'Americans'. The dead are reclaimed as belonging to the state. Like First World War conscripts, their deaths are written off as sacrifices for the greater good. We rapidly reach the point where a commentator can write: 'If September 11 and America's response to it had not happened, think of the world we would still be living in.'[26]

The rush to war and the imposition of even greater state control in the name of security are surely not to reorder the world in any new way. As a response to trauma they are perhaps understandable. But survivors' voices in New York, like survivors from past traumas, are most concerned not to repeat the trauma, in other words not to impose on others what they are suffering. An alternative response, and perhaps the only response to the realisation that nowhere is safe, might be to insistently carry on with the mundane activities on which we are mostly engaged most of the time: bringing up our children, engaging in small acts of courtesy, living our lives, dying our deaths. Another lesson we can perhaps take from Primo Levi is his insistence that we not disregard the humanity of those who plan and organise unilateral, deliberate slaughters of innocent and defenceless people. Despite their utter contempt of life, they are nevertheless human like the rest of us. If we demonise them we are taking an easy way out. We need to refuse such a facile understanding – and the polarisation to which it can lead – and try to establish, step by step, the details of their guilt. However, this does not mean that we should criminalise the perpetrators. As Foucault reminds us, criminalisation is another form of depoliticisation.

The turn to criminalisation in the end risks producing a form of closure of its own. It means little more than transferring the rhetoric of war from military to police action. It is a form of internal exclusion. The enemy becomes the criminal. In both cases, political discussion is ruled out. Criminalisation is problematic because it gives rise to what is precisely another form of biopolitical control – control through observational techniques and disciplinary practices – which depoliticises in a different

[26] William Shawcross, 'Let's take him out', *The Guardian*, G2, London, 1 August 2002, 2.

way. It leads to a securitisation of the domestic sphere with massively increased powers of surveillance and a criminalisation of non-violent forms of protest. Disagreement and dissent are outlawed. It can result in the loss of the right to other forms of protest and the criminalisation of any anti-state groups.

Conclusion

Too often what we call politics in the contemporary world is evacuated of antagonism.[27] Most of what is accepted on to the agenda of discussion is already delimited to such an extent that it contains no properly political disagreements. In the discourse of liberal consensus there is no political alternative: those who disagree are either our enemies, or criminals. They are evil and we are good. As happened very clearly in the aftermath of September 11, the contest is scripted as the battle of good against evil, a clash of civilisations, or of civilisation against barbarism, not as a political struggle. The space of the political is evacuated, or in my terms, what we have is a depoliticisation. What we need to retrieve is the properly political domain, and my argument in this book has been that that realm, precisely, is the sphere of trauma time.

What we call politics takes place in the smooth, homogeneous linear time of narrative forms with origins and end points. It takes place in the context of the nation-state, an imagined community of people with a shared history and culture and shared values or goals. Memory and commemoration are important – indeed vital – to the production and reproduction of this context. The ceremonies and the heroes they venerate are the embodiment of the histories and values that constitute the current social order. But if memory is pivotal, so too, of course, is forgetting. Forgetting is essential because for 'politics' to take place, the way in which the current political structures came into being must be overlooked. These structures must appear to have come down from time immemorial – not to have been born out of the traumatic violence of revolutions or wars. They must appear to have firm foundations – not to have been established by a *coup de force*, itself an unfounded, but founding, moment. What we call politics also serves to legitimise the state, with its pretence that all disagreements that count can be aired within, for example, the liberal framework of democracy. Positions that cannot be incorporated within that agenda are delegitimised and outlawed.

Trauma time – the disruptive, back-to-front time that occurs when the smooth time of the imagined or symbolic story is interrupted by the real

[27] Chantal Mouffe, *The Return of the Political* (London: Verso, 1993).

of 'events' – is the time that must be forgotten if the sovereign power of the modern state is to remain unchallenged. And trauma time is exactly what survivors of trauma want to keep hold of, and to which it seems they want desperately to testify. Their testimony challenges sovereign power at its very roots.

In this book I have traced the struggle between memory and forgetting that takes place between survivors of trauma and the sovereign powers that they confront. We have seen examples where the state has normalised and disciplined trauma to reinstate linear narratives; we have also seen how these attempts have been subverted. Trauma survivors have stood against normalising practices, or, perhaps inevitably, the traumatic excess has in any case escaped capture. In Chapter 2, we saw how in Britain years after the First World War, remembrance remains controversial. Although ceremonial orchestrated by the state dominates, we still find those who remember accounts of relatives who survived. Some of those relatives refused to join their memories to state commemorations. They saw the state as responsible for war deaths. And they refused to take part in the giving of meaning where there was none. We saw how veterans are allowed to have certain memories at certain times: fashions in war memories change. And we saw in some detail in the second part of the chapter how US veterans of the Vietnam war were treated for their symptoms of post-traumatic stress. This treatment was a disciplinary practice that required that veterans verbalise their traumatic moment publicly, sharing it with a group of patients and psychiatric staff. They were under considerable pressure to provide detailed and personal information, to undergo extensive psychiatric testing, to produce a designated traumatic experience and, finally, to submit to treatment and 'cure'. Any political voice they might have had was suppressed and their views medicalised and pathologised.

War memorials are often seen as nothing more than monuments erected by the state to reproduce national heroism and glorify the wars fought in the state's name. With their narrative of sacrifice they represent deaths as purposive and meaningful. In Chapter 3, I looked at two memorials in particular: the Cenotaph in London and the Vietnam Wall in Washington DC. In both cases, an examination of the detail of the design and building of the monuments and, crucially, their afterlife reveals that there is more to it than that. Many other stories, some of them linear and closed but many much more open, are enabled by these edifices. In both cases, there was an unexpected response by the public. The Cenotaph became a focus of public grief: the place to which people in their thousands brought floral tributes to the fallen. The plan had been to remove it after a while, but in the end it was set permanently in place as the centre of annual parades and ceremonies. The Vietnam Wall too excited a much greater public reaction than had been anticipated. People brought letters, flags, flowers and objects to the wall: gifts or messages to their loved ones. For them it was not a site that expressed the heroism of those who had died serving the state. Rather it represented an interface with the underworld, a place at which the dead were still alive and could be addressed. It was also a place where those who opposed the war could express their views. Built by the veterans themselves, it brought a war the state wanted to forget to the centre of the Mall – the sacred ground – where it could not be forgotten, and where, at least for the first generations, it could not be remembered with ease either.

In the case of famines and genocides, and particularly the Nazi genocides of the 1940s, it is widely recognised that commemoration cannot bring closure in the way war remembrance is expected to do. The concentration camps represented a new form of evil. Those that survived bore a burden of trauma different from that of combat veterans. Camp inhabitants were not only surrounded by starvation, violence and death; they were precipitated into a 'grey zone' where nothing made sense, a place in which everyday distinctions no longer operated, where people were treated as worthless and where death and other punishments were handed out arbitrarily, on nothing more than a whim. We saw in Chapter 4 that even the Nazi persecutions can be remembered within a nationalistic framework, as unlikely as that seems. However, when we looked in more detail at how people respond to those representations, in the memorial camp at Dachau and in the US Holocaust Memorial Museum, we found that responses exceed the intentions of museum designers. Visitors have their own agendas and respond in individual ways. Although museums may try to impose a linear narrative that suits their strategy of education and moralising, the tools with which that story is told can sometimes subvert it. The images that are used cannot be entirely contained within the narrative frame, and the objects used in displays do more than demonstrate the 'truth' of the story by their authentic presence. Objects bring with them the remnants of the human sentience that formed them and as such can address their viewers directly, over the heads of the museum curators.

The testimony of survivors is often incorporated into museum narratives in an attempt to produce certain, limited and controlled effects while avoiding any excessive impact. However, there is something in the very structure of testimony, as we saw in Chapter 5, that makes this form of remembering subversive of sovereign power. This is to do with the way in which the witness is speaking for someone else, someone who did not survive to bear witness for themselves. It is this address at one remove that is so powerful. What it bears witness to is the indistinguishability of the human and the inhuman, the alive and the dead. Sovereign power can only operate by sustaining the illusion of the separability of these, and in particular by retaining the fictional distinction between bare life and politically qualified life. The sovereign is the one who gets to say who counts politically and who is to be excluded. Or at least that is how the sovereign likes to appear. In contemporary politics, we have reached the stage where no one counts politically: politics has been replaced by biopolitics, politically qualified life by bare life. Or rather, the two have become indistinguishable. The site that instituted this was the concentration camp, and the testimony of survivors is precisely a witnessing of this event: the zone of indistinction. In the events in Kosovo in 1999 we saw Nato control and authority being established both through the organisation of the camp and through the attempt to incorporate testimony from the start. This blunts testimony's radical potential; it is contained within the framework of the legal witness. Trauma is expected: testimony fails.

In the present chapter I have examined how protest returns to the sites of memory, particularly to the cityscapes of power. The force of non-violent protests against state power can be amplified when they take place in the very locations that memorialise violent traumas of the past. Non-violence itself is particularly eloquent in that setting. It turns the forces of commemoration back on themselves, and reclaims the critical voice of survivors.

I have suggested that the events of September 11, 2001 in Washington and New York can perhaps be discussed as the bringing home of resistance to the centre of imperial sovereignty. In this case, however, the explicit and gratuitous violence contrasts starkly with previous non-violent protests. I have argued that the response was in part at least a rush by the state to reclaim its sovereign prerogative to use violence and to produce bare life. It is, of course, far too soon to judge to what extent the events of September 11 mark a shift in or a new form of sovereign power. However, when the instrumental violence that characterises the zone of indistinction or the camp is brought to the centre of metropolitan New York on an ordinary working day, and a sunny one at that, something new has occurred. If September 11 were to symbolise the extension of the zone of indistinction to the whole planet such that sovereign power could no longer sustain the mythical separation of politically qualified life and bare life, *bios* and *zoe*, on which it depends, then we might expect to see the end of sovereign power and the institution of new forms of geostrategic, rather than geopolitical, control. Certainly, the moves to extend security internally and externally, to augment policing and militarisation, to authorise covert actions and to validate secrecy and to promote 'régime change' that have already taken place disable the political sphere. The voices of survivors have already been co-opted to these actions. In a topsy-turvy way, the violence that normally occurs as a result of war preceded it, and trauma, rather than being the result of state action, is the impetus for it.

On September 11, trauma time collided with the time of the state, the time of capitalism, the time of routine. States moved rapidly to reinstate their control over time. But the time they set in place was a curious, unknown time, a time with no end in sight. If this is a new form of time, and one that signals a new form of 'politics', then it seems likely that this new 'politics' may well be even more hostile to 'the political' than the old. Another possibility, of course – and one that is deeply worrying – is that the state, or whatever form of power is replacing it, has taken charge of trauma time.

Bibliography

I MANUSCRIPT SOURCES

Dachau Concentration Camp Memorial Site. Dachau Archive. Visitors' Books:
Book 509 28/12/97–7/1/98.
Book 525 09/9/98–26/9/98.
Book 526 26/9/98–16/10/98.
Book 536 15/5/99–3/6/99.
Book 544, 18/09/99–07/10/99.
Book 549, 10/02/00–08/03/00.
Book 556, 22/7/00–15/8/00.
Book 563, 2 Feb–24 Feb 2001.
UK Public Record Office: Board of Education and Predecessors: Private Office: Papers (Series 1) (ED 24):
ED 24/2035, King's message on first anniversary of the Armistice.
UK Public Record Office: Metropolitan Police: Office of the Commissioner: Correspondence and Papers (MEPO 2):
MEPO 2/1957, 14 November 1919, Metropolitan Police memorandum, Cannon Row Station.
UK Public Record Office: Office of Works and Successors: Statues and Memorials: Registered Files (WORK 20):
WORK 20/139, Cenotaph: Summary account.
WORK 20/139, Copy from 1914–1918 A Journal of Remembrance: The Story of the Cenotaph, told by Sir Edwin L. Lutyens.
WORK 20/139, 29 July 1919, Edwin Lutyens to Alfred Mond.
WORK 20/139, 5 August 1919, Memorandum to Mr Russell.
WORK 20/139, 15 October 1919, Alfred Mond, First Commissioner of Works, to the War Cabinet.
WORK 20/139, 22 December 1919, Alfred Mond to Prime Minister Lloyd George.
WORK 20/143, 25 November 1920, Memorandum to Director of Works.
WORK 20/143, 3 March 1921, Annotated Memorandum to Chief Architect.
WORK 20/255, 15 June 1922, Memorandum No. 154.
WORK 20/255, 23 November 1922, Letter to Private Secretary, Secretary of State for Air.
WORK 20/255, 11 May 1933, Memorandum Secretary 22C.
WORK 20/255, 12 May 1933, Handwritten memorandum.

WORK 20/255, 12 September 1945, Letter from Mrs S. King.
WORK 20/255, 24 September 1945, Superintendent of Works to Mr Clouting, Architect.
WORK 20/255, 3 October 1945, Letter to Mrs S. King.
UK Public Record Office: War Cabinet and Cabinet: Minutes (CAB 23):
CAB 23/11, 1 July 1919, War Cabinet 587, Minute 2.
CAB 23/11, 4 July 1919, War Cabinet 588, Minute 1.
CAB 24/84, 23 July 1919, War Cabinet 279, The Temporary Cenotaph in Whitehall, Memorandum submitted by the First Commissioner of Works.

II BOOKS AND ARTICLES

Agamben, Giorgio *Homo Sacer: Sovereign Power and Bare Life*, trans. Daniel Heller-Roazen (Stanford University Press, 1998).
Remnants of Auschwitz: the Witness and the Archive, trans. Daniel Heller-Roazen (New York: Zone Books, 1999).
The Coming Community, trans. Michael Hardt (Minneapolis: University of Minnesota Press, 1993).
Amery, Jean *At the Mind's Limits: Contemplations by a Survivor on Auschwitz and its Realities*, trans. Sidney Rosenfeld and Stella P. Rosenfeld (London: Granta, 1999).
Anderson, Benedict *Imagined Communities: Reflections on the Origin and Spread of Nationalism*, revised edn (London: Verso, 1991).
Antelme, Robert *The Human Race*, trans. Jeffrey Haight and Annie Mahler (Evanston, Illinois: The Marlboro Press/Northwestern, 1992).
Antze, Paul, and Michael Lambek, eds. *Tense Past: Cultural Essays in Trauma and Memory* (New York: Routledge, 1996).
Aroneanu, Eugene *Inside the Concentration Camps: Eyewitness Accounts of Life in Hitler's Death Camps*, trans. Thomas Whissen (Westport, Connecticut: Praeger, 1996).
Ball, Edward *Slaves in the Family* (New York: Ballantine Books, 1998).
Bardgett, Suzanne 'The Holocaust Exhibition at the Imperial War Museum', Imperial War Museum, http://www.iwm.org.uk/Lambeth/pdffiles/hol bardgett.pdf, accessed 2 February 2003. (Article appeared in *News of Museums of History* (2002).)
Bauman, Zygmunt *Modernity and the Holocaust* (Cambridge: Polity, 1989).
Bee, John D. 'Eros, and Thanatos: an analysis of the Vietnam Memorial', in *Vietnam Images: War and Representation*, ed. Jeffrey Walsh and James Aulich (London: Macmillan, 1989), 196–204.
Benjamin, Walter *Illuminations*, trans. Harry Zohn (London: Fontana, 1992).
Bergson, Henri *Matter and Memory*, trans. Nancy Margaret Paul and W. Scott Palmer (New York: Zone Books, 1988).
Berlin, Ira Marc Favreau, and Steven F. Miller, eds. *Remembering Slavery: African Americans Talk About Their Personal Experiences of Slavery and Freedom* (New York: The New Press, 1998).
Blanchot, Maurice *The Writing of the Disaster: l'écriture du désastre*, trans. Ann Smock, new edn (Lincoln and London: University of Nebraska Press, 1995).

Bourke, Joanna *An Intimate History of Killing: Face-to-face Killing in Twentieth Century Warfare* (London: Granta, 1999).

Bouson, J. Brooks *Quiet as it's Kept: Shame, Trauma and Race in the Novels of Toni Morrison* (Albany: State University of New York Press, 2000).

Bracken, Patrick J. 'Hidden agendas: deconstructing post-traumatic stress disorder', in *Rethinking the Trauma of War*, ed. Patrick J. Bracken and Celia Petty (London: Free Association Books, 1998), 38–59.

Bracken, Patrick J., and Celia Petty, eds. *Rethinking the Trauma of War* (London: Free Association Press, 1998).

Brown, Laura S. 'Not outside the range: one feminist perspective on psychic trauma', in *Trauma: Explorations in Memory*, ed. Cathy Caruth (Baltimore: Johns Hopkins University Press, 1995), 100–12.

Campbell, David 'Why Fight: Humanitarianism, Principles and Post-structuralism', *Millennium: Journal of International Studies*, 27, no. 3 (1998): 497–521.

Campbell, Stephen J. *The Great Irish Famine: Words and Images from the Famine Museum, Strokestown Park, County Roscommon* (Strokestown: The Famine Museum, 1994).

Cannadine, David 'War and death, grief and mourning in modern Britain', in *Mirrors of Mortality. Studies in the Social History of Death*, ed. Joachim Whaley (London: Europa, 1981), 187–242.

Caruth, Cathy *Unclaimed Experience: Trauma, Narrative, and History* (Baltimore: Johns Hopkins University Press, 1996).

'Parting Words: Trauma, Silence and Survival', *Cultural Values*, 5, no. 1 (2001): 7–26.

'Unclaimed Experience: Trauma and the Possibility of History', *Yale French Studies*, 79 (1991): 181–92.

ed. *Trauma: Explorations in Memory* (Baltimore: The Johns Hopkins University Press, 1995).

Cole, Tim *Images of the Holocaust: the Myth of the 'Shoah Business'* (London: Duckworth, 1999).

Coleridge, Samuel Taylor *The Rime of the Ancient Mariner*.

Crownshaw, Richard 'Performing Memory in Holocaust Museums', *Performance Research*, 5, no. 3 (2000): 18–27.

Dannatt, Adrian *United States Holocaust Memorial Museum: James Ingo Freed* (London: Phaidon, 1995).

Dawson, Graham *Soldier Heroes: Britishness, Colonial Adventure and the Imagining of Masculinities* (London: Routledge, 1994).

Deleuze, Gilles *Bergsonianism*, trans. Hugh Tomlinson and Barbara Habberjam (New York: Zone Books, 1988).

Derrida, Jacques *The Other Heading: Reflections on Today's Europe*, trans. Pascale-Anne Brault and Michael B. Naas (Bloomington, Indiana: Indiana University Press, 1992).

'Force of law: the "mystical foundation of authority" ', in *Deconstruction and the Possibility of Justice*, ed. David Gray Carlson, Drucilla Cornell and Michel Rosenfeld (New York: Routledge, 1992), 3–67.

Di Paolantonio, Mario 'Pedagogical Law and Abject Rage in Post-trauma Society', *Cultural Values*, 5, no. 4 (2001): 445–76.

Dillon, Michael, and Julian Reid 'Global Governance, Liberal Peace and Complex Emergency', *Alternatives*, 25, no. 1 (2000): 117–43.

Distel, Barbara, and Ruth Jakusch *Concentration Camp Dachau 1933–1945*, trans. Jennifer Vernon (Munich: Comité International de Dachau, Brussels and Lipp GmbH, 1978).

Distel, Barbara *Dachau Concentration Camp* (Comité International de Dachau, 1972).

Duras, Marguerite *Hiroshima Mon Amour* (Paris: Gallimard, 1960), 6.

Durkheim, Emile *The Elementary Forms of the Religious Life*, trans. Karen E. Fields (New York: The Free Press, 1995).

Edkins, Jenny *Poststructuralism and International Relations: Bringing the Political Back In* (Boulder, Colorado: Lynne Rienner, 1999).

Whose Hunger? Concepts of Famine, Practices of Aid (Minneapolis: University of Minnesota Press, 2000).

'Forget Trauma? Responses to September 11', *International Relations*, 16, no. 2 (2002): 243–56.

'Legality With a Vengeance: Famines and Humanitarian Intervention in "complex emergencies"', *Millennium: Journal of International Studies*, 25, no. 3 (1996): 547–75.

'September 11 and the Timing of Memory', Paper presented at the International Studies Association Annual Convention, New Orleans, March 2002.

Edkins, Jenny, and Véronique Pin-Fat, 'The subject of the political', in *Sovereignty and Subjectivity*, ed. Jenny Edkins, Nalini Persram and Véronique Pin-Fat (Boulder, Colorado: Lynne Rienner, 1999), 1–19.

Einstein, Albert *Relativity: the Special and the General Theory*, trans. Robert W. Lawson (London: Methuen, 1920).

Elshtain, Jean Bethke *Public Man, Private Woman: Women in Social and Political Thought*, 2nd edn (Princeton University Press, 1993).

Emden, Richard van, and Steve Humphries *Veterans: Last Survivors of the Great War* (Barnsley, South Yorkshire: Leo Cooper, 1999).

Enloe, Cynthia *Bananas Beaches and Bases: Making Feminist Sense of International Politics* (Berkeley: University of California Press, 1990).

Ezrahi, Yaron *Rubber Bullets: Power and Conscience in Modern Israel* (Berkeley: University of California Press, 1997).

Feldschuh, Michael, ed. *The September 11 Photo Project* (New York: Regan Books, HarperCollins, 2002).

Felman, Shoshana 'Education and crisis, or the vicissitudes of teaching', in *Trauma: Explorations in Memory*, ed. Cathy Caruth (Baltimore: Johns Hopkins University Press, 1995), 13–60.

'The return of the voice: Claude Lanzmann's *Shoah*', in *Testimony: Crises of Witnessing in Literature, Psychoanalysis and History*, ed. Shoshana Felman and Dori Laub (London: Routledge, 1992), 204–83.

Felman, Shoshana, and Dori Laub *Testimony: Crises of Witnessing in Literature, Psychoanalysis and History* (London: Routledge, 1992).

Ferguson, Niall *The Pity of War* (London: Penguin, 1998).

Field, Frank *British and French Writers of the First World War* (Cambridge University Press, 1991).

Fink, Bruce *The Lacanian Subject: Between Language and Jouissance* (Princeton University Press, 1995).
Finkelstein, Norman *The Holocaust Industry: the Abuse of Jewish Victims* (London: Verso, 2000).
Foucault, Michel *The Archaeology of Knowledge*, trans. A. M. Sheridan Smith (London: Tavistock, 1972).
The Birth of the Clinic: an Archaeology of Medical Perception, trans. A. M. Sheridan (London: Tavistock, 1973).
Discipline and Punish: the Birth of the Prison, trans. Alan Sheridan (London: Penguin Books, 1991).
Ethics: Subjectivity and Truth, trans. Robert Hurley and others, *Essential Works of Foucault 1954–1984*, ed. Paul Rabinow, vol. I (New York: The New Press, 1997).
History of Sexuality: an Introduction. Volume 1, trans. Robert Hurley (Harmondsworth: Penguin, 1978).
Madness and Civilisation: a History of Insanity in the Age of Reason, trans. Richard Howard (London: Routledge, 1989).
'Intellectuals and Power: a Conversation between Michel Foucault and Gilles Deleuze', in *Language, Counter-memory, Practice: Selected Essays and Interviews*, ed. Donald F. Bouchard (Ithaca: Cornell University Press, 1977), 205–17.
'Truth and power', in *Power/Knowledge: Selected Interviews and Other Writings 1972–1977 by Michel Foucault*, ed. Colin Gordon (Brighton: Harvester, 1980), 109–33.
'Two lectures', in *Power/Knowledge: Selected Interviews and Other Writings 1972–1977 by Michel Foucault*, ed. Colin Gordon (Brighton: Harvester, 1980), 78–108.
Freud, Sigmund 'Thoughts for the times on war and death: II: our attitude towards death (1915)', in *The Standard Edition of the Complete Psychological Works of Sigmund Freud*, ed. J. Strachey (London, 1957), 289–91.
Freud, Sigmund, and Joseph Breuer *Studies on Hysteria*, trans. James Strachey and Alix Strachey, The Penguin Freud Library, vol. III, ed. James Strachey and Alix Strachey (London: Penguin, 1974).
Girard, René *Violence and the Sacred*, trans. Patrick Gregory (Baltimore: Johns Hopkins University Press, 1977).
Hacking, Ian *Rewriting the Soul: Multiple Personality and the Sciences of Memory* (Princeton University Press, 1995).
Halbwachs, Maurice 'The social frameworks of memory', in *On Collective Memory*, ed. Lewis A. Coser (University of Chicago Press, 1992), 35–189.
Hartman, Geoffrey H. *The Longest Shadow: in the Aftermath of the Holocaust* (Bloomington and Indianapolis: Indiana University Press, 1996).
Hass, Kristin Ann *Carried to the Wall: American Memory and the Vietnam Veterans Memorial* (Berkeley: University of California Press, 1998).
Heidegger, Martin *Being and Time: a Translation of Sein und Zeit*, trans. Joan Stambaugh (Albany: State University of New York Press, 1996).
Hendrie, Barbara 'Knowledge and Power: a Critique of an International Relief Operation', *Disasters*, 21, no. 1 (1997): 57–76.

Herman, Judith Lewis *Trauma and Recovery: from Domestic Abuse to Political Terror* (London: Pandora, 1992).
Hilberg, Raul *The Destruction of the European Jews*, student edn (New York: Holmes & Meier, 1985).
Hindess, Barry *Discourses of Power: from Hobbes to Foucault* (Oxford: Blackwell, 1996).
Holmes, Richard *Acts of War: The Behaviour of Men in Battle* (New York: Free Press, 1986).
Horowitz, Sara R. *Voicing the Void: Muteness and Memory in Holocaust Fiction* (Albany: State University of New York Press, 1997).
Husanovic, Jasmina 'Promises and incompetencies in the "post-conflict" Kosovo: a view from below', paper presented at Carr Workshop held in Aberystwyth, University of Wales, 20 November 1999.
Hyndman, Jennifer 'A Post-cold War Geography of Forced Migration in Kenya and Somalia', *Professional Geographer*, 51, no. 1 (1999): 104–14.
Ingadottir, Thordis, Françoise Ngendahayo, and Patricia Viseur Sellers 'The International Criminal Court: the Victims and Witnesses Unit (Article 43.6 of the Rome Statute): a Discussion Paper', *ICC Discussion Paper*, no. 1 (March 2000). Project on International Courts and Tribunals, New York University/School of Oriental and African Studies, University of London.
Inglis, Ken 'Entombing Unknown Soldiers: from London and Paris to Baghdad', *History and Memory*, 5 (1993): 7–31.
Johnstone, Diana 'Humanitarian war: making the crime fit the punishment', in *Masters of the Universe? Nato's Balkan Crusade*, ed. Tariq Ali (London: Verso, 2000), 147–70; 147.
Kelleher, Margaret *The Feminisation of Famine: Expressions of the Inexpressible?* (Cork University Press, 1997).
Kipling, Rudyard 'My Boy Jack: 1914–1918', in *Rudyard Kipling: Selected Poems*, ed. Peter Keating (London: Penguin, 1993), 152.
Kofman, Sarah *Smothered Words*, trans. Madeleine Dobie (Evanston, Illinois: Northwestern University Press, 1998).
Kolk, Bessel A. van der, and Onno van der Hart 'The intrusive past: the flexibility of memory and the engraving of trauma', in *Trauma: Explorations in Memory*, ed. Cathy Caruth (Baltimore: Johns Hopkins University Press, 1995), 158–82.
Kraus, Richard Curt *Brushes with Power: Modern Politics and the Chinese Art of Calligraphy* (Berkeley: University of California Press, 1991), 132–5.
Kundera, Milan *The Book of Laughter and Forgetting*, trans. Aaron Asher (London: Faber and Faber, 1996).
Kushner, Tony 'The Memory of Belsen', *New Formations*, no. 30 (1996–7): 18–32.
Lacan, Jacques *Écrits: a Selection*, trans. Alan Sheridan (London: Routledge, 1980).
Lambek, Michael 'The past imperfect: remembering as moral practice', in *Tense Past: Cultural Essays in Trauma and Memory*, ed. Paul Antze and Michael Lambek (New York: Routledge, 1996), 235–54.

Lan, Xiao, ed. *The Tiananmen Poems* (Beijing: Foreign Languages Press, 1979).
Langer, Lawrence L. *Holocaust Testimonies: the Ruins of Memory* (New Haven: Yale University Press, 1991).
Lanzmann, Claude 'The obscenity of understanding: an evening with Claude Lanzmann', in *Trauma: Explorations in Memory*, ed. Cathy Caruth (Baltimore: Johns Hopkins University Press, 1995), 200–20.
Laqueur, Thomas W. 'Memory and naming in the Great War', in *Commemorations: the Politics of National Identity*, ed. John R. Gillis (Princeton University Press, 1994), 150–67.
Laub, Dori 'Truth and testimony: the process and the struggle', in *Trauma: Explorations in Memory*, ed. Cathy Caruth (Baltimore: Johns Hopkins University Press, 1995), 61–75.
Levi, Primo *The Drowned and the Saved*, trans. Raymond Rosenthal (London: Abacus, 1989).
If This is a Man and The Truce, trans. Stuart Woolf (London: Abacus, 1987).
Leys, Ruth *Trauma: a Genealogy* (University of Chicago Press, 2000).
Linden, R. Ruth 'Deportations and Discursive Displacements', *Sociological Research Online*, 4, no. 2 (1999). Available at URL http://www.socresonline.org.uk/4/2/linden.html
Link, Perry 'Commentary: June Fourth: Massacre and the Morality of Memory', *China Rights Forum*, Summer 1999: Special June Fourth 10-year Anniversary Issue, 1.
Lipstadt, Deborah *Denying the Holocaust: the Growing Assault on Truth and Memory* (London: Penguin, 1994).
Lu, Li *Moving the Mountain: My Life in China from the Cultural Revolution to Tiananmen Square* (London: Pan, 1990).
Macdonald, Lyn *The Roses of No Man's Land* (London: Penguin, 1983).
Somme (London: Penguin, 1983).
They Called it Passchendaele: the Story of the Battle of Ypres and of the Men Who Fought in it (London: Penguin, 1978).
Macdonald, Sharon, and Gordon Fyfe, eds. *Theorising Museums: Representing Identity and Diversity in a Changing World* (Oxford: Blackwell, 1996).
Marcuse, Harold *Legacies of Dachau: the Uses and Abuses of a Concentration Camp, 1933–2001* (Cambridge University Press, 2001).
Mayo, James M. *War Memorials as Political Landscape: the American Experience and Beyond* (New York: Praeger, 1988).
'War Memorials as Political Memory', *Geographical Review*, 78, no. 1 (1988): 62–75.
Michaels, Anne *Fugitive Pieces* (New York: Vintage, 1998).
Miller, Alice *Thou Shalt Not Be Aware: Society's Betrayal of the Child*, trans. Hildegarde and Hunter Hannum, new edn (London: Pluto Press, 1998).
Milton, Sybil, and Ira Nowinski *In Fitting Memory: the Art and Politics of Holocaust Memorials* (Detroit: Wayne State University Press, 1991).
Moriarty, Catherine 'Private grief and public remembrance: British First World War memorials', in *War and Memory in the Twentieth Century*, ed. Martin Evans and Ken Lunn (Oxford: Berg, 1997), 125–42.
Morrison, Toni *Beloved* (New York: Plume, 1987).

Mosse, George L. *Fallen Soldiers: Reshaping the Memory of the World Wars* (Oxford University Press, 1990).
Mouffe, Chantal *The Return of the Political* (London: Verso, 1993).
Mulhall, Stephen *Heidegger and Being and Time* (London: Routledge, 1996).
Neuhäusler, Johannes *What was it Like at the Concentration Camp at Dachau? An Attempt to Come Closer to the Truth*, 29th edn (Dachau: Trustees for the Monument of Atonement in the Concentration Camp at Dachau, 2000).
Nora, Pierre 'Between Memory and History: *Les lieux de mémoire*', *Representations*, 26 (1989): 7–25.
'General introduction: between memory and history', in *Realms of Memory: Rethinking the French Past*, ed. Pierre Nora and Lawrence D. Kritzman (New York: Columbia University Press, 1996), 1–20.
Novick, Peter *The Holocaust and Collective Memory: the American Experience* (London: Bloomsbury, 1999).
O'Ciosáin, Niall 'Hungry Grass', *Circa Art Magazine*, no. 68 (1994): 24–7.
Owen, Wilfred *The Collected Poems of Wilfred Owen*, ed. C. Day Lewis (London: Chatto and Windus, 1963).
Palmer, Laura *Shrapnel in the Heart: Letters and Remembrances from the Vietnam Veterans Memorial* (New York: Vintage House, 1987).
Paskins, Barrie, and James Gow 'The Creation of the International Tribunals from the Perspectives of Pragmatism, Realism and Liberalism', *International Relations*, 15, no. 3 (2000): 11–15.
Popovski, Vesselin 'The International Criminal Court: a Synthesis of Retributive and Restorative Justice', *International Relations*, 15, no. 3 (2000): 1–10.
Pupavac, Vanessa 'Therapeutic Governance: Psycho-social Intervention and Trauma Risk Management', *Disasters*, 25, no. 4 (2001): 358–72.
Quigley, Michael 'Grosse le: "The most important and evocative Great Famine site outside of Ireland" ', in *The Hungry Stream: Essays on Emigration and Famine*, ed. E. Margaret Crawford (Belfast: The Institute of Irish Studies, The Queen's University of Belfast, and the Centre for Emigration Studies at the Ulster-American Folk Park, 1997), 36–7.
Rangasami, Amrita 'Failure of Exchange Entitlements Theory of Famine', *Economic and Political Weekly*, 20, no. 41 (1985): 1747–52; no. 42 (1985): 1797–1801.
Richardson, David 'The Bristol Slave Traders: a Collective Portrait' (Bristol Branch of the Historical Association, The University, Bristol, 1997).
Roberts, Guy 'Assault on Sovereignty: the Clear and Present Danger of the New International Criminal Court', *American University International Law Review*, 17, no. 1 (2001): 35–77.
Roth, Michael S. 'Hiroshima mon amour: you must remember this', in *Revisioning History: Film and the Construction of a New Past*, ed. Robert A. Rothenstone (Princeton University Press, 1995), 91–101.
Rowlands, Michael 'Memory, Sacrifice and the Nation', *New Formations*, no. 30 (Winter, 1996): 8–17.
Ryback, Timothy W. *The Last Survivor: in Search of Martin Zaidenstadt* (New York: Pantheon, 1999).
Santayana, G. *Life of Reason* (New York, 1922).

Saussure, Ferdinand de *Course in General Linguistics*, trans. Wade Baskin (New York: McGraw Hill, 1966).

Savage, Kirk *Standing Soldiers, Kneeling Slaves: Race, War and Monument in Nineteenth Century America* (Princeton University Press, 1997).

'The politics of memory: black emancipation and the Civil War Monument', in *Commemorations: the Politics of National Identity*, ed. John R. Gillis (Princeton University Press, 1994), 127–49.

Scarry, Elaine *The Body in Pain: the Making and Unmaking of the World* (New York: Oxford University Press, 1985).

Schmitt, Carl *Political Theology: Four Chapters on the Concept of Sovereignty*, trans. George Schwab (Cambridge, Massachusetts: MIT Press, 1985).

Scruggs, Jan C., and Joel L. Swerdlow *To Heal a Nation: the Vietnam Veterans Memorial* (New York: Harper Row, 1985).

Shaw, Martin 'The Kosovan War, 1998–99: the historical sociology of state, war and genocide in global revolution', paper presented at *Bringing Historical Sociologies into International Relations* (University of Wales Aberystwyth, July 2–4, 1999).

Silverman, Kaja 'Suture: the cinematic model', in *Identity: a Reader*, ed. Paul du Gay, Jessica Evans and Peter Redman (London: Sage, 2000), 76–86.

Skocpol, Theda *States and Social Revolutions: a Comparative Analysis of France, Russia and China* (Cambridge University Press, 1979).

Solomon-Godeau, Abigail 'Mourning or melancholia: Christian Boltanski's *Missing House*', *Oxford Art Journal*, 21, no. 2 (1998): 1–20.

Spence, Jonathan 'The gate and the square', from *Children of the Dragon* (New York: Collier Macmillan, 1990), excerpted on URL http://www.tsquare.tv/links/spence.html. Accessed 18 January 2003.

Staten, Henry *Wittgenstein and Derrida* (Oxford: Basil Blackwell, 1984).

Sturken, Marita *Tangled Memories: the Vietnam War, the AIDS Epidemic, and the Politics of Remembering* (Berkeley: University of California Press, 1997).

Summerfield, Derek 'The social experience of war and some issues for the humanitarian field', in *Rethinking the Trauma of War*, ed. Patrick J. Bracken and Celia Petty (London: Free Association Press, 1998), 9–37.

Sutherland, Cara 'Preface', in *Hunger of the Heart: Communion at the Wall*, ed. Larry Powell (Dubuque, Iowa: Islewest, 1995), ix–xi.

Tal, Kalí *Worlds of Hurt: Reading the Literature of Trauma* (Cambridge University Press, 1996).

Taussig, Michael *The Magic of the State* (New York: Routledge, 1997).

Thomson, Alistair *Anzac Memories: Living with the Legend* (Melbourne: Oxford University Press, 1994).

Vidal-Naquet, Pierre *Assassins of Memory: Essays on the Denial of the Holocaust*, trans. Jeffrey Mehlman (New York: Columbia University Press, 1992).

Villa-Vicencio, Charles, and Wilhelm Verwoerd, eds. *Looking Back, Reaching Forward: Reflections on the Truth and Reconciliation Commission of South Africa* (Cape Town and London: University of Cape Town Press and Zed Books, 2000).

Wagner-Pacifici, Robin, and Barry Schwartz, 'The Vietnam Veterans Memorial: Commemorating a Difficult Past', *American Journal of Sociology*, 97, no. 2 (1991): 376–420.

Walker, R. B. J. *Inside/Outside: International Relations as Political Theory* (Cambridge University Press, 1993).

Weber, Max *Economy and Society: an Outline of Interpretative Sociology*, ed. Guenther Roth and Claus Wittich (New York: Bedminster Press, 1968), vol I, 4.

The Protestant Ethic and the Spirit of Capitalism, trans. Talcott Parsons (London: Unwin, 1930).

Weber: Political Writings, trans. Ronald Spiers, ed. Peter Lassman and Ronald Spiers (Cambridge University Press, 1994).

Weinberg, Jeshajahu, and Rina Elieli, *The Holocaust Museum in Washington* (New York: Rizzoli, in collaboration with the United States Holocaust Memorial Museum, 1995).

Wheeler, Nicholas *Saving Strangers* (Oxford University Press, 2000).

White, Hayden *The Content of the Form: Narrative Discourse and Historical Representation* (Baltimore: Johns Hopkins University Press, 1987).

Wiedmer, Caroline *The Claims of Memory: Representations of the Holocaust in Contemporary Germany and France* (Ithaca: Cornell University Press, 1999).

Winter, Jay *Sites of Memory, Sites of Mourning: the Great War in European Cultural History* (Cambridge University Press, 1995).

'Forms of kinship and remembrance in the aftermath of the Great War', in *War and Remembrance in the Twentieth Century*, ed. Jay Winter and Emmanuel Sivan (Cambridge University Press, 1999), 40–60.

Winter, Jay, and Emmanuel Sivan, 'Setting the framework', in *War and Remembrance in the Twentieth Century*, ed. Jay Winter and Emmanuel Sivan (Cambridge University Press, 1999), 6–39.

Woods, Tim 'Mending the Skin of Memory: Ethics and History in Contemporary Narratives', *Rethinking History*, 2, no. 3 (1998): 339–48.

Yoneyama, Lisa *Hiroshima Traces: Time, Space and the Dialectics of Memory* (Berkeley: University of California Press, 1999).

Young, Allan *The Harmony of Illusions: Inventing Post-Traumatic Stress Disorder* (Princeton University Press, 1997).

Young, James E. *The Texture of Memory: Holocaust Memorials and Meaning* (New Haven: Yale University Press, 1993), 7.

Zelizer, Barbie *Remembering to Forget: Holocaust Memory through the Camera's Eye* (University of Chicago Press, 1998).

Žižek, Slavoj *For They Know Not What They Do: Enjoyment as a Political Factor* (London: Verso, 1991).

The Plague of Fantasies (London: Verso, 1997).

The Sublime Object of Ideology (London: Verso, 1989).

Tarrying with the Negative: Kant, Hegel and the Critique of Ideology (Durham, North Carolina: Duke University Press, 1993).

The Ticklish Subject: the Absent Centre of Political Ontology (London: Verso, 1999).

III NEWSPAPER ARTICLES

The Independent, London, 8 April 1999, AP photograph, 4.
Jewish Chronicle, 14 April, quoted in The Editor, *The Guardian*, London, 14 April 2000, 4.
'100 massacres, 10,000 dead – a catalogue of killing reveals the horror of Kosovo', *The Independent*, London, 18 June 1999, 3.
'Britain at standstill as 43 million observe two-minute silence', *The Guardian*, London, 12 November 1998, 3.
'Britain pays silent tribute to war dead', *The Daily Telegraph*, London, 12 November 1998, 13.
'The Cenotaph', *The Times*, London, 27 July 1922.
'Conflict briefing: Day 14', *The Independent*, London, 7 April 1999, 2.
'Dr. Rosenberg's wreath: removal from Cenotaph: protest against desecration', *The Times*, London, 12 May 1933.
'End of the wreath', *Yorkshire Post*, 12 May 1933.
'Herr Hitler's wreath', *Leeds Mercury*, 12 May 1933.
'Hitler wreath thrown in the Thames: Cenotaph protest by ex-Captain: "Desecration" of memorial', *Daily Telegraph*, London, 12 May 1933.
'Keep it sacred: the Cenotaph is no place for demonstrations', *Daily Sketch*, London, 13 May 1933.
'Milosevic: crimes against humanity', *The Independent*, London, 28 May 1999, 16.
'Operation Safe Haven', *The Sunday Times*, London, 4 April 1999, 13.
Amundson, Amber 'A widow's plea for non-violence', *Chicago Tribune*, 25 September 2001.
Appleyard, Bryan 'The troops we chose to forget', *The Sunday Times*, London, 12 November 2000, 6.
Beaumont, Peter, Patrick Wintour, Stephen Bates and Burhan Wazir, 'Nato's tragic errors', *The Observer*, London, 4 April 1999, 15.
Blom, Philipp 'The impossible monument', *The Independent Friday Review*, London, 4 September 1998, 13.
Boggan, Steve '15 mass grave sites found in Kosovo: war crimes', *The Independent*, London, 16 April 1999, 4.
'From the war rooms of Whitehall to the squalor of Stankovic No. 1', *The Independent*, London, 4 May 1999, 3.
'Victims tell harrowing tales of rape', *The Independent*, London, 13 April 1999, 1.
Borger, Julian, and Owen Bowcott, 'Troops covered up massacres', *The Guardian*, London, 17 June 1999, 2.
Bowdler, Neil 'Faith and rage at Auschwitz', *The Guardian*, London, 2 September 1998, 8.
Branigan, Tania 'Poppy day marches into a new century', *The Guardian*, London, 13 November 2000, 7.
Butcher, Tim 'British troops given new orders to help Kosovars', *The Daily Telegraph*, London, 5 April 1999, 3.
Castle, Stephen 'Milosevic may be charged with genocide', *The Independent*, London, 19 June 1999, 4.

Cesarani, David 'History on trial', *The Guardian*, G2, London, 18 January 2000, 3.

Cornwell, Rupert 'Bush maps out global strategy against enemies', *The Independent*, London, 12 March 2002, 4.

'Cook says Serbs will pay for atrocities', *The Independent*, London, 24 June 1999, 13.

Dalrymple, James 'Like an oil painting of hell and still the dispossessed flood in', *The Independent*, London, 3 April 1999, 1.

'One tiny woman against the war criminals', *The Independent*, London, 12 May 1999, 5.

'Stateless, landless and derelict: the forlorn lost tribe of Kosovo', *The Independent*, London, 1 April 1999, 1.

Dalrymple, James, and Emma Daly 'In just a week, Kosovo is swept clean', *The Independent on Sunday*, London, 4 April 1999, 13.

Daly, Emma 'Numbed by fatigue and fear the refugees flee Serb death squads', *The Independent*, London, 30 March 1999, 1.

'Serbs drive thousands from homes', *The Independent Monday Review*, London, 22 March 1999, 11.

Daly, Emma, and Rachel Sylvester, 'Serbs wreak revenge after raids', *The Independent on Sunday*, London, 28 March 1999, 3.

Davison, John 'Almost the Last Post of all for the old men of Dunkirk', *The Independent*, London, 31 May 1999, 3.

Davison, John and Kim Sengupta, 'Cook pledges "we'll hunt down all war criminals" ', *The Independent*, London, 30 March 1999, 5.

Davison, John, Rachel Sylvester, Steve Crawshaw and David Usbourne, 'Nato urged to hit Serb death squads as massacres spread', *The Independent on Sunday*, London, 28 March 1999, 1.

Dejevsky, Mary 'Cuban prison camp has McDonald's and golf course', *The Independent*, London, 8 April 1999, 4.

Donnelly, Rachel 'Blair admits famine policy failure by British', *The Irish Times*, 2 June 1997, 1.

Dyer, Clare 'Judging history', *The Guardian*, G2, London, 17 April 2000, 10.

Ezard, John 'Discovery that keeps Kipling's soul in torment', *The Guardian*, London, 27 July 1998, 18.

Farrell, Stephen and Andrew Campbell, 'Massacre victims "run to thousands" ', *The Times*, London, 17 June 1999, 13.

Fenton, Ben 'Expert gathers war crimes evidence', *The Daily Telegraph*, London, 6 April 1999, 5.

Ferguson, Niall 'Do today's public rituals hinder our understanding of war?' *The Independent Wednesday Review*, London, 11 November 1998, 4.

Fernández-Armesto, Felipe 'Crimes against truth', *The Independent on Sunday*, London, 4 April 1999, 25.

Fleck, Fiona 'Serb war criminals escaping justice', *The Times*, London, 17 June 1999, 13.

Gilligan, Andrew 'Expert warns of "massive" war crimes', *The Sunday Telegraph*, London, 13 June 1999, 5.

Gittings, John 'Deng's Tiananmen paranoia revealed', *The Observer*, London, 7 January 2001, 20.

Guttenplan, D. D. 'Why history matters', *The Guardian Saturday Review*, London, 15 April 2000, 1–2.

Hanks, Robert 'All go on the Western Front', *The Independent Monday Review*, London, 22 April 2002, 16–17.

Hattersley, Roy 'There was no poetry for Uncle Herbert', *The Independent Wednesday Review*, London, 11 November 1998, 4.

Hooper, John 'Powerless UN looks on as refugee crisis grows', *The Observer*, London, 11 April 1999, 16.

Jack, Ian 'As I paid tribute to Uncle Jack, I thought of something else. That it was memory without pain, at least for most of us', *The Independent*, London, 7 November 1998, 1.

Keane, Fergal 'What Milosevic is doing is evil but it is no Final Solution', *The Independent Weekend Review*, London, 17 April 1999, 3.

Kilcoyne, Fr Colm 'A reek of famine memories', *Sunday Tribune*, Dublin, 27 July 1997.

Knightley, Phillip 'Propaganda wars', *The Independent on Sunday*, London, 27 June 1999, 29.

Laughland, John 'The anomalies of the International Criminal Tribunal are legion. This is not victors' justice in the former Yugoslavia – in fact, it is no justice at all', *The Times*, London, 17 June 1999, 24.

Litchfield, John '£1m visitor centre will salute victims of Somme battlefields', *The Independent*, London, 11 November 1999, 3.

'The memory of war', *The Independent Friday Review*, London, 6 November 1998, 1.

Lloyd George, David 'A humble recognition of heroes', *The Independent*, London, 7 November 1998.

Lloyd Parry, Richard 'Database of hope helps the missing', *The Independent*, London, 14 April 1999, 4.

'Nato acquits itself with honour', *The Independent on Sunday*, London, 18 April 1999, 16.

'Thousands more head for Macedonia', *The Independent*, London, 15 April 1999, 4.

McElvoy, Anne 'Milosevic has caught Nato still living by its cold war creed', *The Independent Wednesday Review*, London, 7 April 1999, 3.

Porter, Henry 'For the media, war goes on', *The Observer*, London, 4 July 1999, 16.

'Ruthless Serbs may yet dodge justice: proving war crimes will be extremely difficult', *The Observer*, London, 11 April 1999, 18.

Rushdie, Salman 'Reach for the sky', *The Guardian Review*, London, 27 July 2002, 3.

Schaefer, Sarah 'Blair rejects criticism of Nato bombing', *The Independent*, London, 30 March 1999, 8.

Sengupta, Kim 'The long trail to justice', *The Independent on Sunday*, London, 20 June 1999, 25.

'"Tragic" statue for the Great War's executed soldiers', *The Independent*, London, 22 June 2001, 6.

Shawcross, William 'Let's take him out', *The Guardian*, G2, London, 1 August 2002, 2.

Smith, Roberta 'A memorial remembers the hungry', *New York Times*, 16 July 2002. Available at URL http://www.nytimes.com/2002/07/16/arts/design/16NOTE.html. Accessed 19 July 2002.

Staunton, Denis 'The art of remembrance: haunted still', *The Guardian*, G2, London, 12 August 1998, 1–3.

Stummer, Robin 'The war we can't let go', *The Guardian Weekend*, London, 7 November 1998, 12–23; 15.

Sweeney, John 'The cleansing of Krushe', *The Observer*, London, 4 April 1999, 17.

Sweeney, John, Patrick Wintour, Stephen Bates and Burhan Wazir 'Finally, the brutal truth of Serb massacres in Kosovo', *The Observer*, London, 4 April 1999, 1.

Sylvester, Rachel, and John Davison 'Nato to set up sanctuaries', *The Independent on Sunday*, London, 4 April 1999, 1.

Tanner, Marcus 'Milosevic charge splits Allies', *The Independent*, London, 28 May 1999, 1.

Usbourne, David 'Tiananmen anniversary: Chinese leaders are sued over the massacre', *The Independent*, London, 1 June 1999, 14.

Vullamy, Ed, 'Allies seek missing hordes', *The Observer*, London, 11 April 1999, 2.

Vullamy, Ed, and Patrick Wintour 'Hawks smell a tyrant's blood', *The Observer*, London, 30 May 1999, 15–18.

Ward, David 'Battle for recognition: shamed soldiers acknowledged', *The Guardian*, London, 10 November 2000, 5.

Waugh, Paul, and Jason Bennetto 'UK opens old prisons to refugees', *The Independent*, London, 7 April 1999, 2.

Wintour, Patrick, and Justin Brown 'Nato bombers open attack on Serbian murder squads', *The Observer*, London, 28 March 1999, 1.

IV WEBSITES

Artists Network of Refuse and Resist 'Artists performance in New York City "Our grief is not a cry for war!" ' http://www.artistsnetwork.org/news/news14.html, accessed 1 August 2002.

Boston Irish Famine Memorial Project 'The Boston Irish Famine Memorial: The Sculpture', http://www.boston.com/famine/resources.stm, accessed 15 July 2000.

CNN 'Bush: America will not forget', http://europe.cnn.com/2002/US/03/11/gen.bush.speech/index.html, accessed 8 March 2002.

Dachau Concentration Camp Memorial 'Dachau Concentration Camp Memorial Site, the History of the Concentration Camp', http://www.kz-gedenkstaette-dachau.de/english/frame/idxgese.htm, accessed 2 February 2003.

Falun Dafa Information Centre 'Tiananmen: Court of Last Resort: a Special Report Examining the Role of Tiananmen in the 2-year Persecution of Falun Gong', http://www.faluninfo.net/devstories/tiananmen/index.asp. 4pp, accessed 20 October 2001.

Holocaust Educational Trust: Future Events, http://www.het.org.uk/FutureEvents.html, accessed 28 January 2001.

International Criminal Tribunal for the former Yugoslavia, text of the indictment against Milosevic, http://www.un.org/icty/indictment/English/mil-ii990524ehtm. Accessed 1 August 2002, but no longer active. Information about the case later summarised on http://www.un.org/icty/glance/milosevic.htm, accessed 18 January 2003.

Irish Memorial 'The Irish Memorial, a National Monument at Penn's Landing, Philadelphia: the Memorial', http://www.irishmemorial.org/memorial.html, accessed 15 July 2000.

Maya Ying Lin. March 1981 Statement as part of her competition submission, Available in *Vietnam: Echoes from the Wall*. The Teachers Guide: Module 5, at URL http://www.teachvietnam.org/teachers/guide/html/module_5.htm, accessed 18 January 2003.

Museum Resource Centre Facility: Vietnam Memorial Collection Narrative, collection overview, http://www.nps.gov/mrc/vvmc/vvmc.htm, accessed 29 December 1998.

Office of the Governor of New York State 'Governor Pataki dedicates permanent "Irish Hunger Memorial"', press release, 16 July 2002, http://www.state.ny.us/governor/press/year02/july16_2_02.htm, accessed 19 July 2002.

UK National Inventory of War Memorials 'History of memorialisation', November 2001, http://www.iwm.org.uk/collections/niwm/history_memorials.pdf, accessed 25 July 2002.

US Army Military District of Washington, Public Affairs Office 'Tomb of the Unknowns at Arlington National Cemetery'. *MDW Fact Sheet* FS-A04, http://www.mdw.army.mil/FS-A04.HTM, accessed 26 December 1998.

US Presidential Address. Scott Cummings, 'World Trade Center and Pentagon Attacks: Presidential Speeches', Emma Booker Elementary School, Sarasota, Florida, September 11, 2001, 9.30 a.m. EDT, http://www.patriotresource.com/wtc/president/address1.html, accessed 8 March 2002.

Vietnam Wall 'Vietnam Veterans Memorial Wall Replica', http://thevietnamwall.com/thestory.html, accessed 26 December 1998.

Westminster Abbey 'The 2000 Field of Remembrance', http://www.westminster-abbey.org/press/release/991111.htm, accessed 15 January 2003.

'The Unknown Warrior at Westminster Abbey', http://www.westminster-abbey.org/library/burial/warrior.htm, accessed 15 January 2003.

V LEAFLETS AND BROCHURES

Bristol Museums and Art Gallery 'Slave Trade Trail around Central Bristol', Bristol City Council, with sponsorship from The Society of Merchant Venturers, 1998.

The City of Hiroshima and the Hiroshima Peace Culture Foundation 'Hiroshima Peace Memorial (Genbaku Dome)' (Hiroshima: Sanko, 1997).

Dachau Concentration Camp Memorial 'Dachau Concentration Camp Memorial Site', small guide, c.2001, 4pp. and folded museum leaflet.
Friends of the New England Holocaust Memorial 'The New England Holocaust Memorial' (Boston: Friends of the New England Holocaust Memorial, supported by Bank Boston, 2000), brochure, 6pp.
'Here is New York: a Democracy of Photographs', publicity flyer, March 2002.
Hikotara Ando, *Peking* (Tokyo: Kodansha, 1968).
Ministry for Foreign Affairs, Ireland 'Minister visits Grosse le, Quebec', Press section, 3 December 1997, press release.
Ministry for Foreign Affairs, Ireland. Speech by the Irish Minister for Foreign Affairs, Mr David Andrews, TD, at a ceremony to mark the twinning of the National Famine Museum, Strokestown Park, Co. Roscommon, with the Grosse le and the Irish Memorial National Historic Site, Québec, Canada.
New York New Visions Coalition for the Rebuilding of Lower Manhattan 'Around Ground Zero: February/March 2002', by Laura Kurgan, folded map, 2002.
Republic of Ireland, Office of Public Works 'Famine', 1997.
A Sketch Map of the Imperial Palace (Beijing: China Esperanto Press, 1998).
United States Holocaust Memorial Museum 'The Holocaust: a Historical Summary' (Washington, USHMM, District of Columbia, n.d.), 32pp.
United States Holocaust Memorial Museum, Visitors' Guide (Washington, District of Columbia, USHMM, n.d.), folded pamphlet.

VI FILMS, AUDIO MATERIAL AND EXHIBITIONS

9/11. Directed by Jules Naudet, Gedeon Naudet and James Hanlon. Goldfish Pictures/Silverstar Productions, 2002. Broadcast on CBS 10 March 2002.
Between Cinema and a Hard Place. Tate Modern, London, 12 May–31 December 2000.
Blade Runner. Directed by Ridley Scott (Warner Brothers, 1982).
Hiroshima Mon Amour. Directed by Alain Renais, script, Marguerite Duras. (Argos Films, Como Films, Pathé Overseas, Paris, Daiei Motion Picture Co Ltd., France/Japan, 1959).
In Memoriam. New York City 9/11/01. Home Box Office (Brad Grey Pictures, 2002), broadcast on HBO 26 May 2002.
Martin. Directed by Ra'anan Alexandrowicz (Israel, 1999).
Memento. Produced by Suzanne Todd and Jennifer Todd. Directed by Christopher Nolan (Newmarket, 2000).
Notowitz, David *Voices of the Shoah: Remembrances of the Holocaust*, with 4 CDs, narrated by Elliot Gould (Los Angeles: Rhino Entertainment Company, 2000).
Out of that Darkness, Institute of Contemporary Arts film season 16–23 July 2000, in conjunction with the conference *Remembering for the Future 2000*.
A Respectable Trade? Bristol and Transatlantic Slavery. Bristol City Museum and Art Gallery exhibition, 6 March–1 September 1999.
WTC: The First 24 Hours. Camera and direction by Etienne Sauret, produced by Etienne Sauret and David Carrara, VHS 40 minutes (Isis, 2001).

Index

Made in the USA
Lexington, KY
16 May 2013